DEDICATED

to the Gibraltarians and

to all the men and women who in any way

helped them in their hour of need.

THE FORTRESS CAME FIRST

The story of
the civilian population of Gibraltar
during the Second World War

T. J. FINLAYSON

GIBRALTAR BOOKS LTD
Gibraltar
2000

Published by Gibraltar Books Ltd
3/3 Governor's Parade, PO Box 816
Gibraltar

First edition 1991
Second edition (paperback) 1996
Third edition 2000

ISBN 1 919657 02 9

Printed and bound by
Antony Rowe Ltd, Chippenham, Wiltshire

Contents

Contents

List of Illustrations

Acknowledgements

The idea for this book was implanted in my head some time in 1980. I began by spending many hours at the Gibraltar Garrison Library looking through the war-time 'Gibraltar Chronicles'. When this source had been exhausted, I was fortunate to become acquainted with the late Mr J W V Cumming, MBE, my predecessor as Archivist to the Government of Gibraltar. He introduced me to the wealth of documentary material available in the Government Archives and he was kind enough to allow me to spend a great deal of time researching this material. Questionnaires were also distributed amongst certain sections of the Gibraltarian community asking for information about the evacuation. To those who took the trouble to reply my thanks; some of the material proved to be most useful and has been used in the text.

I am most honoured that Sir Joshua Hassan, GBE, KCMG, OBE, LVO, QC, JP, former Chief Minister of Gibraltar and such a colossus in the Rock's politics for over forty years, has agreed to write a foreword to this book. My thanks go, too, to Mr Adolfo Canepa, who was kind enough to read the text and who offered valuable advice, and to the Government of Gibraltar for contributing financially towards the cost of publication.

I must also thank the Foreign and Commonwealth Office for the excellent photographs of 'Gibraltar Camp', Jamaica, and the Imperial War Museum for permission to reproduce photographs from their collection.

Finally, my thanks to Mr Tito Benady and Gibraltar Books Ltd for undertaking the publication of the work.

T J Finlayson
1988

Foreword

By Sir Joshua Hassan, GBE, KCMG, OBE, LVO, QC, JP

Gibraltar has, through the ages, suffered plagues, sieges and difficulties of all kinds—many of these since it came under the British Crown. Historically, it is quite clear that from the point of view of the population the one that caused greatest havoc and anxiety and long term effects was the evacuation of the civil population of Gibraltar in World War Two for reasons of defence.

Here was a law abiding, industrious and hardworking, closely knit community, ready to face the hardships and difficulties of war from their own homes, being suddenly told that they were to be uprooted (women, children and the old) from their City for the requirements of war. Hard as this was, the original evacuation to Morocco was to a country the climate of which was similar to ours, though some of the evacuees were sent into the interior in conditions far from hygenic or even civilised.

Difficulties and hardships were caused but the people put up with them with a sense of dignity and to some extent pride in that they felt it was one more effort to help the allies win the war. But that was only the beginning. Within a few months of this upheaval they were literally thrown out of North Africa as the French troops withdrew from Metropolitan France and took refuge in Morocco. Our people were packed anyhow, to be taken to another destination, into ships that had hardly been emptied of withdrawing troops. The conditions of these ships can well be imagined.

The uproar created in the local population when from small boats they saw their dear ones arrive in the Bay crammed in those ships in shocking conditions and which had only anchored to obtain supplies on their way to Britain, the pressure brought upon the authorities to allow the evacuees to land and prepare themselves for this long journey while the ships were repaired and put in tolerable condition, are graphically described in Mr Finlayson's excellent record of these tragic events.

Once in the United Kingdom, he narrates their tribulations and difficulties in the various centres to which they were taken, and the subsequent proposal to take them across the Atlantic to Jamaica at a time when the German U-boats were sinking merchant ships. That their families should be sent across the Atlantic caused great distress to the people who had remained in Gibraltar on essential work, and petitions were organised which changed the intentions of the authorities.

As a recently qualified lawyer having returned to practice before the outbreak of war, I offered myself to help at the time of the first evacuation to Morocco. Sir Edward Cottrell (Mr Edward Cottrell as he then was) who was in charge of the evacuation allowed me to do so. I therefore lived at close quarters through all the anxieties of our people including that of my own family.

Finally after D day i.e. the end of the war in Europe, the will of the people accelerated the repatriation. This made it necessary to find accommodation to repatriate not only those who had been taken away from their homes in Gibraltar but also for the British subjects around Gibraltar mainly in Spain and Morocco who had joined the Gibraltar evacuees and were then sent back to us as if they had been part of our original population.

All these events left scars in the people who went through these experiences. With the passage of time many of them have by natural process been reduced, and it was urgent to obtain their testimony to record for future generations these tragic events. Mr Finlayson has researched them accurately and with vividness and compassion for posterity to know what the people of Gibraltar went through.

I am glad that at last the book is seeing the light of day so that the world may learn what our people suffered with loyalty and dignity in their firm determination to help the Mother Country in her hour of need.

We must be grateful to the author for giving us this detailed account of such tragic circumstances and bringing back to some of us the memories of such difficult times, which then seemed endless.

Sir J A Hassan

Introduction

'We had a long, last sight of Gibraltar from the decks ... The ship weighed anchor at 5 pm. and it was two hours before the Rock faded from our view. We just leaned on the rail and kept our eyes glued on the towering monster that has always been our home—our beloved home. For the Rock is harsh and forbidding only to the stranger. For us who knew her intimately, she was sweet and amiable—the loving Mother of us all. Do you wonder that we wept as she slowly faded in the distance, becoming at length a blurb just barely visible, and then ... We have many pictures of her, and we often take them out and look at them.'

(An evacuee)

' 'Mid pleasures and palaces
Though we may roam,
Be it ever so humble,
There's no place like home.'

'Peñoncito querido
lejano Gibraltar,
el corazon herido
por ti se va a quebrar.
Que intacto Dios te guarde
para a ti regresar;
aunque volvamos tarde,
te amamos sin cesar.'

'Gibraltar streets are silent
All gone those little feet
But their high-heeled tinkling clatter
On my heart shall ever beat,
As I stood at my embrasure
I hear those little feet.'

In 1940, the implications inherent in living in a Fortress were brought home most forcibly to the civilian inhabitants of the Rock of Gibraltar. The exigencies of war, the needs of the military garrison became paramount. Women, children and old men were turfed out, initially to French Morocco, then to London, Jamaica and Madeira. Several thousands of those who were sent to the United Kingdom were later transferred to Northern Ireland. Some of the evacuees were not to return until five years after the ending of the

Second World War, a period of exile amounting to close on a decade! It proved to be a long and sometimes painful exile. THE FORTRESS, INDEED, CAME FIRST.

This book, the result of about four years of research through countless Gibraltar Government files, newspaper articles published in Gibraltar, the United Kingdom and Jamaica, and interviews with people who experienced the evacuation, traces the story from the ominous developments of the late 1930's in Europe, through the nightmare that was the brief evacuation to French Morocco, the hazards endured as a result of air raids in London, the subsequent ordeal in Northern Ireland camps, the relative peaceful existence of those who were sent to Jamaica and Madeira to the protracted saga of repatriation. A look is also taken at life in Gibraltar itself during the war years whilst the opening chapter looks in general terms at the problems posed by the presence of a civilian population in a military fortress.

T J Finlayson

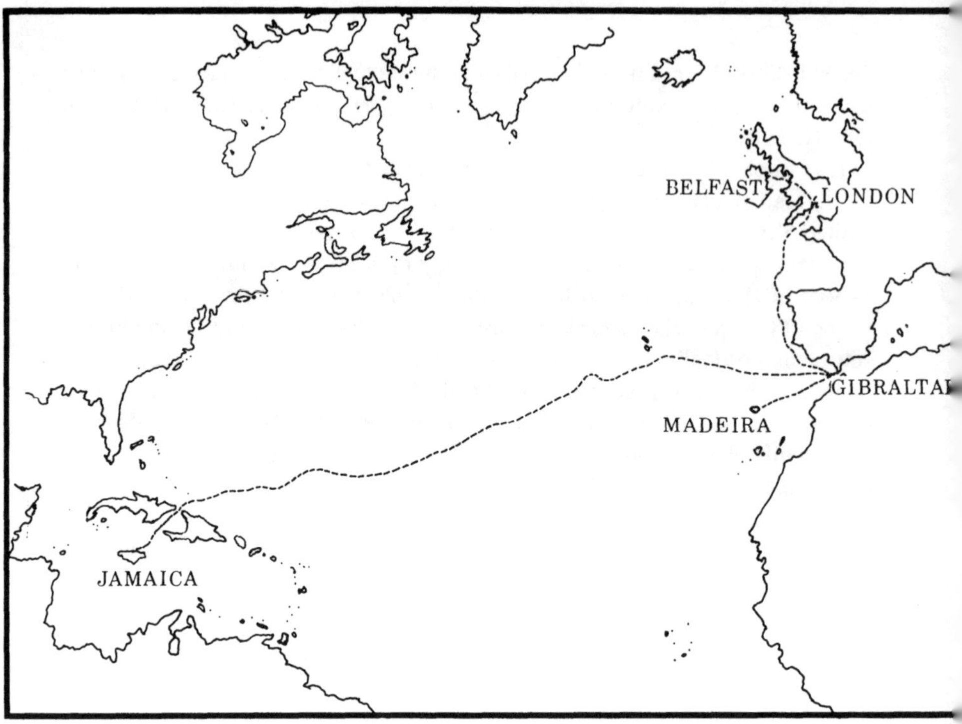
BELFAST
LONDON
GIBRALTAR
MADEIRA
JAMAICA

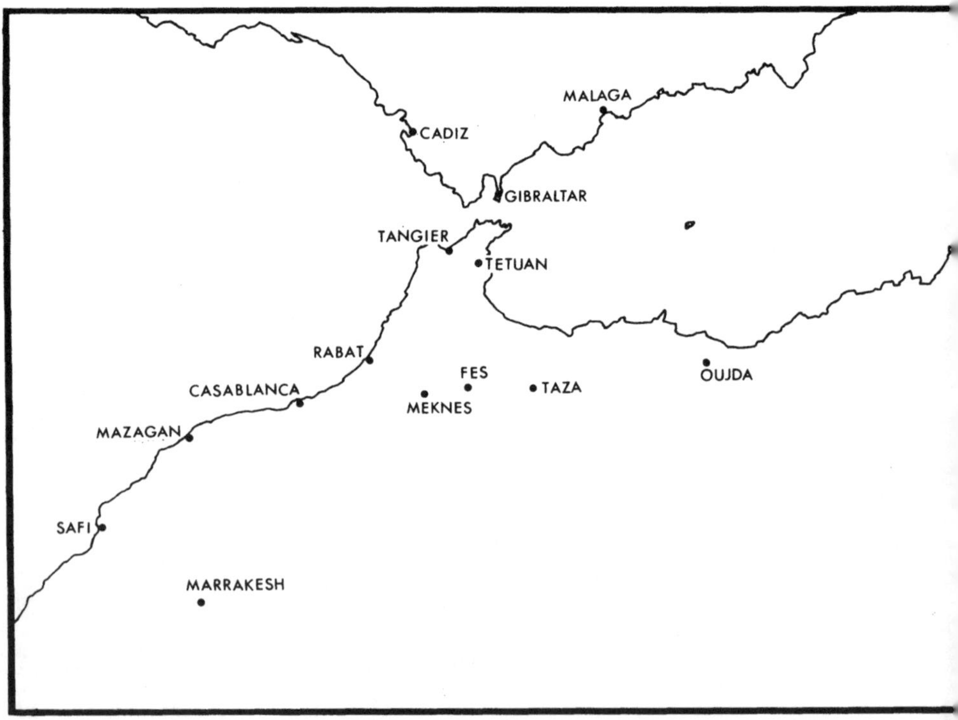
MALAGA
CADIZ
GIBRALTAR
TANGIER
TETUAN
RABAT
FES
TAZA
OUJDA
CASABLANCA
MEKNES
MAZAGAN
SAFI
MARRAKESH

CHAPTER ONE

The Problems posed by a Civilian Population in a Military Fortress

War clouds gathered ominously over Europe as the year 1938 unfolded. In March, Hitler marched his troops into Austria, and a State with more than a thousand years of history behind it disappeared to become part of the German Empire.

A few months later, in September, it was the turn of Czechoslovakia to feel the effects of Hitler's expansionist policies, as German forces occupied the Sudetenland areas of that country.

The fears aroused by such events were hardly allayed by Chamberlain's attempted policy of appeasement, and his claim to have achieved 'peace in our own time' at Munich in September 1938. By the spring of the following year, Nazi jackboots were again trampling across Europe, with Czechoslovakia the victim in March and Poland in September. World War Two broke out on the 3rd September, 1939.

How would such events affect the Rock of Gibraltar and its inhabitants? The presence of a civilian population within the confines of a military fortress had not presented insurmountable problems during the early years of British occupation for the simple reason that at the time of the eighteenth century sieges that population had barely exceeded 3,000. It was thus a relatively easy matter for the military authorities to have this element removed in times of crisis. Indeed, most civilians left voluntarily at the first signs of Anglo-Spanish hostilities!

As the nineteenth century progressed, however, and as Gibraltar entered into a long period of peace and a certain amount of prosperity, so commercial activity increased with a consequent rise in the numbers of civilians residing there. By the mid-nineteenth century there were almost 16,000 of them, which prompted the Governor of Gibraltar, Sir Robert Gardiner, to pose some very pertinent questions in 1853. 'What is to become of this overgrown population in the event of War? What shall we do with it? How dispose of it? Where send it?' Such questions were to remain purely academic for a long time, though in the meantime the British Government did consider such problems and came up with various solutions ranging from enforced expulsion to intimidation and persuasion.

Gibraltar was not in the front firing line during the First World War (1914-1918) so the problem did not then arise. With most of the heavy fighting well away from the Western Mediterranean and with Spain remaining neutral, no mass evacuation of civilians was envisaged.

The situation was to be very different twenty years later. Gibraltar was an important Fortress to the Western Allies, and in the case of Italy and/or Spain entering the conflict, it would clearly be in the front firing line. In such eventuality, what was to become of the 20,000 civilians living on the Rock? Some could well be absorbed in essential defence work, but there remained the 13,000 or so women, children and aged, whose presence in a Fortress at war was likely to become a hindrance and an embarrasment to the defending forces. If they were to be evacuated, where could they go?

Such questions were clearly under the consideration of the British Government's representatives at quite an early stage. On the 17th March, 1939, the then Colonial Secretary, Alexander Beattie, produced a memorandum investigating the possible alternatives. Spain, he said, was the obvious choice, but the possibility of that country being hostile made it necessary to consider other alternatives.

The first such alternative considered was the international zone of Tangier, just across the Strait. Several sites had already been investigated, and the suggestion was that a refugee camp should be set up on one of these. In the event of the Tangier Zone proving impracticable, the Colonial Secretary suggested the French Zone in Morocco and Portugal as other alternatives. The United Kingdom was mentioned *as a last resort.*

The Governor, General Sir Edmund Ironside, studied the memorandum and decided that no further action was called for. However, the matter was not forgotten, as a memorandum from Fortress Headquarters to the Colonial Secretary, dated the 25th May, 1939, illustrates. This urged the Colonial Secretary to draw up a scheme showing order of priority of evacuation, and citing the example of London where plans for the speedy evacuation of children without their parents but accompanied by their schoolteachers had been made. A great deal of work appears to have gone into this last suggestion, but in the end force of circumstances led to its abandonment.

By August, the Governor had sought clarification concerning his powers on the matter, a Major Pidsley had been sent to Morocco (Tangier had by then been discarded in favour of French Morocco) to investigate the question of facilities for any evacuated civilian population from Gibraltar, and it was being estimated that the numbers involved would be in the region of 13,000 (women, children and aged men). The French Protectorate authorities did not appear to be very keen on the idea but not totally opposed to it. An alternative area suggested was Algeria.

On the 14th August, the Local Defence Committee discussed the matter fully and instructed that the City Council should prepare a scheme of evacuation as far as the details of the Gibraltar end were concerned; i.e. marshalling of evacuees ready for embarkation, allotment of baggage, arrangements for supply of currency, etc. It was at this meeting that the term 'useless mouths' was used for the first time to refer to the 13,000 souls scheduled for evacuation. No doubt, in the military sense, the phrase was technically correct, but it was nonetheless an unfortunate choice of words. The new Governor, Lieutenant-General Sir Clive Liddell, and others took up the phrase in later exchanges.

At this stage (August, 1939), the attitude of Spain was a key factor. The authorities in Gibraltar clearly felt that the envisaged evacuation would only be necessary if Spain became hostile. By September, the fact that Italy had so far kept out of the war and that Spain had declared a policy of neutrality had introduced some changes vis-a-vis the proposed evacuation of civilians from Gibraltar. The possibility of evacuation to Spain was now investigated by the Colonial Secretary in talks with the Spanish Consul-General, but the Spanish government vetoed such an idea.

On the 6th October, 1939, the Secretary of State informed the Governor that the Overseas Defence Committee had considered the evacuation scheme and had concluded that, since Spain had declared herself neutral, in their opinion an evacuation scheme for Gibraltar had become, for the moment at any rate, somewhat academic. The 'useless mouths', unknown to themselves, had been temporarily reprieved! There the matter stood until April, 1940, when changes in the international situation again brought it to the forefront.

For a while, things had been quiet on the Western Front; so quiet, in fact, that the war was being dubbed 'the phoney war'. All that was to change in April, 1940. In that month, Germany attacked and occupied Denmark and Norway, and in May she attacked Belgium and Holland, conquering the latter in five days. The British Army in France soon found itself surrounded and forced to retreat to the port of Dunkirk from where the Royal Navy, assisted by hundreds of little ships, managed to rescue many of the troops so trapped. By mid-June, the French had capitulated to the German advance and a puppet government under Marshal Petain and M Laval had been set up with headquarters at Vichy. Mussolini, dictator of Italy, now joined Hitler as an ally, and things seemed desperate for Britain.

It is against the background of such international developments that the next phase in the Gibraltar story must be viewed. By May, 1940, the Governor was pressing London for a decision to evacuate the civilian population to French Morocco, and he was given the go-ahead to investigate the matter further, though warned not to put the scheme into operation without a decision by the War Cabinet. At the same time, he was asked for details of emergency arrangements in hand for the protection of the civilian population in the event of air attack or bombardment from the sea. The assumption was made that local bomb-proof shelters accommodating over 8,000 had been completed. The Governor replied that shelter accommodation was behind time due to labour shortage and that there was only at present ample spacing for 6,500 for short periods only owing to the non-arrival of a ventilating plant.

The Governor then proceeded to make further enquiries as to the possibilities of evacuation to French Morocco, and to this end he decided to send there Lieutenant-Colonel Hay, Officer Commanding Royal Engineers, and Mr Charles Gaggero, a member of the firm of Messrs Bland and Company and a leading official in the Passive Defence organisation, a body which would be responsible for the details of any evacuation scheme. At this stage it was being estimated that the number to be evacuated would be in the region of 13,000, consisting of women, children and a few aged and unfit males.

At the same time, the Admiralty was requesting information as to whether there was local shipping available to cope with a possible evacuation of 13,000 people. In response, the Captain of the Port, Gibraltar, informed that the number of ships available was well under the total required and that in the circumstances the evacuation would take some time to carry out (subsequent estimates from the Admiralty, based on this information, were that the evacuation would require at least five separate trips or about a fortnight to complete).

A few days later, Lieutenant-Colonel Hay and Mr Gaggero were reporting back the results of their investigations in French Morocco. The Hay Report makes interesting reading, particularly in the light of subsequent developments. After stating that the French authorities had been very helpful, Hay made the following points.

With regard to accommodation, lodging under cover could be provided, partly in hotels, partly in empty houses and billets. Most evacuees would stay in Casablanca, but some would have to be taken elsewhere. Families in hotels would pay their own bills. On this matter of accommodation, Hay conceded that difficulties would be encountered and he informed the French authorities that the bulk of Gibraltarians were used to roughing it, sometimes living six to eight to a room. L H Hurst, His Britannic Majesty's Consul-General in Rabat, quotes Hay as having said that 'the Gibraltarians were used to a pretty lowly standard of life for the most part.' Hay claimed that he had made this statement to simplify the reception of evacuees.

The provision of food was another problem tackled by Hay, who stated that there would be 'no difficulty about food supply, but (that it was) probably best to give ration allowance in cash and let the evacuees shift for themselves.'

Bedding and furniture could not be provided by the French authorities, so the evacuees would have to take their own blankets and cutlery. Hay also suggested that since mattresses would take up shipping space, the possibility ought to be investigated of sending over a stock of army biscuits.

Hay also stated that the French medical organisation was sufficient to look after the evacuees, an opinion certainly not borne out by subsequent events!

The matter of the few Spaniards residing in Gibraltar was to prove a difficult one to resolve, given the reluctance of the authorities in French Morocco to accept any but British subjects from Gibraltar. In his report, Hay stated that Spaniards could, with difficulty, be squashed into a concentration camp, but that a new one might be necessary.

On the 10th May, 1940, the British Consul-General in Rabat informed Hay that less accommodation than hitherto believed would be available in Casablanca so that some of the evacuees might have to be lodged in camps. Mr Gaggero's report from Casablanca added the ominous note that some of the places ear-marked for housing the evacuees lacked sufficient sanitary arrangements.

Some inclination of what was going on behind closed doors was given to the public on Friday, 17th May, when a Government Notice in the *Gibraltar Chronicle* warned that circumstances might arise which could force the Governor to order the evacuation of women, children and aged and infirm men. Meanwhile those who could afford it were urged to make their own arrangements for departure. The effect of such an announcement on a closely-knit community with strong family ties may well be imagined. Many of those concerned had never set foot outside Gibraltar!

Meantime, some confusion in communication between London and Gibraltar seems to have arisen. The War Cabinet in London met on the 16th May and decided that the evacuation of civilians from Gibraltar to French Morocco should be carried out. The Governor, on the other hand, appeared to assume that this decision was merely an approval of the scheme and not orders to carry it out forthwith. At this point, the Governor was strongly against the evacuation of civilians from Gibraltar provided that there was no probability of Spain entering the conflict. His chief concern was that a premature evacuation would create a wrong impression in that country.

This apparent confusion in the interpretation of the War Cabinet's decision of the 16th May was further evidenced when the Director of Sea Transport, in a naval signal dated the 17th May, assumed that the Cabinet had issued an executive order for the evacuation to commence, an assumption which the Admiral Commanding North Atlantic questioned in another naval signal of the same day. The latter, quoting the Governor's message to London deprecating the evacuation so long as Spain remained neutral, expressed the opinion that the War Cabinet's statement was merely an approval of the evacuation scheme and not an executive order for it to be carried out immediately. The Admiral concluded his message by saying that 'whilst considering that all arrangements should be made for quick evacuation I entirely agree with the Governor's views.'

The confusion was clarified two days later when the Secretary of State informed the Governor that 'in view of the disturbed situation in the Mediterranean generally and the time needed to complete evacuation, it has been decided as a precautionary measure that evacuation is to proceed immediately upon shipping becoming available.' The decision was also taken to evacuate Service families direct to the United Kingdom, not to French Morocco.

The news was broken to the public by means of a Government Notice issued on the 21st May, 1940. The evacuation of families with children under the age of fourteen was to be carried out under the scheme prepared by the City Council, and the 'Mohamed-Ali-Kebir', an Egyptian vessel chartered by the British Government, was to be used to transport them to French Morocco.

The Notice concluded: 'His Excellency fully realises that these steps will cause a great deal of anxiety and inconvenience, but they are being taken in the interests of the persons concerned and in those of the Fortress. He feels sure that all citizens will abide loyally by his instructions, and cheerfully endure such sacrifices as they are called upon to make.'

'Operation Evacuation' was under way!

CHAPTER TWO

The Problems of Mass Evacuation

The uncertainties over, the process of evacuating civilians from Gibraltar finally got under way on Tuesday, 21st May, 1940. Matters were to proceed very rapidly over the ensuing few weeks: sometimes too rapidly for those who had to make the reception arrangements at the other end!

On Tuesday, 21st May, 1940, the s.s. *Gibel Dersa,* a vessel of 1,226 gross tons employed in the Gibraltar-Tangier service, set out from Gibraltar bound for Casablanca. On board were Mr Charles Gaggero, a medical officer and other control staff, including Police, and several hundred persons (328 adults and 166 children) who could be classified as independent evacuees; ie in a position to pay for their own passages and to arrange their own accommodation.

Those not in such a fortunate position set out the following day, Wednesday 22nd May, on board the ss *Mohamed Ali Kebir,* an Egyptian ship of 7,000 tons specially chartered for the task. This first contingent of Government evacuees comprised 950 women and children and a few old men. They came under Category A of the City Council scheme: ie women and children under the age of fourteen. It is not difficult to imagine the anxiety suffered by these souls and the relatives whom they had to leave behind so suddenly, and the effects of this were to become apparent in the subsequent report of the Medical Officer on board, Dr J J Giraldi.

Meanwhile, the *Gibraltar Chronicle* of Friday, 24th May, 1940, tried to make light of the problems involved, no doubt in an attempt to maintain the morale of those yet to be evacuated and of those who would have to stay behind.

'Over 900 evacuees belonging to Group A of the City Council Scheme, consisting of women and children under fourteen years of age, and a few elderly and infirm persons left Gibraltar on Wednesday evening for Casablanca by the ss *Mohamed Ali Kebir,* which had been chartered by His Majesty's Government for that purpose. The *Mohamed Ali Kebir* arrived at Casablanca early on Thursday morning.

Cheers and greetings were exchanged between those on the ship and friends ashore as the steamer left the wharf. Certainly the younger element regarded the evacuation as a great adventure and for many of them it was their first experience of travel. Lorries were provided by the City Council for the conveyance of the belongings of evacuees from convenient points to the wharf in the Dockyard.

The evacuees appeared to have carried out the instructions issued by the ARP organisation to whom the detailed work was delegated, and embarkation arrangements worked satisfactorily.

It should be remembered that in the carrying out of a large scheme of this nature, some hardship to individuals cannot be avoided, particularly in view of the short time available. A few of the inconveniences of the first day will doubtless be averted in the light of experience gained in the initial stages.'

Three days later, the same periodical stated that 'according to those in a position to judge, the first embarkation went off most satisfactorily, and the greatest credit is due to the City Council and its ARP organisation, and others responsible, not overlooking the evacuees themselves for their orderly and cheerful behaviour.'

The report of the Medical Officer on board the *Mohamed Ali Kebir* on that fateful day paints a rather different picture! He stated that of 800 persons taken, 100 were allotted to cabins, the rest having to travel on troop decks. The ventilation of these quarters had been quite efficient and the atmosphere did not become unpleasant until the next morning at about 4 am., when it was markedly 'heavy', the place then being thoroughly messed by vomited matter and evacuations of children.

The sanitary arrangements had been good and close at hand, but by early morning most children had been too sick to ask for, or to go to, the lavatories provided.

The evacuees, continued the report, had come on board rather tired and in low spirits. They had apparently been kept on the quay for about three hours. From the start some people had refused to go down to the decks and had loitered about the promenades. They had been down and stated that they could not stand it. As the boat left the quay there had been a few hysterical fits and other expressions of emotionalism. (The 'cheers and greetings' of the *Chronicle* report!)

The thirteen-hour journey must have been a nightmarish experience. Six hours after leaving port about ninety per cent of the evacuees were seasick and from midnight until about 6 am there was a continuous demand for medical attention. The two midwife nurses also went sick and the aid of the three special constables on board and their officer had to be enlisted. In addition to their own duties, these men had to carry people from troop-decks to the fresh air and others who had fainted in the open and were chilled had to be carried below. Not surprisingly, these men were overtaxed to the point of exhaustion.

Apart from sickness due to the ship's movements there was a series of cases of collapse. The Medical Officer attributed this to exhaustion due partly to lack of food (especially hot food) and cold. Some of the evacuees, owing to worry, had not been eating well prior to embarkation and once on board had had very little. In addition, some people had tied their blankets with their belongings so that they could not get at them when they were most needed. During the night the Medical Officer had to attend to between 200 and 300 cases, some requiring the administration of medicines.

Such, then, was 'the great adventure' described by the *Gibraltar Chronicle!* There were to be many more over the ensuing weeks. Nor was the ordeal over once the ship had berthed at Casablanca, for this contingent was destined for Rabat and this entailed a further hour's journey by train.

The majority of these evacuees were distributed in three old hotels (the 'Transatlantique', the 'Guessous', and the 'Annexe de France'), the remainder going to numerous small villas and apartments, which numbered about sixty and were spread all over the peripheral areas of the town.

According to Dr Giraldi, who took charge of the medical department in Rabat, the accommodation was ample but the sanitary conveniences were to some extent deficient, owing to disuse. Instructions had been issued to repair this and the work was proceeding satisfactorily. The Consul-General in Rabat reported that once the mattresses had been distributed, the main fault had been that many of the buildings had not been properly cleaned in advance, combined with insufficient overhauling of sanitary arrangements and the fact that there had been some delay in making electric light and water again available where they had been disconnected. Such occurrences, he added, had only been temporary.

The villas and apartments were situated in healthy surroundings with plenty of open space for children, and the sanitary conditions were good except for minor details which were being seen to.

The French authorities, however, were worried that the arrival of 3,000 evacuees was going to throw some strain on the Bureau d'Hygiene of Rabat. On public health in general in the area, Dr Giraldi reported that the water supply was good and safe to drink, typhus amongst Europeans was very rare, and little or nothing was seen of malaria. However, trachoma (an eye disease) was frequent among the Moorish people; in fact, the disease was endemic in Rabat with 1,000 new cases in 1939.

The question of the milk supply to babies presented problems, with 59 bottle-fed babies already in Rabat. According to Dr Giraldi's calculations, this would require about 150 tins of condensed milk a week. Since this was difficult to obtain, the City Council of Gibraltar had been asked to send a weekly supply. Dr Giraldi advised some mothers to use 'Mont Blanc' milk, but he said that he dared not recommend the fresh milk of Rabat. The doctor concluded his report by saying that he had gained a good impression of health conditions there and that he did not anticipate great difficulties.

Whilst this first contingent of evacuees was being settled in, preparations were already under way for the next batch. The idea was to gradually absorb the evacuees into the town, but meantime temporary quarters were being prepared. These consisted of three huge hangers situated at the port. They were well ventilated, had five closets with running water attached and drinking water was plentiful. Feeding arrangements were to be looked after by a Ladies' Committee at the expense of the Gibraltar authorities. Portable kitchens belonging to the Army were to be taken to the Port to ensure a supply of hot meals plus hot water day and night, particularly important for the feeding of babies.

The month following the departure of this first contingent of Government evacuees was a hectic one both at the departure and reception ends. Between the 22nd May and the 24th June, the *Mohamed Ali Kebir* made twelve trips to Casablanca taking a total of 12,105 evacuees. In addition, the *Gibel Dersa* made two journeys, taking a total of 846 voluntary evacuees, and a further trip on the 19th June carrying 544 passengers. In all, 13,495 people were evacuated from Gibraltar in that time. Whilst those responsible for organising reception arrangements in French Morocco kept urging the Gibraltar authorities to slow down the rate of exodus, the latter insisted on the necessity of speeding it up! Inevitably, problems cropped up.

One such problem arose from the French Authorities' fear that undesirable elements might enter their Zone under cover of the evacuation. At the very outset of the exercise they were demanding lists of evacuees in quadruplicate, insisting that the ships should arrive off Casablanca by 6.00 am., and asking that lists of evacuees be presented to the French Consul in Gibraltar for visas before sailing. The French Consul, M Neuville, wrote on the 24th May complaining that the batch of 950 evacuees who had sailed on the *Mohamed Ali Kebir* on the 22nd May had had no visas and he threatened that 'if in the future the formality of the visa was not complied with, the French Authorities would be obliged to take steps to drive back the evacuees to Gibraltar.'

The Gibraltar Authorities replied that the demand for visas was impractical since the lists of evacuees were only completed as they embarked. At the same time, an assurance was given that every individual embarking for Morocco would be carefully scrutinised and would be well known to the Police and officials accompanying the ship.

The French Authorities eventually agreed to a collective visa but then began to express concern at the inclusion of many undesirables, both Spaniards and other nationalities, amongst the evacuees, an allegation denied by the Authorities in Gibraltar.

Of particular concern were the Spaniards residing in Gibraltar. These fell into two distinct categories. There were those technically Spanish by birth but who had lived in Gibraltar all their lives and by marriage connection or long association could be considered members of Gibraltar families. They were nearly all women, and the French Authorities agreed to admit them.

The second category posed a more difficult problem. These were Spanish refugees in Gibraltar as a legacy from the Spanish Civil War. They refused to return to their country on the grounds that if they did they would be shot immediately or at any rate suffer long imprisonment. According to official sources in Gibraltar, there were 1,073 men, 102 women and 38 children in this category.

The Gibraltar Authorities negotiated with the Governor of Algeciras in an effort to allow some of these people to return to their own country in safety, but to no avail.

The attitude of the French Authorities was that they preferred these refugees to be sent somewhere else other than French Morocco. If this proved impractical, the French Zone would accept them on the condition that they were all sent as an isolated homogeneous group in a ship conveying no other evacuees. On arrival they would be interned in Casablanca, and sorted out. Some might be usefully employed but the bulk would be interned for the duration of the war. The French Authorities added that their Zone was already full of 'red' refugees of all sorts. This statement was made in early June, after which no further reference to these people is to be found in the official records of the evacuation.

To return to the process of evacuation of Gibraltarian civilians, the second contingent (850 women and children and a few men) left Gibraltar aboard the *Kebir* on Friday, 24th May. On arrival the following day they were billetted in the environs of Casablanca in four main locations: Ocean Plage, Luna Park, Park Beaulieu and Guingnette Fleurie. All four places were dance and entertainment halls converted for the purpose of receiving the evacuees.

327 evacuees went to Ocean Plage which was adequately roofed and glass-windowed all round, with a terrace and adjoining small rooms and out-houses. The situation was good, being by the seashore. However, there were no cubicles in the main hall, the kitchens were in an unsatisfactory state, and the lavatory annexe was poor and inadequate. The latter two were being improved and movable huts with buckets were in the process of being supplied. The food was satisfactory, except for infants, but flies were particularly bad in the area.

In Luna Park, which took 227 evacuees, the main pavilion had been curtained off into cubicles, but once again the lavatories were bad and movable huts with buckets had been promised. In this place, water had to be piped 120 yards.

At Park Beaulieu (110 occupants) there were no cubicles but wires had been stretched across to enable curtaining off. Electric light and a bathroom had just been added but the lavatory situation was as in the other sites.

The fourth location, Guingnette Fleurie with 123 occupants, was cubicled off with makeshift curtains. There, the large kitchen was run by a French woman as caterer with five Moorish assistants. This caterer also supplied the food for Beaulieu and Luna Park from the same kitchen. When the Colonial Secretary visited this place on the 2nd June, the meal being prepared consisted of roast meat, roast potatoes, petit pois and carrots. He noted that specially built cooking places for mothers to cook food for young children were under construction—this to remedy a justified complaint that meals of the type above described were not suitable for young children.

Such, then, were the living quarters provided for this second contingent of Gibraltarian evacuees. On their arrival, on Saturday 25th May, they were supplied with clean straw to sleep on as mattresses could not be supplied. Some of the evacuees did not take too kindly to this but the great majority settled down on being told that mattesses would be forthcoming next day.

Dr Durante, the Medical Officer in charge of the Evacuation, expressed the view that it would take some time for the evacuees to become acclimatised to communal life, and he feared that the chosen localities would not be suitable as winter quarters since there were no facilities for heating the buildings. He also regretted the fact that the sites were isolated and difficult to control without a motor car. On the whole, the Medical Officer was dissatisfied and apprehensive about the whole situation, and he concluded with a strong plea for the rate of evacuation to be slowed down—otherwise, he said, the risk of ultimate chaos was very real. The whole of the organising staff were showing signs of exhaustion and the risk of epidemic diseases was a very real one.

M Sicot, Director of Political Affairs in French Morocco, also expressed the view that the evacuees were coming in faster than they could be dealt with; he complained that 'they were getting swamped'. Mr Gaggero, too, was requesting that the arrivals scheduled for Monday should not exceed 800, and that those due on Wednesday should be limited to 700.

The response from Gibraltar to these pleas was that, whilst appreciating the difficulties being encountered at the reception end, advantage had to be taken of the ship's capacity, that even at the present rate the evacuation of Category A would not be completed before mid-June, and that it might prove necessary to accelerate!

Meanwhile, the *Gibraltar Chronicle* of Saturday, 25th May informed its readers that His Britannic Majesty's Consul at Casablanca had intimated that there was a shortage of accommodation there. Consequently, voluntary evacuees proceeding to French Morocco under their own arrangements were encouraged to go to some other town unless they had friends in Casablanca.

A third contingent of evacuees, totalling 908 and including 668 children, left Gibraltar aboard the *Kebir* on Sunday, 26th May. A further batch followed on Thursday, 30th May, totalling 920 and including 437 children and 8 hospital cases. These evacuees were also accommodated in the environs of Casablanca, again in large halls with lofty ceilings.

Two of these, the Robinson (capacity 400) and L'Hermitage (capacity 200) were dance halls. The former, more inland and of a more permanent character than those described above, had a restaurant hall with long tables attached and a kitchen. Cubicles were in the process of being erected, and lavatory and washing accommodation and cooking facilities for infants' food could be provided. L'Hermitage, being circular, was more difficult to cubicle off.

A third 'camp' was Ain Chuk. This was some distance out of town, somewhat isolated but healthy. Single, storied barrack rooms formed three sides of a square all enclosed by a wall. The barrack rooms had been specially turned into cubicles by wooden partitions. Forty four rooms had been cubicled into five cubicles, each with a small dining space provided with trestle tables. Since each cubicle could hold forty five persons (if mainly children) the total accommodation available was about 900. Kitchens, lavatories and washing places had been provided, and there was the possibility of erecting additional buildings nearby to accommodate a further 800 persons. It was estimated that this would take three months to complete, but the French authorities subsequently vetoed the idea.

Meanwhile, Dr Durante and his staff in Casablanca were coming under increasing pressure, and the Medical Officer warned that the premises being used to accommodate the evacuees were unsuitable. He pointed out that the sanitary conditions were totally inadequate, that the heat of summer was intolerable whilst there were no heating facilities for winter, there was overcrowding, the evacuees were scattered over a large area and communications between them for medical purposes and the supervision of hygiene were very difficult, there was no provision for the disposal of refuse and there were already signs of accumulation, and the French Municipal Services could not devote adequate attention to the evacuees.

If the use of such quarters was to be continued, added the doctor, a large staff would be required to keep them in order and clean. In the long-term a suitable site would be necessary. Dr Durante concluded with the ominous statement that 'the perseverence in the use of these localities will almost certainly end in serious epidemic outbursts.' It was not the first time that he had uttered such a warning!

To make matters even more difficult, some of the evacuees had been sent from Casablanca to Mazagan, Saffi and Ouadzen right in the interior where shortage of staff made it impossible for the Medical Services to be extended.

Whilst those responsible for the medical welfare of the evacuees were making such pleas for more assistance, the Medical Officer of Health in Gibraltar was complaining to the City Council that, whereas he had initially been given to understand that the French authorities would be able to cope with the medical attention of the evacuees, there were increasing demands being made upon staff from Gibraltar. He concluded that, 'desirable as it may be that we should do all we can for our people there, both for their own sake and for the assistance of the French, we must essentially remember our position here where the risk of casualties from both military and normal causes is at least as great and the consequences of deficiency in our medical and sanitary services might be vastly more catastrophic to the general effort we are now engaged in.'

The MOH further recommended that the evacuees should be encouraged to help themselves. There were amongst the evacuees many individuals who were capable members of the St John Ambulance Association and of the ARP Casualty Service, and plenty of adult males and females with little else to do who could devote themselves to the ordinary internal economy and welfare of the individual communities and thc maintenance of the cleanliness and sanitation of their environs. Indeed, the MOH considered 'the organisation of employment within these little colonies to be almost equally important as the provision of food and shelter', and that if this was not done rapidly 'they will deteriorate into useless dissatisfied and sickly communities for whom nothing can be done.'

Meantime, some efforts were being made in Gibraltar to help out. On the 28th May, the appointment of a Committee by the Governor to establish a voluntary fund to provide additional amenities for the poorer people amongst the evacuees sent to French Morocco was announced in the *Gibraltar Chronicle.* The fund was also to be used to help the same class amongst the men left behind without their wives and no adult to look after their houses. Amongst other things, the committee hoped to establish for the men left in Gibraltar a canteen or canteens for the provision of meals at moderate prices.

Arrangements were also announced by which husbands or other relatives could remit small amounts of money to the evacuees in French Morocco. This had nothing to do with the scheme, later to be evolved, by which persons left in Gibraltar who were responsible for the maintenance of evacuees, would be required to contribute towards such maintenance. To this purpose, a temporary office was opened in the Exchange and Commercial Library Building.

On the 31st May, a further announcement was made that a Flag Day would be held on Saturday, 8th June, the proceeds of which were to go to assist poor people affected by the evacuation scheme.

The month of June, 1940, opened with a Government Notice warning people of the dangers of spreading false reports and statements in relation to the war. On the same day, students from Madrid University demonstrated before the British Embassy shouting 'Gibraltar is Spanish'. The demonstration, which followed upon a recent press campaign for the return of Gibraltar to Spain, was timed to coincide with the arrival of the new British Ambassador to Madrid, Sir Samuel Hoare.

A fifth contingent of Government evacuees left Gibraltar on the *Kebir* on Saturday, 1st June; there were 1,111 evacuees on board, including 509 children and six people in the ship's hospital. On board, too, was the Colonial Secretary, and he must have witnessed some of the problems caused by certain groups of evacuees.

According to the Admiral commanding North Atlantic, in a memorandum to the Governor, the departure of the *Kebir* that day had been delayed for almost three hours, which had caused a corresponding delay in work on another ship waiting to occupy her berth. The Admiral attributed the following causes to the delay:

a. The amount of baggage on the quay was greatly above that expected and took four and a half hours to load. It included heavy crates of goods, and even sewing machines! This, the Admiral pointed out, was contrary to instructions.

b. The police families to be embarked had been formed up by the police in a position where they obstructed the loading of the baggage. Requests that they should be moved had been ignored.

c. Because they remained in this position and because only the aft gang-plank could be used at this time, this party could not be embarked until after the baggage had been loaded.

d. Although visitors were not allowed to accompany evacuees on board, members of the police force had accompanied their families on board, and berthed them where they thought fit, thereby confusing the proper berthing plan of the ship. Very few of them moved when requested to do so.

e. Having gone below, the police remained with their families, and at one time eleven were counted in the forward and midship decks, seated at tables with their families.

The Admiral concluded that it was 'most unfortunate that this delay should have been caused by the conduct of the members of the Police force.'

The *Kebir* eventually left at 6 pm. in calm seas. The Colonial Secretary inspected the troop decks and commented on the excellent work being performed by St John's Ambulance Nurses and Men's detachment and Special Constables. The passengers, he said, were all quiet, cheerful and obedient, and children were sleeping in rows. At the same time, clerical staff of Specials were busy until the late hours preparing and classifying lists, while the military staff and the ship's staff were very helpful and considerate. The boat arrived at Casablanca at 9 am., where the disembarkation proceeded smoothly. In the Custom House opposite French Red Cross ladies dispensed hot tea and other refreshments and worked hard helping the children.

On Monday, 3rd June, the Colonial Secretary held a meeting in Rabat with the French authorities. The latter were now insisting on having advance estimate of probable numbers in three categories:

X: those who could afford to pay for their own better class accommodation;
Y: those who could pay for cheap lodgings;
Z: those who would have to be accommodated communally.

They were also suggesting that a 'camp' should be constructed in or near Casablanca to consist of 500 houses with water, sanitary and cooking arrangements. The houses would have concrete floors, walls of rubble and flat roofs and would be capable of accommodating a family of 5 or 6 persons. The estimated cost of the whole project was 3½ million francs and it was considered that it could be put up in under three months. We shall return to this project later.

The Colonial Secretary, for his part, raised the question of the settlement at Andrea Del-pit where 83 Gibraltarians were 'camped' in workmen's houses, which belonged to a derelict phosphate factory. He said that it had been reported to him that this settlement was some 130 kilometres from Casablanca and 15 kilometres from the nearest small town, that there was no electric light which had necessitated oil lamps being sent, that water and food were scarce, and that the Evacuation Committee had had to go to great expense in sending supplies there by lorry. To the suggestion that this 'camp' should be closed and the inhabitants transferred elsewhere, M Morize, the Secretary General at the Residency, had asked for the matter to be left in abeyance until the evacuation from Gibraltar was complete as then some general 'sorting out' could be arranged.

There had been many complaints about this particular 'camp', and it is therefore interesting to note what Mr A M Dryburgh, subsequently appointed Controller of the Evacuation Scheme, had to say about the place when he visited it. Dryburgh described Andre Del-Pit as a long, wide village street, flanked by double rows of shade trees. On either side were rows of trim, brand new cottages, set in fairly large gardens, with white walls and red tiled roofs. The gardens, of course, were still bare earth since the village had only just been completed. Each house had a comodious kitchen with a large tiled charcoal cooking range and tiled floor, like all the rest of the house, one good-sized living room and two bedrooms. In front of each house was a verandah about six feet by eighteen feet. In the garden there was an outbuilding containing a WC and a washhouse. Dryburgh remarked that he 'would be happy to spend a long holiday in the country in such an ideal cottage.'

Everything in the food-line was ridiculously cheap, and what the local Moors could not supply the Evacuation Commission's lorry would bring from Kourigha and Ouedzem. The former was a large town with several thousand Europeans in it where everything from Lipton's Tea to English cigarettes could be purchased. These goods were bought in bulk at wholesale rates by a Mr Cruz, the officer in charge, who retailed them at cost price—less than Casablanca retail prices.

Most of the people, continued the Controller, were happy and contented but there was a minority who were most disgruntled and anxious to get away. They all wanted to go to Casablanca—which (with Rabat) was just where the French authorities would *not* permit them to go. These malcontents, said

Dryburgh, were largely of the worst class of our people. 'I recognise some of the Shorthorn Farm squatters, others were from La Linea. It is most unfortunate that, by the luck of allotment and owing to the fact that red card (aliens) had to be sent out of Casablanca, these beautiful trim little houses have fallen in too many cases into the hands of people who do not appreciate them and would rather be 'pigging' it ten or twelve in a room in a Casablanca slum.'

The Phosphate Company was pressing on with the pipe-line bringing the water supply. Meanwhile, the Company was providing a squad of Moors and a water cart to do the pumping from the well and deliver the water at the houses. Dryburgh suggested that His Excellency the Governor, through the Consul-General, should most warmly thank the directors of this Company for all that they had done and were doing *free of cost* for the evacuees from Gibraltar.

Dryburgh concluded his report thus: 'We listened patiently to all the grousing and it boils down to discontent with the isolation. This apparently, with many of the people, completely neutralises all the advantages of housing such as they have never enjoyed before and never will again, and cheap and plentiful food which enables them, on 10 francs a day, to feed as they have never done before, on fresh country produce brought to their door. Even the sheep are brought to the outskirts of the village alive, and the mutton sold immediately after slaughtering. The place is very free from mosquitoes and there are far more flies in my Casablanca hotel than there are in the village of Del-Pit.'

Dryburgh added that Cruz had done a good job of work and that he hoped that the mischief-makers (who had been slandering him after all he had done for them) could be transferred to some other place. 'They will miss the cheap living of Andre Del-Pit, which is quite the best of our Stations for cheap and good local produce. Cruz, by buying in quantities and retailing at cost, has made living there exceptionally cheap. The thanks he gets is that slanderers say he is profiteering.'

Returning to the Colonial Secretary's meeting with the French authorities, the former reminded the French that they had initially agreed to provide medical services for the evacuees, whereas subsequent developments had made it necessary for the Gibraltar authorities to retain for duty in Morocco certain doctors needed in Gibraltar. M Morize had replied that the situation had altered since the first discussions as at that time only Casablanca had been contemplated as an evacuee district, whereas circumstances now demanded that the Gibraltarians must be spread over various parts of the country.

Whilst these discussions were taking place, a sixth contingent of evacuees left Gibraltar. The *Kebir* conveyed 1,279 evacuees, which included 626 children and 5 in the ship's hospital; the batch was destined for Fez and Meknes.

On Wednesday, 5th June, 1940, the completion of the evacuation of Dunkirk was reported.

The seventh contingent of Gibraltar evacuees, destined for Rabat, Casablanca and Mogador, left Gibraltar on Thursday, 6th June—1,183, including 572 children and 10 in the ship's hospital. The eighth contingent followed three days later—1,020, including 474 children and 7 in the ship's hospital.

This chapter should not end without a tribute to the 'silent men' who worked so hard to ease the problems arising from such a massive exercise. All too often, their efforts were taken for granted, and rarely did they get the thanks they so richly deserved! Quite the reverse!

Mr Charles Gaggero had been asked by the Governor, at very short notice in late April, to go to Casablanca with Lieutenant-Colonel Hay to investigate the possibilities of an evacuation of civilians to French Morocco. He was still in the process of preparing his report when the Governor informed him that the decision had been made to proceed with the evacuation immediately, and asked him whether he was prepared to lead a committee to organise the whole venture! His acceptance was followed by a hectic period, getting his family to pack, recruiting suitable volunteers to do the work, being briefed by the Colonial Secretary and the Treasurer, and looking after the shiploads of evacuees as they arrived in French Morocco. For Gaggero and his Committee this meant getting up at 5.30 am every time a ship carrying evacuees was scheduled to arrive: the ships usually berthed between 6.30 and 7 am. After an indifferent breakfast in an equally indifferent bar, there followed a full day's work getting the evacuees to their destination and sorting out their luggage and bedding. The Committee would finish at about 5 or 6 in the evening having been on their feet all day. By then they would be too tired to eat and most of them would lie down to sleep with no supper! All they received from the evacuees in exchange was an endless stream of enquiries and complaints; most of them were not paid a penny for their unstinting efforts!

The Camp.

The Camp.

Camp Entrance.

Typical Hut.

Dental Parlour and General Scene.

The Matron's Quarters.

Administrative Staff.

The Kitchen.

The Pantry.

The Luncheon Hour.

At Lunch.

Children at Lunch.

Washing Day.

CAMP GIBRALTAR

WARNING!

Attention is drawn to the Evacuees (Defence) Regulations 1940 made by the Governor and published in the Jamaica Gazette of October 18th, 1940, and to the Rules under these regulations.

Members of the public are warned that no persons may enter Camp Gibraltar without a valid pass signed by the Commandant or a person duly authorised by him.

The penalties for breaches of the above-mentioned Regulations and Rules provide for a fine not exceeding £25.0.0. or imprisonment for a term not exceeding three months or to both such fine and term of imprisonment.

Passes to enter the Camp will not normally be granted to members of the public except in special cases where the purposes of the visit are approved by the Commandant of the Camp.

J. L. WORLLEDGE
Chairman
Gibraltar Camp Committee.

29th October, 1940.

Cabinet Making and Carpentry Shop.

The Sewing Room.

The Canteen.

General Dry Goods Department.

The Fire Station.

The Police Station.

Bound for the City.

Group of Gibraltar Evacuees.

Special Constables.

Jamaica Military Band Entertains at The Camp.

TO NIGHT!!

You Have A Definite Date At The

WARD THEATRE AT 8.30,

To See "Gibraltar Comes To Town"

GRANDIOSO!! MAGNIFICO!!

MUY PRECIOSO!!

FOR THE WAR FUND.

SEATS 3/-, 2/6 and 1/-.

Space donated by "ISSA'S" of King St.

CHAPTER THREE

The War hots up

The events of the next few weeks represented a worsening of the international situation. At the same time, the evacuation of civilians from Gibraltar was extended to include four further contingents.

On Monday, 10th June, 1940, Mussolini declared war on the Allies, and that same evening six Italian ships (the *Collina*, *Pollenzo*, *Libano*, *Levono*, *Olterra* and *Pagao*) attempted to scuttle themselves in Gibraltar Bay. The prompt action of Naval Ratings and Dockyard tugs enabled the majority of them to be successfully beached and one remained afloat and undamaged. Only the *Pagao* succeeded in sinking herself. This was the official version given by the Gibraltar authorities. According to sources from Madrid, the *Collina* had been sunk by a number of bombs placed in different parts of the vessel, and another Italian ship named *Numbolia* had also succeeded in scuttling herself.

Italy's entry into the war did not alter Spain's policy, Madrid announcing an attitude of 'non-belligerency' a few days later. Nonetheless, Malta and Aden were soon to feel the effects of this new development in the war as the Italians proceeded to carry out bombing raids on both places.

In Gibraltar, the Governor announced at a meeting of the Executive Council held on the 11th June, that he had decided to send Mr A M Dryburgh, the Assistant Colonial Secretary, to Morocco to take charge of the Evacuation Scheme. Mr Gaggero, due to his excellent work in connection with the evacuation, would remain 'Head of the Gibraltar Evacuation reception committee.'

The appointment of Dryburgh created problems vis-a-vis the position of Gaggero; the latter, to use his own words, 'obviously decided to resign my commission.' However, Dryburgh persuaded him to change his mind. At a discussion held on Friday, 14th June, it was agreed by the two that the Evacuation Scheme in Morocco should be under a Commission consisting of the following:

Controller, and Chairman of Commission:	Mr A M Dryburgh
Commissioner for General Administration:	Mr C Gaggero
Commissioner for Medical Services:	Dr J A Durante
Commissioner for Finance:	Mr H E Bacarisas
Commissioner for Staff & Outdoor Administration:	Mr P Coll

Dryburgh described Gaggero's attitude as 'most public-spirited and generous.' In recording his personal appreciation of Gaggero, Dryburgh pointed out that 'had he refused to co-operate, in the full and wholehearted manner he is doing, the Scheme at the Moroccan end would have been plunged into chaos, for the success which it has had to date has been entirely due to the initiative and organising ability of Mr Gaggero and to his tact and zeal in putting the Gibraltar point of view and requirements to the French authorities.'

On Wednesday, 12th June, the ninth contingent of Gibraltar evacuees was dispatched to French Morocco. This batch, mainly from the Nectar Factory, Imossi's sheds, North Front Hutments, and Catalan Bay, was described as 'suitable . . . for communal camps.' This was the last sailing scheduled for the meantime. Indeed, the Director of Sea Transport had informed three days earlier that the *Mohamed Ali Kebir* was required for urgent movement to Malta and Alexandria.

On board was Dryburgh to take up his new appointment. The ship arrived at Casablanca at 9.00 am, and the evacuees were despatched to Saffi and Mogador and to the Ain Chok camp in Casablanca. At noon, Lady Liddell gave a Reception on board the ship to the members of the French Red Cross, various French officials who had been most closely connected with the evacuation work, and members of the Gibraltar Committee.

At 6.30 pm. Dryburgh went to the Ain Chok Camp. A difficulty had arisen there regarding the alien (red card) evacuees who were supposed to be going to Rabat. It was found that owing to many of them being members of British families (white cards) it would be impossible to accommodate all these (alien mixed) families in Rabat.

Dryburgh and Gaggero then went to see M Rablot at the Municipality. He made no difficulties about permitting the familites containing aliens going to Del-pit, and the accommodation at Rabat being re-allotted to wholly British families. The only stipulation he insisted on was that the families including aliens should all go to one destination.

Further serious international developments had meanwhile taken place. Paris had fallen to the Germans on the 14th June, and on the same day 1,200 Spanish-Moroccan troops had occupied the International Zone of Tangier. According to Madrid, the occupation had been carried out in the name of the Sultan of Morocco to safeguard the neutrality of the zone. The French authorities had been advised before the occupation took place, and the International status of the zone would continue. (The convention under which the International Zone was administered had been signed by Britain, France and Spain in 1923, with Italy adhering in 1928).

The following day (Saturday, 15th June) more Spanish troops entered Tangier, bringing the estimated total there to 3,500. A Spanish cruiser patrolled in Tangier Bay, and the Spaniards had occupied the aerodrome.

Such developments caused some uneasiness among the British and French population in Tangier, owing to the size of the force, and the additional fear of a food shortage. The British Consul-General in Rabat also expressed concern at the possibility of an invasion of the French Zone from the Spanish Zone or capitulation by France, and the effect this would have on British subjects there. The normal numbers of British in the Zone was about 2,000, but, of course, the situation was now complicated by the recent arrival of 12,000 Gibraltar evacuees. In the circumstances, the Consul-General asked that the possibility of detailing or deviating shipping to the area be studied urgently.

Instead, the Governor of Gibraltar informed Rabat and Casablanca on the 14th June that the situation now required that one more contingent of evacuees be sent to French Morocco! This was to consist mainly of elderly adults, invalids and voluntary evacuees from Category B.

The following day, Dryburgh was informed that suitable accommodation would be required for the entire transfer of the Council Home (for destitutes), comprising a superintendent cook, 48 males, 20 females and three children. Such a home would have to be run as a self-contained independent household. Dryburgh was also asked to consider similar possibilities for the Mental Hospital, consisting of 20 male and 24 female inmates, a matron nurse and staff. The evacuation of these groups was to cause untold problems!

At the same time, the British Consul-General in Tangier was informing Gibraltar that there were 700 Gibraltarians or descendants of Gibraltarians who might wish to leave Tangier, and he asked whether they might be shipped to the French Zone and linked up with the evacuation scheme. About one hundred or more of these people were destitute. The response from Gibraltar was clear enough: 'no useless mouths from Tangier should be allowed to return here!'

The French authorities in Morocco were by now insisting on the erection of a permanent camp of 500 huts to hold 2,500 to 3,000 persons, because important war-production establishments were to commence work at Casablanca and most of the available accommodation being occupied by the evacuees would be required for the workmen and staffs of these establishments. A site at the Roches Noires quarter of Casablanca was suggested, the cost of erection to be borne by H.M. Government.

Dryburgh reported that the Roches Noires Quarter was in the most dangerous part of the town, should there be an air attack or a naval bombardment. It was (a) near the port; (b) surrounded by industrial undertakings, an electrical power plant and oil tanks; (c) near a native hutment area.

Dryburgh expressed doubts about the scheme in the following terms: 'The huts will take about six months to complete if sufficient labour and materials are available. There is said to be an acute shortage here of building material and labour. Who knows what the situation may be in six months time? Who is to supervise the building contract? No one on the Commission is a Civil Engineer or is capable of taking out quantities, or of judging the quality of materials and workmanship, nor, indeed, overworked as we are, will we have much time to visit the site very often.' All these problems were to prove purely academic as things turned out!

On Monday, 17th June, the tenth batch of evacuees set out for French Morocco—896 people, including 59 approved Spanish aliens of whom 28 were children, 56 Gibraltar children and 28 Hospital cases. Many of this contingent had made accommodation arrangements with relatives already in Morocco. The French authorities decided that this additional contingent should be sent to Azemmour (a small village near Mazagan) and to Ain Chok camp in Casablanca. By this time, the only camps still occupied in Casablanca were at Ocean Plage, Le Guingnette and Ain Chok; over 4,000 evacuees had left for private accommodation.

Dryburgh sent an agent to investigate the Azemmour accommodation, and his report was a grim one. The place was a military prison, three kilometres from the village, with barbed wire fence, barred windows and the general aspect of a prison. The Civil Controller was expecting to receive 'dangerous persons' and was arranging accordingly. The accommodation was sufficient only for 650 persons (the French wanted to send 800 there!)

Dryburgh and Gaggero managed to persuade the French authorities to send the evacuees to the camps in Casablanca instead, where there was now ample room available. However, Dryburgh added that the French authorities would not admit that the Azemmour Prison was unsuitable for evacuees, and he feared that they might insist on its being used for future parties. He was to be proved right!

In this contingent were included the Christian Brothers, the Nuns of the Loreto Convent and Jews—they went to accommodation reserved privately. The rest went to Ain Chok.

As this contingent was leaving, the Governor was informing Rabat and Casablanca that the 'interests of the Fortress' required yet more civilians to leave the Rock! The true reason for this can be gauged from the following telegram sent to the Secretary of State in London on the 17th June, 1940: 'In view of deterioration of situation am sending further contingent today comprising women and men regarded as useless. Situation now demands that British subjects women and children from La Linea must be sent to Morocco and if ship available this will be done Wednesday. Please press Admiralty to leave transport available here until this is complete. Women and children La Linea are definite menace to safety of fortress. First sign of trouble they will rush in here or be sent in and nullify evacuation scheme. If refused admission at frontier it will create serious embarrasment to defence and they might be used as shield by unscrupulous enemy.'

By then, France was on the point of capitulation, the Germans were behind the Maginot Line, the Italians were raiding Tunis, Corsica and Malta, and German planes were bombing Malta. In Britain food rationing had begun.

The *Gibraltar Chronicle* of Tuesday, 18th June, 1940, included an announcement setting out the procedure to be followed by the remainder of the persons to be evacuated:

1. ALL parents or guardians with children under 14 years of age who have *NOT* complied with His Excellency's compulsory order as to evacuation, for any reason whatsoever, must report forthwith at the City Hall. (Underlined passages appeared in bold type).

2. All persons in Category 'B' (i.e. females and men over 60 years of age), who have not submitted a certificate of exemption from evacuation, must report forthwith to register their names at the City Hall. They must bring with them family identity cards. These persons will be given a number and their evacuation will take place as speedily as possible as and when shipping is available. A further sailing may take place tomorrow, Wednesday.

In fact, two sailings took place on Wednesday, 19th June. The *Gibel Dersa* took 544 evacuees including 299 children, and the *Mohamed Ali Kebir* transported 924 persons, including 24 children, 39 approved Spanish, and 12 hospital cases. Amongst those on board were Gibraltarians recently arrived from Spain.

310 Gibraltarians had arrived from La Linea on the 18th June and had been accommodated at North Front. From 3.30 pm onwards, they had been supplied with tea, bread and butter, and the children with milk. At 8 pm supper had been given; this had consisted of sandwiches, tea, bread and butter.

On the following day about 355 more people had arrived from La Linea, and they too had been accommodated at North Front. At 8 am all had been served tea, bread and butter, and at 12.30 pm a meal consisting of a meat stew with rice and potatoes had been supplied.

The new arrivals had been registered, all their Evacuation papers prepared and their luggage labelled. At 2 pm. the embarkation had begun, the evacuees being transferred from North Front to the embarkation quay by buses and private cars (placed at the disposal of the City Council by their owners free of charge).

The *Kebir* arrived in Casablanca at 10 am. the following morning and disembarkation commenced at once. Disembarkation from the *Dersa* took place at 2 pm. The passengers were transported to the Casablanca camps. The camp population in Casablanca was now 942 and decreasing rapidly as people found private accommodation outside. Only half of the Ain Chok Camp was by now at the disposal of the Evacuation Commission, the other half having been requisitioned by the French authorities for refugees from France.

By Thursday, 20th June, 1940, the Governor of Gibraltar could inform London that over 11,000 British subjects had been evacuated to French Morocco, but that there were still in Gibraltar about 200 or 300 women and unfit men not employed on war or essential work and who could be classified as 'useless mouths'. There were also some 300/400 British subjects, women and children, left in La Linea who had refused the present opportunity of evacuation but whom the Spanish authorities were threatening to turn out. The Governor added that in every case where wife and family had been evacuated the Spanish Government had turned out the men. There was no accommodation for them in Gibraltar.

On the same day, there was an air-raid warning sounded in Gibraltar at just after 10 am., the ninth air-raid alarm in Gibraltar since the outbreak of war. Most people had made for the nearest ARP shelter, but they had scarcely taken cover when the 'all-clear' was given. It was later officially announced that the alarm had been due to a technical hitch in the air-raid system. A classic case of a 'false alarm' if ever there was one!

On Friday, 21st June, Dryburgh informed that the French authorities had agreed to accept the inmates of the Mental Hospital and that suitable accommodation had been found. More information was forthcoming from Dr Durante who had visited Ber Rechid, a hospital 45 kilometres from Casablanca, to interview the Medical Officer in charge of Neuro-Psychiatrique, a Dr Donnadieu. The latter had informed Dr Durante that the violent cases would be detained there and the milder inoffensive ones would be sent to Ben Ahmed, a Moorish country village about 90 kilometres from Casablanca and 45 kilometres from Ber Rechid. There, there was a Moors' Decrepit Home, and the Gibraltar patients would be permanently housed, together with their attendants, in two wards.

The proposed billets consisted of a large one-storeyed building divided into six compartments each capable of accommodating six (or eight if necessary) patients. They were well ventilated and there was ample ground for exercise. There were only two WC's, which Dr Durante considered insufficient. The pavilion formed part of an institution for poor aged Arabs, but it had been recently built (in fact, added Dr Durante, it was not quite finished and there was no glass on the windows yet). Assurances had been given that there would be complete separation between the Gibraltar inmates and the Arabs. According to Dryburgh, the place was 'not ideal for lunatics, being practically unenclosed and having too many glass doors and windows, but there is no prospect of getting anything more suitable.' Dr Durante was also assured that water was good and abundant, but he himself saw no evidence of any provision for running water. The kitchen was ample and well kept. There was a room which was to be used as a living room for some of the attendants; this was separated from the main pavilion. The rest of the attendants would have to be housed in the same pavilion as the patients, some of the sections being reserved for this purpose.

If a matron accompanied the contingent she would have to be billetted outside. There were two British missionaries who Dr Durante thought might be helpful in this matter. There were beds, but mattresses and bed clothes had to be brought by the patients. Dr Durante emphasised that it was imperative that a nursing staff should accompany these patients and stay to attend to them. Due to the exigencies of the situation, he thought that this locality could be utilised for the purpose of housing the patients, but improvements would probably have to be carried out to render them fit for permanent habitation. Ben Ahmed was to bring untold problems as will be seen!

Whilst the Consul-General in Rabat was informing Gibraltar that Casablanca was now full up, the Governor was informing Rabat and Casablanca that he was endeavouring to arrange a final shipment of evacuees by the *Gibel Dersa.* This shipment was to include the Mental Hospital patients, inmates of the Council Home, and more British subjects from La Linea. Rabat replied that the ship would land the mental cases at Casablanca and the rest at Saffi for Saffi and Mogador.

The *Gibel Dersa's* departure with this contingent, scheduled for Sunday, 23rd June, had to be postponed because of weather conditions. By then, civilians as well as British military and naval servicemen who had recently left Marseilles had been accommodated at Gibraltar and all were reported to be well and determined to fight on.

On that same day, 23rd June, the Casablanca Hospital Authorities informed Dryburgh that all the chronic cases would have to be evacuated from the hospital—these included people unable to walk, or to look after themselves, and Dryburgh predicted that their life in the camps would be an utter misery to them and a terrible burden to their relatives.

These lonely, helpless, chronic invalids or cripples, in Dryburgh's words, 'should never . . . have been submitted to the inhuman purgatory involved by their evacuation. Better, perhaps, that they should have died by violence than endure the hardships they have encountered.' Some of these unfortunates could not even walk to the latrines, and those without relatives had to depend on strangers for assistance. For these incurable and decrepits 'death was the only release from their present misery.'

On Monday, 24th June, 1940, France accepted complete capitulation. The *Gibel Dersa* finally got away from Gibraltar, though the suggestion that she should sail on to Saffi had been vetoed on the grounds that she had neither sufficient coal nor the necessary charts for such a journey. On board were 593 evacuees, including 56 Mental Hospital cases, 73 from the Council Home, 293 British subjects from La Linea, and 225 Gibraltar evacuees from various districts. The Governor announced that no further evacuation was envisaged for the present.

Having dispatched these evacuees to French Morocco, the Governor sent the following telegram to London: 'In event now likely that French Morocco will not continue struggle what steps are proposed regarding 13,000 evacuees from Gibraltar scattered over nine different towns. Quite impossible do anything here.' It would seem that the Gibraltar civilian population had been moved from the frying pan into the fire!

The French authorities refused to allow the latest arrivals to be accommodated in Casablanca, where all accommodation was required by the French themselves for refugees, etc. They insisted on sending them to the Azemmour Camp (the prison described earlier!). By the time the *Dersa* had reached Casablanca, the French authorities had again changed their minds: the new arrivals were to be sent to Saffi and Mogador, except for the inmates of the Mental Hospital and the City Council Home who were to go to Ben Ahmed. The Evacuation Commission had previously made arrangements for the City Council Home inmates to stay in two old dance halls in Rabat, but the French authorities were not now willing to tolerate any more people going to Rabat owing to overcrowding.

The ship arrived at 2 pm. on Tuesday, 25th June, and the Saffi and Mogador contingents left on buses, accompanied by Messrs. Gaggero and Coll and Dr Triay. Mr Dryburgh and Dr Durante attended to the Council Home and Mental Hospital cases. The latter were sent off first to Ber Rechid where the Medical Officer in charge of the Asylum decided to keep about half of them—the more violent cases. The rest were sent on to Ben Ahmed.

The buses failed to return for the City Council inmates and it was 8 pm. before transport could be found for them for the 90 kilometre journey to Ben Ahmed. They had had no meal since leaving Gibraltar, and owing to its being the Day of Mourning in Morocco, with all shops shut, it was impossible to get them a meal whilst awaiting transport. The French Red Cross gave them coffee and biscuits.

At 9 am the following morning, Wednesday 26th June, the Matron and Nursing Sister of the Mental Hospital arrived in Casablanca by bus from Ben Ahmed demanding to go home at once! They appeared to be completely demoralised, the Matron was in tears and both were on the verge of a breakdown. They complained that they had been given to understand in Gibraltar that they were being sent to a properly equipped Mental Hospital, not to a new entirely unfurnished building, with no facilities for restraining the patients (all glass windows and doors, and no unscalable wall). They also complained that Ben Ahmed was unhealthy, full of mosquitoes and entirely without amenities.

In view of this latest development, Dryburgh dropped all other work and, accompanied by Dr Durante and the two women, went to Ben Ahmed to see conditions there at first hand. Although conditions were far from ideal, Dryburgh found that things were not as bad as the sisters had made out. The

Controleur and his wife had done everything possible for the evacuees; both were working very hard. They had arranged an excellent hot meal for the inmates of both Institutions on their arrival late the previous night, and they had also taken bedsteads from the other buildings (occupied by Moorish paupers) and given them to the Gibraltarians.

Seeing the condition of the two nurses the Controleur had put them up in his own house for the night. Dryburgh further observed that the Male Attendants were behaving very well, as was the Superintendant of the Decrepit Home. However, the female Mental Hospital Attendants had taken their cue from the Nursing Sisters and were completely demoralised. The patients were quiet and seemed quite at home, but the City Council Home people were full of complaints—mainly that the food, though good, was not the kind they were accustomed to and that they objected to Moors handling and cooking their food. The City Council Home men had apparently been a bit out of hand and quarrelsome, so Dryburgh arranged for them to be under the discipline of the mental Male Attendants if necessary. There was, of course, overcrowding, and part of the City Council Home people were in the pavilion allotted to the patients. Before leaving, Dryburgh arranged for the sisters to be accommodated in a small hotel.

Whilst these events were taxing the Evacuation Commission in Morocco, security was being tightened up in Gibraltar. On Tuesday, 25th June, 1940, a Government Notice informed that all residents who wished to leave the Fortress for the night would require an Exit Permit. In addition, persons resident in Gibraltar who wished to visit Spain for a period under 24 hours would be required to fill up particulars of their visit in a book kept for the purpose by the police at Four Corners and Waterport. Furthermore, as from Wednesday, 26th June, 1940, Landport Gate (Casemates Square) would be closed at 10 pm. each night.

In London, where bombs were already falling, the question of conditions in Tangier was raised. Mr R A Butler, Under-Secretary for Foreign Affairs, in reply to a question, stated that 'services in the Tangier Administration are reported to be functioning normally.' Asked if the Government was alive to the grave responsibility of trusting a country which was non-belligerent, and harboured at the same time so many of the enemy, Mr Butler said: 'We have been notified by the Spanish Government that they intend to respect the neutrality of Tangier.' Mr Shinwell (Labour) then asked: 'Can we trust the Spanish Government in this matter?' Mr Butler replied that His Majesty's Government accepted the honourable declaration of the Spanish Government.

On Wednesday, 27th June, Dryburgh was informed by the French authorities that all Gibraltar evacuees would have to leave the camps in Casablanca by the following Monday, and that they should go to Azemmour. As the Controller observed, this would involve a further journey for the chronic invalids in crowded buses: a simple matter for the young and fit, but a painful one for old people, some of whom could only sit up with difficulty.

Two days later, the two Nursing Sisters of the Mental Home were back in Dryburgh's office demanding to be sent back to Gibraltar at the first opportunity! They insisted that they could not live in Ben Ahmed—their hotel was poor, the food was bad, there were mosquitoes and rats, and no running water. Dryburgh commented that they seemed to be very little interested in the patients and that their own trials and privations seemed to occupy all their thoughts. Dr Durante was of the opinion that they should be allowed to return to Gibraltar as otherwise they would upset the rest of the staff and completely break down themselves. As Dryburgh said: 'They are useless for work in their present condition and have given the Commission more trouble, and wasted more of our time, than the disposal of a thousand evacuees!'

The month of June, 1940, ended with a report in the *Gibraltar Chronicle* stating that shortly after 5 pm. on Sunday, 30th June, a French plane, which had been manoeuvring to land on the Neutral ground (the area between Gibraltar and the mainland of Spain) had been shot down by machine-gun fire from the Spanish frontier and had crashed into the sea near Western Beach. The report stated that the two occupants of the plane had been killed (the Coroner's Report of the 5th July referred to four dead). It was understood, continued the report, that the plane may have inadvertently infringed Spanish territorial waters or territory.

CHAPTER FOUR

The Unwanted Evacuees

The first days of July 1940 witnessed further dramatic developments in the situation, and these were to have profound effects upon the Gibraltar evacuees. The French no longer wanted their presence in Morocco, the Governor of Gibraltar refused to have them back, and London was determined not to allow them to be sent to the United Kingdom. They had, indeed, become 'the unwanted evacuees.'

Following the capitulation of France, the British Government had decided to prevent the French warships falling into the hands of the Germans. The Vichy Government was therefore presented with three alternatives:

1. that these warships should continue to fight alongside Britain with their own crews on board;
2. that they should sail with reduced crews to British ports—the reduced crews would be repatriated as soon as possible and full compensation paid at the end of the war in either of these two events if the ships were damaged;
3. that they be sailed to the island of Martinique, a French colony in the West Indies, and dimilitarised.

If these terms were not accepted, Britain would attack and destroy them.

When Vichy refused these three alternatives, Force H, the naval force based in Gibraltar under Admiral Sir James Somerville, attacked the French ships at Mers el-Kebir, the military port of Oran in North Africa on the 3rd July, 1940. Force H included the battlecruiser *Hood,* battleships *Valiant* and *Resolution* and the aircraft carrier *Ark Royal.* In the course of the action the French battleship *Bretagne* had blown up and a number of French sailors had been killed.

Whilst these events were taking place, 8,166 French soldiers and 5,196 French sailors were being repatriated in British ships. These men had given up the fight against Germany and had decided to toe the line of the Vichy Government. Since they were not prepared to make any contribution to the war effort and they had to be housed and fed at Britain's expense when food was short (they had been living in camps in the Liverpool district) the British Government had decided to get rid of them. They could not be taken back to France since her ports were either controlled by the Germans or within easy reach of their bombers. The nearest piece of French territory to which they could be shipped was Casablanca in French Morocco.

They were shipped in fifteen freighters, 1,000 men in each, and for the first part of the journey they were attached to another convoy of twenty-four bound for Gibraltar under the command of the senior Commodore, Admiral Sir Arthur Crooke. It was whilst this convoy was at sea that the Oran incident occurred.

Some sixty miles south of Cape St Vincent the convoys separated. Crooke with his twenty-four ships altered round to the eastward and with all escorts proceeded to Gibraltar. The fifteen freighters bulging with French troops and heading towards an unfriendly port and a very uncertain reception, were on their own! We shall return to them shortly.

The worsening of relations between Britain and Vichy France could clearly have some effects on the 13,000 Gibraltarians in French Morocco. On Tuesday, 2nd July, the day before the destruction of the French ships at Oran, the Governor of Gibraltar was informing London that he was concerned about the situation of the Gibraltar evacuees in Morocco and that there was a great deal of anxiety amongst the relatives remaining in Gibraltar. On the 3rd July, the Governor warned London that the possibility of having to evacuate the Gibraltarians had to be faced, and that arrangements ought to be made immediately to have them transferred elsewhere at short notice. However, the Governor was quite adamant that that 'elsewhere' could not be Gibraltar.

The War Cabinet in London was equally adamant that the Gibraltar evacuees should not be sent to the United Kingdom, and they seemed prepared to go to great lengths to prevent this. They even instructed the Admiralty to give orders for only one or two of the ships carrying the French troops to enter Casablanca at a time, and that, until these ships had come out empty, the other ships carrying troops should not be allowed to enter the harbour. It was hardly a realistic suggestion given that the ships carrying the French troops were defenceless freighters in a hostile environment.

Commodore Creighton, in charge of the convoy,who was on board the *Balfe*, gives a graphic description of what happened when his ships were five miles south of Casablanca: '. . . I found a varied assortment of French naval craft heading towards us at high speed from Casablanca. Two destroyers circled us and one hoisted: Stop instantly or you will be sunk.'

I signalled the convoy to stop. Two submarines that had evidently been covering our approach from a submerged position now surfaced close by while a squadron of light bombers roared over almost at masthead height. Things were going to be interesting.

A motor boat was lowered from the destroyer which had signalled the convoy to stop. This brought a party of three sailors, armed with Tommy guns, and a hefty-looking Capitaine de Frégate with a very blue chin, over to the *Balfe*. A jumping-ladder was lowered over the side and they scrambled on board. They marched straight to the bridge where the Capitaine was most disagreeable. He asked me if we had a wireless office. I replied that we had.

Whereupon he ordered one of his men to lock it up. He then strode across the bridge elbowing my dear old master, Captain Woods, out of the way as he did so. This made me see red.

I rushed up to him, grabbed him by the lapels of his coat and said that I objected to his insulting attitude towards the master and took strong exception to the way he was behaving. I pointed out that we had come from England at considerable risk to bring the French soldiers and sailors who did not want to fight any more out to Casablanca to be repatriated.

He began to burble about: 'Assassination criminel des matelots francais à Oran.' He continued a diatribe in this vein which I ignored. When he was spent he asked me if I wished to go into the port.

I replied: 'Certainly, I want to disembark the troops as soon as possible and get my ships away.'

One of the French sailors signalled the destroyer with a lamp and an answer came back to say we could get under way and enter the port. Just before reaching the breakwater we were boarded by a pilot, who was just as unpleasant as the Capitaine and his men, and handled the *Balfe* with deliberate carelessness, bumping her twice against the jetty and badly denting the hull.

After we had berthed, the remainder of the ships came into port in batches of three and I could not help wondering if we should ever be allowed to leave.'

Meanwhile, the War Cabinet continued to insist that the Gibraltar evacuees must not go to the United Kingdom, and they looked around desperately for alternatives. Other parts of the Empire presented great practical difficulties both as regards provision of transport and as regards the selection of a suitable area and arrangements for their reception. An approach to the Government of the Union of South Africa was considered, but nothing seems to have come from this.

On the question of whether they should return to Gibraltar, some difference of opinion arose between the War Cabinet and the Governor. The former stated, on the 4th July, that 'the purpose of evacuation, as far as it was intended to secure the safety and welfare of evacuees, has been to a large extent frustrated by course of events.' The message also assumed that underground shelters already constructed would provide a substantial measure of protection for the evacuees should the need arise.

The Governor replied that 'the purpose of evacuation is primarily to avoid handicapping the Garrison in many obvious respects in the defence of the Fortress. It has always been understood here that in the event of probability of attack the majority of the Civilian population would have to be evacuated. Shelters were designed to give protection against sporadic air attack only and accommodation available in them for 9,000 sitting and standing or less than 3,000 lying down. Moreover some of these shelters must now be taken over for certain essential Military purposes . . . Further, since evacuation started accommodation vacated has been filled by reinforcements to the

Garrison, ammunition and supplies, and if my demands are complied with further reinforcements will arrive.

'The total area of the Rock is only one and seven eighths square miles and of which less than half is habitable and it is impossible to contemplate herding over 20,000 civilians mainly women and children as well as the increased Garrison and Dockyard in this Fortress which is now liable to heavy and sustained air attack as well as attack from land and sea. In this event so small a target is almost certain to be completely gutted by fire, the inhabitants meanwhile being unable to escape.' Indeed, the Governor informed London that he wanted more civilians evacuated from Gibraltar! He concluded by saying: 'I cannot press too strongly for arrangements to be made to transfer the evacuees to some other part of the Empire and for a further 1,000 from here. I would point out that Gibraltarians have a greater claim to sanctuary in England or other parts of the Empire than so many Aliens already accepted.' So much for the War Cabinet's suggestion!

Two days later, the 6th July, the Governor informed London that he had been given to understand that some eighteen ships sent from England to Casablanca with French troops were arriving on the 8th and 9th July. The French authorities in Morocco were likely to insist on these ships taking the Gibraltar evacuees away (they subsequently did!). The Governor now requested an immediate decision as to the destination, repeating that it was quite impossible to accept them in Gibraltar.

The response from London was immediate: the ships in question could only be used for the evacuation of the Gibraltar evacuees to Britain and this was not desirable. The Secretary of State even went to the extent of suggesting that it was difficult to see how the French authorities could insist on their evacuation in the absence of transport facilities. It would appear that London preferred to leave the Gibraltar evacuees at the mercy of the French if the alternative was to take them to Britain!

The Governor pointed out on the following day (the 7th July) that anti-British feeling was growing in French Morocco, that further trouble was bound to occur there, that Spain or the Moors could take advantage of the situation, and that whatever happened the evacuees would be in a dangerous position, whilst their husbands, fathers and relatives in Gibraltar would be in a constant state of anxiety detrimental to morale.

With regard to transferring them to the United Kingdom, the Governor had the following comment to make: '. . . these people are all very trusting in His Majesty's Government, simple and well behaved. They will give far less trouble than many of the English evacuees from London. The children are friendly and polite and not undisciplined and spoilt. I should prefer to have them in my house than many English town children.' The Governor ended with a strong plea for the evacuees to be sent to the United Kingdom—'I cannot accept them here even in transit as I am doing utmost to prepare this place against the scale of attack to which it is now liable, and arrival of evacuees would seriously retard this work as has the arrival of evacuees from south of France.

The fears expressed regarding the safety of the Gibraltar evacuees in Morocco were substantiated by a message from the Consul General in Tangier to the effect that the Rabat Authorities were insisting on their removal at the earliest possible moment as otherwise measures would have to be taken for their protection against a rising tide of anti-British feeling.

Whilst the future of the Gibraltar evacuees was being discussed in these terms, the Rock itself had its first taste of war activity. Three air raids were carried out on Friday, 5th July, but according to official sources in Gibraltar no damage or casualties were reported, and all the bombs dropped into the sea. For the next three days unidentified aircraft were spotted and the anti-aircraft batteries brought into action. No bombs were dropped. The Vichy Government claimed responsibility for this activity as a reprisal for 'the cowardly attacks' on the French Navy. It claimed that at least one large British vessel had been hit, but the Gibraltar authorities insisted that no damage had been done.

In Morocco, the French authorities were now insisting that the Gibraltarians must leave their Zone—indeed they threatened that they would not allow the British ships which had brought the French troops to leave unless they took the evacuees away with them! The Governor suggested to London that approaches should be made to the Portuguese Government with a view to sending them to Madeira and the Azores.

On the 8th July, London telegraphed Gibraltar as follows: 'It has been decided that evacuees in Morocco should be removed on ships now at or about to reach Casablanca. Ultimate destination not yet settled but unlikely to be UK. Urgent enquiries being made as to possibility of reception in Jamaica or South Africa or Azores or Madeira. We understand that ships will take several days for revictualling and this should give them time to collect and embark evacuees and to settle destination.'

It was being assumed by the British authorities at this point that the French would allow the ships to be cleaned and victualled before departure. Commodore Creighton provides an eye-witness account of what actually happened: 'No sooner had the repatriated soldiers disappeared from view than a mass of civilians poured through the dock gates and spilled out across the road leading to the jetty. Black troops forced them forward with rifle buts. I saw as they came closer that they were Europeans; men, women and children of all ages, they stumbled along the baking dusty quayside. Old men and women were collapsing in the heat, young mothers were trying to shield their babies from the sun. Clutching battered suitcases and parcels roughly tied with string these people—there were thousands of them—were a pathetic sight.'

The Commodore was then informed by the Vichy admiral in charge of the port that his ships were under arrest and would remain so until each ship had embarked 1,000 of the civilians now squatting miserably on the quayside. The young French Lieutenant who had brought this message told the Commodore that these people had been driven out of their billets in Casablanca and that they were British subjects. They were the women and children, the old and infirm, of the population of Gibraltar who had been evacuated to French Morocco some weeks ago. 'It was plain', continues the Commodore, 'that the French Admiral, livid after Oran, was intent on using these helpless scraps of humanity to embarrass the British.'

Commodore Creighton insisted that his ships were totally unfit to put to sea with these people. The stores were exhausted, the galleys designed to cater for the score or so officers and crew were quite inadequate for cooking meals for 1,000 people, the field kitchens used by the French troops had been taken ashore when they landed, and there were no lavatories apart from the few for officers and crew.

Not only that, the holds themselves were in a nauseating state and the smell was indescribable. The troops had hardly poked their noses out from below during the fourteen days at sea and the highly insanitary state in which they had left them would have been very dangerous to the health of the evacuees particularly the small children. Furthermore, the Commodore pointed out that the only access to the holds was by vertical iron ladders from the upper decks. While these were adequate for able-bodied troops they were quite impossible for decrepit old people, invalids and children.

These points were conveyed to the Admiral by the British Consul (who was already packing his bags following orders from the French that he had to leave), but to no effect—the ships would remain under arrest in Casablanca until the Gibraltarians had been embarked. Meanwhile, the evacuees, with no food or water, were suffering increasing distress from the sun blazing down on them. A request to the Admiral that they should be allowed to go into some empty cargo sheds nearby until the holds of the ships had been cleaned out was met with a blunt refusal.

Presented with this situation, the Commodore wrote to Admiral North (Admiral Commanding North Atlantic) saying that he intended to send the ships to Gibraltar, to which the Admiral replied 'For Heaven's sake don't—we had enough trouble getting them out.' A Naval Message to the Admiral from Casablanca, dated the 10th July, was more explicit:

'Commodore Creighton and Dryburgh consider convoy ships in their present condition cannot possibly be used for conveyance of women and children for a period of more than 24 hours without serious loss of life. Doctor agrees. French naval authorities now categorically refuse allow departure of ships unless they take away Gibraltarians and won't consider suggestion that these ships should leave pending other arrangements for removing Gibraltarians.

They see no reason why Gibraltarians should not be sent back to Gibraltar by these ships and further onward arrangements made for them there.

Gibraltarians from other places are being continuously sent to Casablanca under new agreement where there is now no accommodation or possible arrangement for them. Return to Gibraltar seems only solution and we suggest should be adopted.'

Despite this, the Governor insisted that the evacuees should not be brought back to Gibraltar. Defence interests, the food situation and lack of accommodation were given as the reasons.

Commodore Creighton then took the law into his own hands and decided to send his ships to Gibraltar anyway! In the circumstances, he had little choice! The French tried to cram on board more than could safely be carried on the upper decks of the first three ships. However, the officers and crews quickly put a stop to this by mingling with the evacuees and getting them to obstruct the efforts of the troops prodding them on board with their rifles. The ploy worked as the evacuees crowded round the gangways screaming, yelling and shoving with the result that the French officer in charge of the black troops was forced to give up the struggle.

Creighton subsequently reported that 'the attitude of the French and the vindictive spirit in which they inflicted great suffering on women, children, the aged and infirm, constitutes a grave blot on the honour and decency of a so called civilised nation that will never be forgotten by any who witnessed it.'

At last, the ships were on their way. Fortunately, the weather was calm and sunny for the six-hour journey to Gibraltar, so having to stay on the upper deck did the evacuees no harm. The Gibraltarians were heading back for home. But what reception awaited them there?

CHAPTER FIVE

Planning for Re-Evacuation

The first three ships, carrying 3,200 evacuees, arrived at Gibraltar on the morning of Thursday, 11th July, 1940. The excitement of seeing the Rock once again after the recent trials and tribulations was soon to be dampened by the news that the evacuees would not be allowed to land!

This news was announced in a press communique in *the Gibraltar Chronicle* under the heading 'Gibraltar families leaving Morocco.'

'His Excellency the Governor regrets to announce that circumstances have arisen necessitating the immediate withdrawal from Morocco of all the Gibraltar families.

It will be realised that had they remained there any longer under present circumstances they would have been liable to undergo extreme discomfort and hardship.

Arrangements are being made for their immediate transfer to another destination, calling at Gibraltar only for replenishment of ships.

IT WILL NOT BE POSSIBLE TO ALLOW ANY LANDING. (my block capitals and underlining), . . . but lists of passengers will be published for information as early as possible.

The public are assured that everything practicable will be done for the comfort and welfare of the passengers, and they are particularly requested not to make personal enquiries which can only hamper and delay the organisation.

It must be borne in mind that it is only by full co-operation of all and some personal sacrifice that it will be possible to avoid many of the dangers and hardships which have and are being experienced by many thousands of families in other parts of Europe.'

In a communication to the War Office, the Governor put the matter rather differently:

'Three ships due from Casablanca tomorrow morning . . . and further ships will follow at short notice. French authorities are filling ships regardless of hygiene and comfort, great anxiety and discontent amongst male relatives here and situation may become ugly as streets full of angry crowd. IN VIEW OF SITUATION ABSOLUTELY IMPOSSIBLE ALLOW EVACUEES TO LAND (my block capitals and underlining), and unless I am in a position to give immediate and definite information of His Majesty's Government's intentions, I shall be faced with a very discontented civil population in the Fortress.'

In actual fact, by the time the press communique had been published London had decided that there was no alternative but to evacuate the Gibraltarians to the United Kingdom and to this end arrangements were already afoot for the provision of additional shipping.

The news that the evacuees were not going to be allowed to land and that their destination was not yet known caused great consternation in Gibraltar. On the morning of the 11th July nearly all shops were closed and many men did not go to work. Crowds assembled in Mackintosh Square (the town centre) where several speeches were made. There was no disorder. Along a Main Street bristling with armed troops a deputation consisting of Mr A J Baldorino and Mr S Benady, City Councillors, and Mr A B M Serfaty, Acting President of the Exchange and Commercial Library, went to Government House to see the Governor.

Commodore Creighton was now stressing very strongly that radical alterations had to be made to the holds of his ships if the evacuees were to make an ocean passage in them.

The Secretary of State in London was also advising the Governor to change his mind about not allowing the evacuees to land in the following terms: 'This question (of evacuees) has been under continuous Ministerial consideration and I want to assure you that we have been doing everything possible to help you. Our difficulties have been much increased by the attitude of the French who have given us practically no time to make adequate arrangements. I am very sorry that (entirely unexpectedly so far as we are concerned) some of the ships for Casablanca have been sent to Gibraltar. *But now that they are at Gibraltar, I cannot help feeling doubt whether in all the circumstances, especially as there appears to be such strong local feeling, it would be wise to prohibit evacuees from disembarking unless they can be transhipped almost immediately for re-evacuation to Madeira or to this country.*' (my italics)

In the face of such pressures, the Governor had no option but to agree to the evacuees landing. This was officially announced on Thursday, 11th July, together with details of plans for further evacuation to the United Kingdom:

'. . . His Excellency the Governor has now been notified by His Majesty's Government that evacuees from Gibraltar should proceed to the United Kingdom. Arrangements are being made accordingly.

2. Gibraltarians from Morocco are now arriving in various ships.

3. As soon as practicable they will be permitted to land *temporarily* but on the clear understanding that they will be reembarked as soon as ships are ready for further journey. This will be in the course of the next few days. For those who have not their own accommodation temporary accommodation will be provided as far as is possible and they will be notified of this on disembarkation.

4. It is hereby impressed upon all concerned that the evacuation to the United Kingdom is now *compulsory* for all those persons in Categories A and B, including those who did not go to Morocco.

(Category A: mothers or guardians and children under 14 years of age. Category B: all females, and males over 60 years of age or who are physically unfit.)

5. Any persons in the above categories employed in an essential service or willing to undertake such essential service, must apply to the Evacuation Committee at the City Hall to be placed in a new evacuation Category C. The numbers in this new category will be kept to an absolute minimum.

6. His Excellency in announcing these revised arrangements calls upon the citizens of Gibraltar to do everything in their power to assist the authorities in carrying out these orders, and feels sure that he can rely on their patriotism and loyal co-operation.'

It will be noted that, whilst giving in to the demands for the evacuees to be allowed to land, the Governor was now extending the categories to be re-evacuated. Many not sent to French Morocco would now find themselves dispatched much further afield!

The announcement that the evacuees would be allowed to land (if only temporarily) relieved the tension in the town. Buses, taxicabs, private motor-cars and gharries were placed at the disposal of the evacuees who showed the effects of their enforced journey from Casablanca and the shortage of food and sleep. There were hundreds of relatives waiting at Waterport Wharf entrance and in Casemates to greet their families. Those without homes were temporarily accommodated at Gavino's Asylum, St John of God Orphanage and elsewhere, and voluntary workers were kept busy in supplying the needs of the evacuees in food and clothing.

A further development in the situation had been the agreement of the Portuguese Government to accept a maximum of 2,500 evacuees in Madeira subject to the express condition that no republican Spaniards could be admitted. London suggested that the number should be limited to 2,000.

Whilst appreciating the offer of the Portuguese Government, and only too happy to accept it, the Governor pointed out to London the difficulties in the way of selecting 2,000 out of a total of 14,000 evacuees to go to Madeira. He added that it was possible that the number could be made up of families in a position to pay for their own accommodation and expense and would volunteer to go to Madeira on that condition, if they knew facilities existed. Lisbon subsequently confirmed that they would prefer if said evacuees were made up of families in a position to pay their expenses.

Subsequent to this, the Gibraltar firm of Messrs. Smith, Imossi & Co. announced in the *Gibraltar Chronicle* that, with the approval of the Government, they were in a position to arrange passages to Madeira for persons and families prepared to furnish a guarantee that whilst in Madeira they would be responsible for the cost of their own accommodation and maintenance. Such passages were only available for people eligible for evacuation under the Civil Evacuation Scheme to the United Kingdom. Passage rates would be £6 First Class; £4 Tourist Class; £2 Third Class. Children from three to twelve years of age would travel at half rate, one child under three years of age would travel free, and additional children under three years of age would pay one quarter fare.

By Saturday, 13th July, the evacuation from Morocco had been completed. The old and infirm and mental hospital cases embarked on the 11th July aboard ss *Bactria,* and they were not allowed to land. Amongst the additional shipping which had by now become available for re-evacuation to Britain was the passenger liner *Athlone Castle*.

A group of Gibraltar women petitioned the Governor on the 15th July along the following lines:

'The inhabitants of this historical and valuable Fortress are very thankful to His Excellency for his good will in connection with the evacuees from Gibraltar.

The public fully sympathises with His Excellency for the huge difficulties he is now facing in respect with re-evacuation. We humbly beg to expose before His Excellency the following which we know quite well would be the only way out of the difficulty.

As it is well known, it is the women principally who object going on a fresh evacuation. This is chiefly due to their not being open to separate themselves from their husbands, their sons, brothers and other relatives. The immense majority of women continue saying that they would rather die in Gibraltar than be re-evacuated.

Having gone through the above with various groups of women of all categories, we have come to the conclusion that the only way out of the said difficulty would be as follows:

1. That H E passes a Law ordering the complete evacuation of ALL the Gibraltarian inhabitants in general, men and women whether fit or unfit for local service, irrespective whether working for Civil, Military or Naval or Airforce.

2. That all the above be evacuated to CANADA, or any other safe place under British flag, and that those persons capable of doing any work for their Country be given such occupation in the same place as they and their relatives be evacuated to.

3. That the Gibraltar Fortress, which is now playing such an important task to our beloved Mother Country, be properly defended by first-class, extra-trained capable men, chosen from the very best throughout the British Empire, thoroughly experienced with War defence and who are apt of handling arms and ammunition. H. E. will evidently realise that, notwithstanding the fact

that Gibraltarians are very patriotic, they have never had the experience of war, and still less to a Fortress attack. In such a case, as their spirit is poor, they would prove to be a nuisance at such a critical period, rather than a help. Due to their lack of courage, they would faint in case of a heavy bombardment.'

It is impossible to assess how representative these views were of the women of Gibraltar since no list of signatures was appended to the petition, but it does show the lengths to which some of them were prepared to go to avoid a further separation from their men. The petition was never made public, which was just as well as it did not reflect too well on the attitude of its authors at a time when so many sacrifices were having to be made in so many countries of the world. One does not suppose that the men of Gibraltar would have taken too kindly to some of the references by their womenfolk to their lack of courage!

Work was proceeding on improvements to the cargo ships due to re-evacuate the Gibraltarians to the United Kingdom. Carpenters were taken off other work in the dockyard to build proper accommodation ladders. Cooking ranges, lavatory buckets and wash-basins were taken on board. Stores and provisions were loaded. Nonetheless, the Governor admitted in a secret telegram to the Secretary of State on the 16th July that '. . . conditions will remain hard for the hundreds of women and children on each vessel.' In a further communication of the same date the Governor admitted that 'whilst bulk of people realise necessity for leaving they are practically certain to refuse to sail in cargo ships in which they were transported from Casablanca in such trying circumstances. Forcible evacuation will be difficult and may be impossible.' For this reason, he pleaded for some passenger liners to be made available.

No doubt with such problems in mind, the *Gibraltar Chronicle* of Thursday, 16th July published an article on 'The Necessity for Evacuation', which seemed to be very much of a propaganda exercise! Under the title 'How People of Gibraltar can show their loyalty', the article went as follows:

'Perhaps one of the cruellest trials of warfare is the necessary separation from their families of those concerned in the defence of their homes, a trial to which the people of Gibraltar have already been subjected, and which they have faced with a most praiseworthy fortitude.

Unfortunately when the first shock of this separation had begun to wear off, the change in the political situation necessitated a return to Gibraltar under conditions of unavoidable discomfort and hardship.

Although this further trial was again overcome with cheerfulness and courage, the experience, still so fresh and all too vivid in the minds of many, has inspired a natural horror and foreboding at the thought of facing yet another breaking of family ties.

Such reactions are understandable but the people of Gibraltar must be called upon to give yet another proof of their well-known level-headedness and loyalty to the sacred cause for whose victory the whole Empire is battling.

They must try to picture to themselves the terrible destructive power of the modern bombing planes and guns, and not be lulled into a sense of false security by the apparent harmlessness of the reconnoitring planes which have recently appeared over the Rock.

SOLDIERS WILL FIGHT HAPPILY IF THEIR FAMILES ARE SAFE.

After one hour of really intensive aerial attack with high explosive and incendiary bombs this town would be in the same plight and conditions as most of the beautiful cities of Northern France, that is to say, a chaotic heap of fiercely blazing ruins.

Although the air-raid shelters provided cannot be too highly praised, it can well be realised that herded together for weeks, perhaps even months, life for the thousands of people concerned would become intolerable.

This totalitarian war which has been forced upon us affects not only the soldier but the entire civil population. The women have their part to play, and one of the most important is to ensure that the morale and the courage of the fighting man remains high and it is certain that every woman knows that those who are fighting for her will do so with brave heart confident that she is safe, and well cared for, rather than wondering whether every crash of exploding bomb or shell had not spelt death or injury to his loved ones.

Sacrifices must be made by all.

It is our privilege to make them with a loyal heart, and if these sacrifices involve hardship and sorrow we must comfort ourselves that they are made in the splendid cause for which we are fighting—the liberty of mankind and the rebirth of an era of peace and prosperity freed from the perpetual menace of brute force and destruction.'

Could there possibly be any connection between this article and the petition by some women of Gibraltar of the previous day?!

In the same edition, a Government Notice announced that the Governor had directed that the following persons had to be evacuated from Gibraltar within the next few days:

a. All children of both sexes under the age of 17 years on the 1st August, 1940.

b. All women except those who, on the recommendation of the Controller of Man Power, are considered by the Gibraltar Evacuation Committee to be in an essential service.

c. All men who are physically unfit.

d. All men above the age of 45 years except those who on the recommendation of the Controller of Man Power are considered by the Gibraltar Evacuation Committee to be in an essential service.

2. All men between the ages of 17 and 45 on the 1st August, 1940, may apply to the Committee to be evacuated. Applicants will be evacuated if not engaged in essential services and not required for such services.

Also in this edition, the *Gibraltar Chronicle* published a much deserved 'thank you' to the officers and crews of the ships which had brought the Gibraltarian evacuees from Casablanca as follows:

'Many readers have asked us through the medium of the *Gibraltar Chronicle* to express their sincere thanks and deep gratitude for the kindness, attention and sacrifice of personal comfort shown by the officers and crew of the British ships in which they were evacuated from Morocco.

One correspondent writes: 'In such circumstances when duty demands the sternest attention, they could find it possible to dispense the human touch, doing all they could to alleviate and make easier our adversities. We can never forget this and hope and trust that these men of the sea, who so faithfully serve their Empire, may have their reward.'

The name of Commodore Creighton ought to have been inscribed at the top of this article! Gibraltarians should never forget this man's name!

The problems created by the need to re-evacuate the Gibraltar civilian population were capitalised upon by the propaganda agencies of the Axis Powers. On the 16th July, 1940, a German broadcast aimed for North America announced that, according to the Italian agency Stefanie from Madrid the situation in Gibraltar was becoming increasingly serious because of the approaching date fixed for the evacuation of the population. According to the report, the transports were ready to sail but the whole population of Gibraltar was strongly protesting against the plans of evacuation measures. The fleet and military authorities had had to intervene time and time again in order to disperse demonstrating crowds. Similar reports of discontent among the population on account of the evacuation were being made in German and Italian broadcasts. A broadcast from Rome on the 14th July had stated that as a reprisal for the demonstrations of discontent the British authorities had had to suspend all work and had to order the shops to be closed down. The report continued that in view of the total stoppage of the town's life activities all would have to be evacuated because of the lack of food.

Such reports were described by the Governor of Gibraltar as 'greatly exaggerated.' Certainly the people were upset by the recent trying experiences, caused largely by the antagonistic treatment from many of the French people, particularly officials. However, every sympathy had been shown to these people in their distress, and reports as to reprisal were without foundation.

The realities of war were brought home to the inhabitants of Gibraltar in the early hours of the morning of Thursday, 18th July, 1940, when two aircraft raided the town dropping fifteen heavy bombs on the Catchment areas and buildings on the southern half of the Rock. These brought the first civilian casualties of the war—three died: Sister Lorcan O'Connor (aged 71), Luis Dallia (aged 51) and his wife Maria Dallia. The nun had been in Gibraltar for fifty years. Also killed was one RA Gunner, and several other slight injuries were incurred.

London was by now complaining that the numbers to be evacuated to the United Kingdom kept on increasing. The original figure of 13,000 had now gone up to 16,000! Because of accommodation difficulties in the United Kingdom it was only possible to accept 11,000 (i.e. the original figure of 13,000 less the 2,000 going to Madeira).

In addition, the British Government insisted that:

a. No aliens should be included amongst the evacuees.

b. It would be desirable that on arrival in the United Kingdom the evacuees of similar social standing should be accommodated together, and that it would greatly facilitate arrangements if such persons as far as possible travelled in the same ships.

c. Every person over sixteen years of age should be provided with an Identity Document including a photograph attached to it.

d. All evacuees should be medically examined before embarkation, that seriously ill people should not be sent, and that persons suffering from infectious or contagious diseases should be segregated on a single ship with adequate medical supervision. The *Athlone Castle* was suggested for this purpose.

The Governor replied to the complaint about increasing numbers to be evacuated thus:

'Situation is that this is a Fortress liable to heavy and immediate attack and there should be no civilians whereas there are 22,000. The 13,000 was the number evacuated to Morocco and more would have been sent had situation there not altered. Am sending available ships to full capacity which will absorb 10,000 and endeavours being made to send 2,000 to Madeira. That will still leave 4,000 who will be a serious handicap to defence if left here.'

By Friday, 19th July, thirteen ships with a total capacity for 6,250 evacuees were ready to sail. A further six ships with accommodation for 2,200 would be ready by the 27th July. With the *Athlone Castle* capable of taking 1,672 evacuees, the total accommodation available would be 10,122. The stage was set for the re-evacuation!

CHAPTER SIX

The Re-Evacuation and Reception in Britain

The term 're-evacuation' is not, strictly speaking, the correct one to use when referring to the mass exodus of civilians from Gibraltar which took place in the months of July and August, 1940, since many of those evacuated had not endured the trials and tribulations of French Morocco. Nevertheless, for the bulk of those now sent to the United Kingdom and Madeira it was their second departure from home in a very short space of time. Between the 19th July and the 20th August just over 11,000 civilians were sent to the United Kingdom, where ironically they were to suffer the horrors of 'the Battle of Britain' whilst the Fortress of Gibraltar remained relatively free from war action, and under 2,000 (the lucky ones!) went to Madeira.

On Friday, 19th July, 1940, the *Royal Ulsterman* set off on the two-day journey to Madeira. On board were 89 men, 250 women and 110 children (a total of 449); these were families who could afford to pay for their own accommodation and upkeep. All were British subjects with the exception of three technical Spaniards who had lived in Gibraltar most of their lives, and three Portuguese. Also on board was the wife of the Governor of Gibraltar, Lady Liddell.

Whilst this journey was under way, the Governor was informing Lisbon that indications now were that it might not be possible to make up the complement of 2,000 for Madeira from persons able to support themselves. He asked whether it would be acceptable to the Portuguese authorities for the numbers to be made up by a contingent of families who would have to be maintained in camps or at the cheapest possible rate of expense to the Gibraltar Government.

Two days later, Sunday 21st July, the movement of civilians to the United Kingdom began with the departure in convoy of the *Avoceta* (146 Gibraltar evacuees and about 100 refugees from Lisbon who had arrived on the ship), the *Clan McBean* (213 evacuees), and the *Bactria.* On board the last named ship were the Mental Hospital inmates consisting of 19 men, 24 women accompanied by a staff of two nurses, six male and four female attendants. Also on board were the inmates of the City Poor House, comprising 43 men, 15 women, 4 children with a Matron in charge and the families of the attendants consisting of 5 men, 10 women and 7 children. On board the *Avoceta* was Dryburgh, the Chief Assistant Secretary who had been the Controller of the Evacuation Scheme in Morocco—he was to act as liaison Officer between the Colonial Office and other Home authorities and the evacuees. On the same day, the *Ulster Monarch,* with 282 evacuees on board, set off on the much less hazardous journey to Madeira.

Dryburgh, with his usual penchant for detail, described his voyage on the *Avoceta,* a most unpleasant voyage lasting sixteen days. 'On boarding the *Avoceta* I found there was no accommodation for me—her cabins were all occupied by people who got on at Lisbon—Poles, Czechs, French, British from Geneva (League Secretariat), and from Spain, etc. I managed to get a 'cubby hole' in the stern under the gun—in other times probably the ship's carpenter's bunk. This I shared with a Lance Corporal of the Royal Engineers going home on a course.

'The food was deplorable. Irish stew twice a day whilst the fresh meat lasted; thereafter bully beef and biscuits for the last five or six days. The Captain had a long story to tell of Curton keeping him and his Chief Steward hanging about outside the door of the Food Control office for seven hours and then refusing all supplies. The lack of any fresh fruit or vegetables was particularly unpleasant. So was the complete absence of all liquor except ship's tea! The evacuees fared better, as they had their own supplies of food, and fared better in the holds than we did in the saloon.

'There were only 146 evacuees aboard so conditions were pretty good and there was no sickness. They all landed in good shape—but lousy, owing to the careless habits of one or two families which of course infected the rest.'

Already, the polemic between London and Gibraltar was going on as to the number of evacuees which could be accepted in the United Kingdom. On the 22nd July, the Secretary of State for the Colonies informed the Governor that no more than 11,000 evacuees could be accepted in Britain. 'I am sorry it has not been possible to go further forward meeting your representations, but the decision, which arises from the situation as regards accommodation here has been reached after full consideration of military factors by the War Office who concur in it.'

With the first and preliminary batch of evacuees away, the Gibraltar authorities then proceeded to the main task of evacuation in earnest. A Government Notice of the 22nd July informed the public that embarkation of evacuees would commence on the 25th July. Those concerned were warned that failure to comply with any of the Orders made under the Defence Regulations rendered the offender liable on summary conviction to a fine of £100 as well as imprisonment for a term of three months.

The first ship scheduled for departure was the *Athlone Castle* (code letter 'D'), and evacuees earmarked for this voyage were instructed to be with their baggage, which had to be clearly marked with name, address, registration number and the letter 'D', at one of the three following places: Casemates Square, Line Wall opposite 'The Haven', the taxi stand at the bottom of Scud Hill.

Mattresses and blankets were not required on the voyage but would have to be taken for use later. Knife, fork, spoon, plate, cup or mug would also be required later and should therefore be carried in the hand baggage. The evacuees were advised to take light refreshments for the day of embarkation as the first meal on board would be supper. The conveyance of evacuees to Waterport would be by bus, and their luggage would be taken by lorry. All the necessary work would be done by military personnel, and no private cars would be allowed in the vicinity of Waterport.

The *Athlone Castle* left Gibraltar on Friday, 26th July, in the evening, carrying 198 men, including eleven control staff with Mr John Haynes in charge, 769 women including a midwife and ten Voluntary Aid Detachment, and 630 children. The bulk of this contingent were aged and invalids, maternity cases and families with babies. The ship's doctor was in medical charge as no doctors could be spared from Gibraltar. Included in the above numbers were one youth and two women technically Spanish aliens vouched for. The journey was relatively uneventful, and despite the long detours necessitated by the exigencies of war, the *Athlone Castle* arrived safely in Liverpool on Friday, 1st August, at noon, after just under a week at sea.

On the very day that these evacuees were being embarked on the *Athlone Castle,* Gibraltar had some unwelcome visitors! In the early hours of the morning of the 26th July, about four aircraft approached Gibraltar from the north and were engaged by all AA guns. The raid lasted 22 minutes and bombs were dropped in the following places:

(a) six bombs on the west side of the road to Four Corners between the Cross of Sacrifice and the remaining buildings of Blands foundry;
(b) one bomb fifteen yards north of the cross of Sacrifice;
(c) one bomb on the north face of the Rock just below Rock Gun;
(d) two bombs in the sea near the Commercial Mole;
(e) two bombs on the east side of Europa Road near the Pumping Station;
(f) one bomb on the Europa Road Tank;
(g) two bombs on the road just south of Europa Road Tank;
(h) three bombs on Engineer's Road thirty yards south of Europa Road Tank;
(i) four bombs in the sea off Eastern Beach;
(j) four bombs in the sea off Europa Point;
(k) one bomb in the Holy land;
(l) one bomb on the sandbank directly below the Holy Land.

Casualties included one civilian female killed, 21 wounded and taken to hospital and 15 slightly wounded, as well as three wounded soldiers. Damage was sustained to the Pumping Station on Europa Road and to buildings in that area. The Naval W/T station at North Front sustained slight damage.

The Detached Mole reported that Algeciras had blacked out as soon as the first searchlight had been exposed, the lights being put on again shortly after the firing had ceased. At 11.30 pm more aircraft approached but they did not succeed in flying over the Rock, and this time no bombs were dropped.

In the evening of the following day, Saturday 27th July, three more vessels set off for the United Kingdom with evacuees. The *Ulster Monarch* and the *Royal Ulsterman,* back from their recent trips to Madeira, were joined by the *Royal Scotsman.* The *Ulster Monarch* carried 640 evacuees, the *Royal Ulsterman* 650, and the *Royal Scotsman* 633. All the ships arrived safely at their destinations on Monday, 5th August, after a ten-day journey.

There was another air raid on Gibraltar on Sunday, 28th July, and a mysterious explosion at North Front shortly after 11 am on Monday, 29th July, in the vicinity of the naval Wireless Station. This 'accident', the cause of which was not given, resulted in the death of three Black Watch 'other ranks'. The Gibraltar Museum was closed on the following day, the 30th July, and in the evening another batch of ships sailed for the United Kingdom.

In a convoy of 24 ships were the 15 which had taken the French troops to Casablanca and the Gibraltar evacuees from there to Gibraltar. Amongst these were the *Euryades* (481 evacuees), the *City of Evansville* (496), the *Dromore Castle* (364), the *Beckenham* (391), the *Belgravian* (363), the *Balfe* (413), the *Strategist* (505), the *Baharistan* (303), the *Swinburne* (250), the *City of Windsor* (467, including diabetic cases and other persons requiring medical attention, and maternity cases), the *Brittany* (718), and the *Calumet* (259), including eleven prisoners detained under Defence Security Regulations).

It was a precarious journey. Escorts were scarce as they were needed for convoys more vital to the prosecution of the war. The main thing which haunted Commodore Creighton, on board the *Balfe,* on the twelve-day voyage was the lack of life-saving gear. Two lifeboats designed between them to carry the normal crew of thirty would not be much use among all the evacuees! Although every raft and lifebelt that could be found in Gibraltar had been collected and distributed amongst the ships these 'were about as useful among so many as a lorry would be for evacuating a battalion of soldiers in a hurry.' Moreover, added the Commodore, 'I did not fancy the chances of these excitable people, young, old, women and children of every age and mentality, doing the right thing and not panicking in an emergency, on board freighters that would sink in a matter of seconds—engulfing them before ever they got out of the holds. If this convoy was attacked, and it had only one escort, it could result in one of the worst maritime disasters in history.' Fortunately, there was no attack!

There were no doctors in any of the ships to attend to the old and sick or to bring the babies into the world. The Commodore observed: 'This last job was done by women. The mother-to-be was screened off with canvas and at the first cries of the new infant a cheer would go up from the rest of the company in the hold.' One morning a signal was received from the master of the *John Duncan* (incidentally, a ship not mentioned in the official list of vessels carrying evacuees). The message read: 'Good morning, Commodore. Happy to inform you that Master Alfonso Duncan Alvarez arrived this morning. Mother and son doing well.'

The following day the commodore was able to retaliate with a signal of his own. 'We too are fruitful. Master James Balfe Gomez has put in an appearance. Mother and baby doing well.' Luckily, the weather remained fine and all the new-born babies (twelve were born on this trip) survived. On the other hand, the anxiety, strain, discomfort and fear took its toll on the old people, five of whom died en route).

As the convoy passed Rathlin Island off the north coast of Ireland and nearing the Isle of Man, the master of the *City of Windsor* requested permission to put in to Liverpool as he was desperately in need of sugar essential for the diabetics on board. The request was refused on the advice of the commanding officer of the sloop escorting the convoy. He said that he did not think it a good idea for the ship to leave the convoy as the enemy had a habit of sending a bomber flying up and down the Irish Sea on the lookout for stray merchant ships. The Gibraltarian evacuees were eventually landed in South Wales.

By the end of the month of July, 1940, 9,200 persons had been evacuated to the United Kingdom, and 731 to Madeira. Still to go were 1,800 to the United Kingdom, and 1,300 to Madeira. Even after the latter had gone, reported the Governor, there would still remain in Gibraltar more than 1,700 women and children and old and unfit men, with the prospect of further 'useless mouths' to come! London again expressed regret but there could be no question for the moment of admitting any more evacuees to the United Kingdom, and little prospect of finding an alternative place in the immediate future.

At the same time, the Governor was informed that the *Neuralia* would be sent to Gibraltar. This vessel was to be used to take the balance of evacuees to Madeira, then return to Gibraltar to transport more evacuees to the United Kingdom. It had also been intended to use the *Mohamed Ali Kebir* for the transportation of evacuees to Britain, but this ship was torpedoed and sunk in the Atlantic before it could reach Gibraltar.

The *Neuralia* sailed for Madeira on Saturday, 10th August, with 1,248 evacuees on board. She then returned to Gibraltar, and on Thursday, 20th August she set off for the United Kingdom with 1,786 evacuees; she arrived safely at her destination on Wednesday, 4th September.

At the end of August, 1940, the Governor of Gibraltar informed London that since the departure of the *Neuralia* he had been carefully reviewing the situation, and that there were still in Gibraltar 1,650 registered for evacuation. He again insisted that it was of the utmost importance that these be evacuated at the earliest opportunity. He added that a further 1,400 could become redundant as civil and commercial acitivities in Gibraltar continued to decline. He proposed to London that the Argentine be investigated as a possible destination—'language and other conditions there are suitable and there is already a Gibraltar colony in that country as some years ago emigration from here was a regular feature.'

How was Gibraltar itself standing up to the war? The air raids of the 26th and 28th July have already been noted. On Friday, 2nd August, the BBC announced that enemy stations were broadcasting tales of havoc at Gibraltar caused by air raids. The true facts, stated the BBC, were that the damage caused had been negligible.

A report by Reuter's news service, published on the 9th August, was headlined: 'GIBRALTAR STANDS READY. Italian Raiders have tasted its mettle.' The report continued:

'As the war in the Mediterranean gathers momentum, the fortress of Gibraltar stands ready for any eventuality from land, sea or air. Italian raiders have already tasted its mettle. Hitherto they have been able to cross the Rock only three times, dropping bombs which caused negligible damage—none at all to military objectives.

With the evacuation of thousands of civilians, the Rock is daily assuming a more purely military aspect. Activity is intense as innumerable workmen labour in the great heat to make Gibraltar even stronger. All the troops are in the highest spirits.'

Six days later, the 15th August, Reuter's special correspondent gave the following eye-witness account under the headline 'ITALIAN MERCHANTMEN SWEPT FROM THE SEAS.'

'I have just returned from a 48-hour cruise in the straits of Gibraltar on board a British warship. The experience has convinced me that no ship can pass into or out of the Mediterranean unless the Royal Navy so desired. Italian merchant vessels, like Italy's 'fighting' ships, have been swept from the surface. Before Italy declared war the Contraband Control was stopping at least twelve Italian merchantmen every day. They have now vanished and traffic to and from Italian ports has ceased. During 48 hours' steaming only six vessels appeared. They were all Spanish plying between Spain and Spanish Morocco.'

Italy was at this time expressing the hope that Spain would seize Gibraltar and close the western exit of the Mediterranean thus trapping the British Navy in the Mediterranean!

On the 20th August, further bombing raids were carried out on Gibraltar. In the first raid bombs were dropped in the sea and the aircraft was brought down in the sea off Europa Point. In the second raid bombs were dropped on the Rock causing a fire to break out. This was quickly brought under control and no appreciable damage was caused, and no casualties were reported.

An intensified campaign was being conducted in the Spanish press in early August for the return of Gibraltar, whilst in Gibraltar itself an order from the Governor was published to the effect that all hotels, taverns, beershops, clubs and canteens had to close by 9.30 pm.

Whilst those who remained on the Rock, then, enjoyed a relatively trouble-free life, those evacuated to the United Kingdom were not so fortunate! As the Gibraltar evacuees reached the United Kingdom, fierce air battles were taking place over that country—the 'Battle of Britain' had begun! From mid-August, throughout September, Britain, and London in particular, was being pounded by German bombs.

The arrangements for the reception of the evacuees in the United Kingdom were placed in the hands of the Ministry of Health and, according to Dryburgh, were being very well handled. The ships were arriving at various places on the West Coast from Glasgow to Avenmouth. They were met by Ministry of Health officials and doctors, medically examined, fed, put up for the night and de-loused, and when clean, forwarded to London and billetted in various centres where further disinfection and medical examination took place.

Many of the evacuees were billetted in the Kensington area: 800 in Kensington Palace Mansions (North Block), 1,000 in the Royal Palace Hotel in Kensington High Street, 1,000 in Marlborough Court, 300 in the British Empire Hotel, 250 in the Broadwalk Hotel, and 550 in Star Block B, North End House. One thousand went to Fulham Road Receiving Centre, 800 to the Grafton Hotel in Tottenham Court Road, 750 to the Empress Hall, 750 to Anerley Receiving Centre, 750 to Dr Barnardo's Homes in Barkingside, 500 to the Empire Pool in Wembley, 1,850 to the National, Shelbourne and Raglan Hotels in Bedford Way, and 1,543 to Lancaster Gate. (This was the distribution as reported by Dryburgh on the 17th August—a further 1,786 evacuees arrived in early September on board the *Neuralia*—see above, page 48).

Dryburgh remarked that from conversations he had overhead he had gathered that the residents of Kensington were not very pleased at this invasion of the sacred precincts of De Vere Gardens. The hanging out of the washing from the windows and the sitting about on the pavement in front of the buildings was trying Kensington hard!

On the 8th August, 1940, the *Evening Standard* published an interesting story on how Gibraltar families were settling down to their new life in London:

'GIBRALTAR ARRIVES AT KENSINGTON'
HIGH STREET FILLED WITH CHEERFUL STRANGERS

'A thousand civilian refugees are being housed in the Royal Palace Hotel, Kensington, and today, High Street, Kensington is thronged with olive skinned strangers, most of them very cheerful. They like the look of London, especially Kensington Gardens. And, unlike the refugees from the South of France, they had a pleasant and comfortable voyage, even though it did take fifteen days instead of five.

But that does not mean that Mr Forbes, the manager of the hotel, has an easy problem in catering for them, nor that the 120 members of the South Kensington's Women's Voluntary Service, who are helping him, have an easy task.

WORKING HARD

Miss Anderson, head of the South Kensington WVS, and her second-in-command, Mrs H John Lewin, have been on their feet from early morning until late at night for days past. Their working day at the moment is dawn to midnight. But they hope soon to get fully organised help from the refugees themselves. Pillie Fuller, Nieves Bowden and Helen Bossano, three jolly, laughing, devil-may-care young women who went to the same school in 'Gib', are already getting down to work at the hotel. They scrub and clean, they help in the kitchen and in the dining-room, which used to be the ball-room. They take milk upstairs for the babies and interpret for the mothers. Pillie, aged 23 and Helen, aged 19, are unmarried. Nieves is 26. Her name means 'Snow' and she has a husband in the Gibraltar police.

A LOVELY TRIP

They were all educated at the Loreto Convent in Convent-street. 'There are two Loreto Convents in Gibraltar', said Pillie, 'so don't say we were at the other one. I was working in the Imperial Censorship before I came away, and before then I was a draughtswoman in an architect's office.' Helen should be useful, for she was a St John Ambulance worker. 'We had a lovely trip', said Mrs Bowden. 'None of us has been to England before, and the delightful green fields, with the animals and houses looking like toys, were a joy to see.'

All three girls wanted me to mention two Christian Brothers from the College of the Sacred Heart in Gibraltar, Brother Russell and Brother O'Brien. 'How they worked!', said Mrs Bowden. 'They were simply wonderful with everybody on board.'

LAUGH AT RAIDS

Pillie and Helen hope to get work here before very long. Mrs Bowden hopes her husband may be able to join her soon. These Gibraltar people laugh at the air raids they have had here. 'Bombs cannot hurt the Rock', said one man, 'nothing can hurt it.'

Most of the catering in the various 'hostels' was in the hands of 'Lyons'. Both Dryburgh and Major Patron, Chairman of the Gibraltar Advisory Committee formed by the Ministry of Health, reported that the only complaints about the food had come from the few places in which the Hotel

Manager had been allowed the catering contract. Dryburgh seemed to think that the Ministry of Health would soon be cancelling all these and giving the whole show to Lyons.

Reporting on the 4th September, Dryburgh stated that 'going round the billets the only serious complaint one hears is about food, and on further enquiry it is the kind of food and the way of cooking it that gives rise to complaint. The quantity and quality is on the whole quite good though, of course, catering being on such a large scale, there is bound from time to time to be one dish put up which has "gone off" a bit.'

Dryburgh visited most of the 'hostels' and found that the people were comfortably housed and provided with good camp beds with excellent Government linen and blankets (their own mattresses were stored at central depots). The evacuees were visited daily by a doctor and nursing staff, and the Women's Voluntary Service had done sterling work in cleaning up the hotels, arranging beds and making the places ready generally for the reception of the evacuees. They were still working there after the arrival of the evacuees, mostly in a supervisory capacity. The idea was that the evacuees would keep their own quarters clean, and serve and look after themselves, and according to Dryburgh, this was being done in most billets without any trouble. However, there were a few cases of people who imagined that the ladies of the WVS were going to be their servants for the duration of the War! Patron added that the 'WVS rendered excellent help at all billets, especially with the children, and a large debt of gratitude is due to them by the inhabitants of Gibraltar.'

Patron described the medical arrangements as excellent; 'in fact, too good, as they involved a much stricter discipline than many have been accustomed to.' Conditions, he said, varied at the different billets; for example, the Empress Hall, which was one of the London County Council Centres, was only really suitable for the rougher and less educated of the evacuees. There was no privacy, which greatly increased the hardships, due to people of all classes being together, and the sleeping accommodation was specially poor. No visitors were allowed in to see them and there was a much stricter discipline than in other centres. On the other hand, due to the space available and the entertainments organised, people with no objection to leading a communal life were quite happy there, which, claimed Patron, emphasized the need for a certain amount of segregation to be tactfully carried out.

This matter of the segregation of people according to their standard of cleanliness and education was one in which Patron strongly believed. The United Kingdom authorities had asked Gibraltar to despatch the evacuees in groups of similar social standing, but the rush with which the re-evacuation had taken place had made this impracticable. This, said Patron, had greatly complicated matters at the reception end and he now hoped that gradually a small amount of moves would be made so that friends and relations could be kept together as far as possible.

Another problem which arose at this stage was over the question of payment of those officers who had been placed in charge of the billets. The British authorities held firmly to the view that the administration work in each billet should be done voluntarily, and some of the men, accustomed to payment in Morocco, were not too happy at this decision. Dryburgh hoped to persuade them to keep on working on a voluntary basis, and in the meantime he had arranged for the payment of £5 for the voyage to the Head Man on each ship and £3 to his assistants. 'From all accounts I have received, and my own experience on the *Avoceta,* this money was well earned, for most of the people are terribly bad sailors, with no idea of making any effort, and would have died from starvation, filth and neglect, if not looked after by somebody with energy and initiative.'

Archbishop Amigo, the Roman Catholic Bishop of Southwark and a Gibraltarian, interested himself in the welfare of his compatriots, particularly in the matter of arranging educational facilities for the children of the evacuees. The idea was, if possible, to have a School in the Kensington area and another in the Bloomsbury area, where most of the billets were. The Loreto Nuns had already gone off to Ireland, but most of the Christian Brothers were still in England and efforts were being made to enlist their aid. Such a hope never materialised, as will be seen later!

The question of the evacuees going out to work created considerable problems. Initially, the authorities took the view that they should not be allowed to take on jobs, the reasons for this being three-fold:

a. it would cause them to disperse and render re-evacuation difficult;

b. if some went out and worked for wages it would cause discontent amongst the others who had to do the house cleaning and kitchen work of the billets without salary;

c. to start trying to assess how much persons earning money should contribute for maintenance in cases in which they and/or their families remained in the hostels was a formidable task the Ministry of Health wished to avoid.

It was therefore decided that anybody who found employment had to leave the Scheme and had to give a guarantee that he would not call for further assistance. This was also to apply to people leaving the billets for any reason whatsoever.

Pressure from the evacuees, however, proved too strong, and in early September the Ministry of Health had to change its mind and, in consultation with the Colonial Office and the Ministry of Labour, agreed to allow the evacuees to seek employment. It was felt by the authorities that evacuees who earned sufficient money to be self-supporting should live outside the

Centres. If they preferred to stay in the Centres, it could be that they would have to contribute towards the cost of their maintenance.

A Ladies' Committee was formed, of ladies who talked Spanish and knew the people, and arrangements were made that one should visit each billet and talk to the evacuees and try to keep them happy and give as much assistance as possible.

A Fund was also raised to get the evacuees small amenities and comforts such as cots, toys and Kindergarten supplies for the small children and contributing to the payment of assistants to look after them. Outings were arranged, cigarettes and radio sets were provided, materials were bought to give employment to some of the women. Cases of special hardship were helped with funds for visiting sick relations or rejoining relatives. Thanks to the generosity of Mrs Mackintosh, who contributed £2,500, the Fund soon passed the £3,000 mark. However, Patron expressed some disappointment at the little support for the Fund being received from Gibraltar, and he asked for some publicity to be given to it there.

The practice of making deductions from the salaries of wage earners in Gibraltar to help defray the cost of maintaining their families in London gave rise to practical difficulties. The people in the Centres, other than the five County Council places, were expected to do all the housework. Many of the women were refusing to carry out this work on the grounds that their husbands were paying a lot of money for their maintenance. They argued that the work should all be done by those evacuees whose husbands were paying nothing. (Many of the husbands were in the Centres). Others, who belonged to the better-off classes, argued that they should not work at dirty jobs (scrubbing and kitchen) as their husbands were contributing a lot of money; let the dirty hard work be done by those whose husbands were not paying so much. To add to the problem, the Ministry of Health were not asking the men in Britain to contribute, even though some of them, for example the Government Pensioners, had means.

From the very outset, Patron had urged the abandonment of contributions from husbands, etc., left in Gibraltar on the grounds that the whole system was unfair and that such relatively small sums were thus obtained. The Ministry of Health and the Colonial Office sympathised with this view. On the 11th October, in a letter to the Colonial Secretary, Patron stated:

'I am all in favour of the Colony contributing anything it can towards the help of the Home Government, but I do not think the contributions are the right way of doing it. It would be much more fitting and right that the monied classes and the larger firms, who have not suffered to the same extent as the poor evacuees, should contribute more liberally, either by increased taxation or any other method.'

Patron concluded his initial report by saying that 'with few exceptions the evacuees have behaved with dignity and restraint. It is a pleasure to see how attached the families are to each other and how natural the children are, and how grateful they are for what little can be done for them.'

The position of the doctors who had come from Gibraltar with the evacuees also created problems in the initial stages. These doctors assumed that they had been sent to the United Kingdom to work on a salary basis, but on arrival there they found that there was no work for them as the Medical Inspection of billets had all been arranged by the Ministry of Health long before their arrival!

However, by early September Dryburgh was reporting that it was very probable that Drs Dotto, Vasquez and Riera would be engaged by the Ministry of Health to assist with the vaccinations and inoculations prior to the re-evacuation. Their powers of persuasion, it was felt, would be useful in this connection since the Ministry of Health doctors had already found difficulty in persuading parents to have their children inoculated against measles, and they therefore were anticipating resistance to the wholesale anti-typhoid injections and the vaccinations which it was proposed to carry out.

In the midst of all this work to get the Gibraltarians settled in to their new environment came the bombshell—the British Government was planning to re-evacuate them elsewhere! But that is a story which must wait for the next chapter.

CHAPTER SEVEN

Evacuation to Jamaica

The months of September and October, 1940, witnessed further significant developments both in the progress of the War and in the situation of Gibraltarian civilians. The bombing of London continued mercilessly whilst the Royal Air Force retaliated by dropping bombs on Berlin, there were a number of air raids on Gibraltar, and contacts between Spain and the Axis Powers were giving cause for concern. The British Government was now proposing to re-evacuate the Gibraltar evacuees from the United Kingdom to the West Indies, and more civilians were evacuated directly from Gibraltar to Jamaica.

The first indication which the Gibraltar authorities had of the proposed re-evacuation to the West Indies was a reference which Dryburgh made in his Report of the 17th August, in which he said that amongst other things he had to decide whether the evacuees would require an issue of topees before going on their travels again to Jamaica, Trinidad and Mauritius!

The last mentioned place was soon discarded much to the relief of Dryburgh since the plan had been to house them in Port Louis, the capital—'a malarious cesspool where no European ever willingly spends the night. They would have been all right up on the inland plateau where the European Residential quarter and Military Camp are situated, but Port Louis would I fear have proved a death trap to people "unsalted" to tropical conditions.'

The Evacuation Committee in Gibraltar expressed concern at the possibility of further evacuation when shown Dryburgh's Report. In early September the matter was still confidential though many rumours were circulating both amongst the evacuees and in Gibraltar. Archbishop Amigo and Cardinal Hinsley were strenuously opposing this re-evacuation and claiming that if London was not safe, the Gibraltarians should be sent to some other part of the country. The official answer was that there was no place where accommodation could be found for 13,000 people, that it was dangerous in the circumstances for the evacuees to spend a winter in the British climate, and that they would be safer and more comfortable in every way in Jamaica and Trinidad.

On Friday, 6th September, the Governor received a deputation of leading citizens who argued against such a move. They saw no reason to doubt that the majority of the evacuees would be able to withstand the English winter. The deputation pointed out that winter in Gibraltar could be cold since the houses and the usual clothing were not adapted to such conditions as they were in England.

It may well seem strange that there should have been such opposition to a move which would have taken the Gibraltarian evacuees out of damp, war-torn London to the war-free tropical bliss of the West Indies. However, as the deputation pointed out to the Governor, some of the evacuees had already endured three sea voyages within a few months and under the most adverse conditions in many cases. A further move so soon was bound to have a disquieting effect upon those relatives remaining in Gibraltar in essential services. One may understand the reluctance of these evacuees to embark once again on a long and hazardous journey. The Governor concurred with the views of the deputation and this was relayed to London.

So much for the case against re-evacuation. The British Government had already made up its mind to send the Gibraltarians in London to the West Indies, the reasons for this decision being transmitted to the Governor on the 12th September. They may be summarised as follows:

1. It had never been intended that the evacuees should remain in Britain.

2. Difficulties of accommodation meant that the Gibraltarians could only be housed in the London area.

3. The conditions under which they were living there were far from satisfactory as a permanent arrangement, particularly during the winter: communal conditions with little privacy for individuals or families in public buildings, requisitioned hotels and mansion flats.

4. Apart from the danger to health, especially from respiratory diseases which the retention of the evacuees in the United Kingdom during the winter would necessarily involve, an outbreak of epidemic disease such as influenza among them could have very serious consequences.

5. The situation was further complicated by the air raids being carried out on London.

All these disadvantages would be almost absent in the West Indies where special arrangements were being made for the welfare of evacuees and much more suitable accommodation was being provided. Such was the case for re-evacuation!

As if to underline these arguments, London continued to endure nightly bombing raids with Buckingham Palace suffering a hit of Saturday, 14th September. On the same day the first fatal casualty amongst the Gibraltarian evacuees in London occurred: a fourteen-month-old male child named Mario Massetti.

To reinforce its case, the British Government prepared a Notice which was put up at all the billets where Gibraltarian evacuees were staying. It read as follows:

MESSAGE TO THE PEOPLE OF GIBRALTAR IN LONDON

His Majesty's Government greatly regret that it has been necessary for you to leave your homes in Gibraltar on account of the threat of enemy action, and they have given very careful consideration to the arrangements which should be made for your safety and welfare. It is their desire and intention that you and your children should be able to live comfortably and safely for the remainder of the war under conditions as similar as possible to those to which you have been accustomed in Gibraltar.

These conditions are unfortunately not available in England where danger from enemy action will persist, the winter is damp and cold, and the accommodation available is limited. But in the British West Indies the Governments of Trinidad, Jamaica and St Lucia have generously offered to provide temporary homes for you while the war lasts. Some of you may be reluctant to undertake another journey, but in the West Indies the climate is warm and sunny like the climate of Gibraltar; suitable accommodation with greater privacy for each family can be provided and facilities will be available for the education of your children. His Majesty's Government are fully satisfied that it will be in your best interests to go to the West Indies and that you will be assured of a warm welcome from the people of the loyal British Colonies to which you are sent.

Arrangements for your journey to the West Indies are being made and will be notified to you later. Suitable ships will be provided and you may be sure that you will not be called upon to endure the hardships of your previous journeys. The organisation for the transfer of more than 10,000 people is a complicated matter and His Majesty's Government feel certain that you will do your best to assist the authorities, and to comply with the instructions which will be issued to you from time to time.

Another notice from Mr J. Patron, Chairman of the Gibraltar Advisory Committee, urged the evacuees to support the British Government's decision:

TO MY FELLOW CITIZENS OF GIBRALTAR

We are citizens of one of the World's chief fortresses and have all appreciated that though while living there we enjoyed many advantages, in time of War our interests must be subordinated to those of the defence of the Empire.

The Evacuation of all non-combatants not engaged on essential work is, obviously, necessary, not only in the National interest, but in that of the inhabitants. It is quite true that so far the attacks on the Town have been of little importance but modern war is swift and ruthless, and in a small crowded place like Gibraltar, conditions might well come about at a moment's notice when the Civilian population, if left there, would be decimated in a few hours. It was necessary to move you at short notice from Morocco and the shipping available was not suitable to take you to your ultimate destination. Moreover, the accommodation and arrangements for you had to be got ready. It was necessary to find you a home temporarily and due to the crowded state of this country, this could only be done in London. The billets available are not suitable for the winter months, and London, as you have seen for yourself, is being heavily attacked.

It is necessary to move a community consisting mostly of women and children to a more suitable climate and a safer place. The most eminent doctors have advised the Government as regards the most suitable places, and you will see from the official notice the steps that are being taken. The climate in Jamaica, as well as other Islands, is excellent, but as an extra precaution you should take advantage of the facilities for inoculation that will be given to you.

The Authorities being fully convinced that they are acting in your best interest are determined to carry on with their plans, and we can get the best results and best help ourselves by behaving with dignity and restraint, and co-operating loyally with the plans made for us, and proving ourselves worthy of our ancient Rock.

I have endeavoured to lay your views and your needs before the authorities and am convinced I can best help by endeavouring to raise funds to help the more needy amongst you; by acting as your unofficial representative in this country, and putting forward any reasonable complaints or suggestions to the Authorities; by keeping in touch with the many friends of Gibraltar in this country, so when better times come, you are not forgotten.

At the same time, Patron was cabling the Colonial Secretary in Gibraltar in the following terms:

'It will not be possible due to large movements of population in this country to send evacuees outside London and as their present billets are unsatisfactory for a long stay both on health grounds and from a safety point of view while every assurance is being given as to the comfort and the safety of the ships to be taken and conditions in their final destination I do not consider in the interests of evacuees to endeavour to oppose the plans being made and instead of petitioning for the plans to be delayed as I gather has been done we should in my opinion ask these to be expedited!

Despite these pronouncements, the evacuees strongly resisted the attempt to re-evacuate them yet again. By early October, Patron was informing the Ministry of Health that the evacuees were very discontented and in an unfortunate frame of mind. He urged that they should be given some assurances otherwise they would have to be compelled to go, and this would not only cause a great deal of dissatisfaction amongst the evacuees, but would also take the heart out of the male members in Gibraltar.

Patron summarised the views of the evacuees thus:

'We quite appreciate the necessity for evacuating us from Gibraltar and that the hardships and great loss which we have had to suffer have been brought about by force of circumstances, but inasmuch as we have been called upon as British Subjects to bear these losses and to do our part in the defence of the Empire, we think once having been evacuated here, we should be treated on the same terms as peoples in this country.

We have noticed that the Evacuation here is not obligatory and that an option is given to the people to leave London if they so desire, and it seems that the same principles should be applied to us and we should be given the option of going abroad or remaining in this country.

We have noticed in the Press that it has been considered advisable to discontinue the Evacuation of children from this country, which, apparently, is thought too dangerous.

We are quite willing to suffer hardships and run the risk of danger in this country if we are given opportunities of doing work, but if it is necessary to evacuate us again (although we do not want to go), we consider it reasonable that we should be given the same assurances that are being asked for the children going from the country and that we should be given definite assurances that the conditions on board the ships will be better than those that brought us here; that the food and medical regulations will be adequate; that the ships will be escorted; that some representative members from amongst us be given the necessary authority to represent us and put forward our views when we arrive on the other side; that such employment as possible should be found for us and as many members of the community as possible should be employed in the work of the Camp and any necessary work in Jamaica.'

The news of the sinking of the *City of Benares* and the consequent stoppage of the evacuation of children from Britain added steel to the resistance of the evacuees to the proposed move to the West Indies. Some of them, described as 'hotheads' by Patron, even talked about seeking an outside opinion to advise them as to their rights. The matter was then referred to the War Cabinet and we shall return to their decision later on in this chapter.

On the 24th September, 1940, Gibraltar suffered its fifth and longest air-raid. It lasted two and a half hours and about forty French aircraft, taking advantage of low patches of Levanter cloud, bombed the Rock from a height of about 20,000 feet. Approximately one hundred bombs were dropped, though many of them ended up in the sea. About thirty bombs dropped on land, mostly in the Dockyard and to the south of it. A number of buildings were damaged, including the Naval Store Buildings, two buildings at the Dutch Shell Store, the South Generating Station, the Married Quarters at Naval Hospital Road, Barrack Block in Europa, Cormorant Wharf, King George V Memorial Hospital, St Jago's Barracks and Scud Hill Post Office. One bomb fell in the middle of South Barracks parade ground, and two more fell at the top of Scud Hill. One bomb fell in King's Yard and caused a fire in the CRE's office, and a fire was caused in No. 5 Coal Shed, South Mole. A six-pounder emplacement was damaged at Europa Pass but there was no damage to the gun. Six people were killed (three Military and three Civilian) and there were many injuries.

Two days later there was a further raid carried out by large numbers of French aircraft, estimated as numbering over one hundred. Some three hundred bombs of varying sizes were dropped, a large proportion of which dropped in the sea and on the barren parts of the Rock. However, many fell on buildings, roads and old defences. Considerable damage was done to private property and Government offices, but there was very little damage to Military works and personnel.

One small ship was hit and subsequently sank in the harbour. There were a number of casualties, including some fatal ones. Several enemy aircraft were shot down: three for certain, and possibly two more.

With typical English 'sang-froid', after an afternoon of such intense air bombardment, the traditional Ceremony of the Keys was carried out in the presence of His Excellency the Governor with full ceremonial!

A few days prior to these events, on Friday 20th September, the Governor had cabled London that he presumed that in view of the plans to transfer the Gibraltar evacuees in London to the West Indies, arrangements would also be made to transfer directly from Gibraltar to the West Indies the 1,650 remaining evacuees. Since the *Neuralia* was expected to arrive shortly in Gibraltar, the Governor suggested that she should be utilised for this purpose. London replied six days later that the *Neuralia* was urgently required to carry evacuees from Britain, which the British Government considered should be given priority.

The Governor replied immediately along the following lines:

'During the heavy air raids of the last two days which on Wednesday was carried out by a hundred aircraft dropping 500 bombs, the urgent necessity for evacuating at least 1,600 women and children registered for evacuation has been conclusively proved. Gibraltar has an area of three miles by one only and attacks on the scale of the last two days could be sustained indefinitely either from North Africa or from Spanish aerodromes. In fact, Gibraltar above ground would soon cease to exist and Gibraltar underground is insufficient to accommodate the necessary Garrison and the existing Civil population. I would remind you that this is the only place in the Empire liable to heavy and sustained air attack which has no fighter defence and is dependent entirely on limited AA Defence. Therefore I feel that Gibraltar should have priority as regards evacuation.'

These arguments had the desired effect in changing the minds of the British Government. On the 3rd October, the Governor was informed that it had been decided that the *Neuralia* would be used for the transference of the evacuees direct from Gibraltar to the West Indies. All on the ship would go to Jamaica. It was estimated that with due allowance for Control Staff, doctors, nurses and the arrangements necessary for the comfort and welfare of the evacuees, 1,150 evacuees could be accommodated on this ship. It was stressed that that number should not be exceeded, but that it was hoped that a second ship would become available. It was essential, continued the instructions from London, that the *Neuralia* should not be overcrowded and that better arrangements should be made for the health and comfort of the evacuees than on some of the ships which had conveyed evacuees to the United Kingdom.

Regarding rations, the needs of invalids and infants would require special consideration. Hammocks as provided on the *Neuralia* were considered unsuitable for the type of evacuee who would be travelling on the ship, so mattresses were being substituted.

On the matter of safety, insistence had been made on life boatage sufficient for *ALL* evacuees; troopship rafts were not thought adequate. It was also understood that the *Neuralia* would leave Gibraltar in a United Kingdom convoy for part of the journey after which protection would be arranged by the Admiralty (this final expectation never materialised!)

Before going to Gibraltar to pick up the evacuees, the *Neuralia* had to call at Lisbon to embark Polish and other airmen bound for the United Kingdom. The ship would take them to Gibraltar where they would embark on a convoy headed for Britain. It was anticipated that this would only delay the departure of the Gibraltar evacuees by a few days.

It was also stressed upon the Governor that the decision to use the *Neuralia* for this purpose had been taken by the War Office 'only because of vital defence aspect', and that this was 'likely to be the final figure (1,650) for evacuation.'

By September, too, Germany's plans regarding Gibraltar, and Spain's relations with the Axis Powers were causing concern and much speculation. Hitler's plans for the invasion of Gibraltar, code named 'Operation Felix', was considered by the Germans to require Spanish approval. Accordingly, General Wolfram Freiherr von Richthofen, Commander VII Air Corps, met General Franco in Spain on the 9th September, and a week later the Spanish Foreign Minister had talks with his German counterpart, Joachim von Ribbentrop, in Berlin. Further meetings throughout September failed to make conclusive progress.

On Sunday, 13th October, Madrid reported that General Franco had been invested with the Italian Order of Annunziata. In a speech, Franco praised the heroic traditions of the Italian army in Africa, and expressed the entire solidarity of the Spanish people towards their Fascist comrades.

A week later, Herr Himmler, the Nazi Police Chief, arrived in Madrid and met the Spanish Foreign Minister, Señor Suñer, and other members of the Spanish Cabinet; he later met General Franco. At the same time, a Spanish expert on air transport went to Berlin to confer with the German authorities on the opening of regular air services between Spain and Germany.

On the 23rd October, Hitler and Franco met at Hendaye on the Franco-Spanish border. None of these meetings brought forth a commitment from the Spanish leader to join the war.

But it is time to return to our evacuees! The *Neuralia* left Gibraltar on the afternoon of Wednesday, 9th October, carrying 1,104 passengers of whom 1,093 were evacuees. In charge of the evacuees was B D Austin-Cathie. About 250 passengers, of a 'better social standing', travelled cabin class; this created problems! As Austin-Cathie later reported, 'very definite jealousies were engendered by the preferential accommodation on board for certain nominees of the Evacuation Committee.' There was one actual stretcher case on board, and six sitting cases had been conveyed to the embarkation point by ambulance.

The *Neuralia* left Gibraltar in convoy. For the first five days of the voyage the sea was very choppy and the majority of the evacuees were sea-sick. This made the keeping clean of the troop decks and the ship generally rather difficult, but Wardens for each deck were appointed, volunteers came forward and fatigue parties were arranged. As soon as the people had found their sea-legs, regular routine was enforced and the Captain and the Troop Officer quickly expressed their satisfaction with the discipline of the evacuees and the cleanliness of the ship. According to one evacuee, most of the time was spent on deck because of the heat; another stated that those who had to sleep in the ship's hold often took their mattresses and blankets and slept on the deck.

The *Neuralia* left the convoy on Sunday evening, the 13th October, and there followed 48 anxious hours. Nothing happened until early morning five days later when a large steamer was sighted and the *Neuralia* commenced to zig zag. There was a certain amount of excitement in the troop decks, but nothing approaching disorganisation. The stranger equally zig-zagged and disappeared. She was then thought to have been an American Express Line Steamer.

At 2.20 am on the 22nd October, a male child was born to Mrs Maria Hall of 63 Prince Edward's Road, Gibraltar. The child was christened in the Camp Church on Sunday, 3rd November and was named Arthur Andrew after the Captain of the ship.

According to Austin-Cathie, an unpleasant incident occurred at the end of the voyage. At the request of one or two evacuees a collection for the crew was made during a dance on deck which had been arranged by the Troop Officer. This had resulted in 858 people over the age of twelve subscribing the paltry sum of £2.14.5½d., which had to be made up to £5 privately before it was even presentable. Worst still, continued Austin-Cathie, the people who had been occupying first and second class state-rooms gave as a reason for not tipping adequately their Indian stewards the fact that a 'large' collection had been made for them. For example, the four 'Control' Officers appointed by the Evacuation Committee, comprising with their families 24 adults, gave collectively 23 shillings to their table stewards and 13 shillings to their bedroom-stewards for a sixteen-day voyage travelling first class throughout.

These figures, said Austin-Cathie, were more remarkable as £3,700 sterling had been changed into Jamaican notes at the Camp after being checked off the ship and £200 had been spent at the Canteens and Beer Bar on board. Apparently, there was grave dissatisfaction amongst the crew and particularly the Indian section of it who were much dependent on tips and who had had a very thin time since the ship had ceased trooping. Austin-Cathie concluded by saying that he felt that the Officer in charge of Evacuees ought to be supplied by the Gibraltar Government with a generous sum (at least £80) for gratuities to obviate this blot in the future.

It must be added here that Gibraltarians, whatever their other faults, are not known for their lack of generosity, witness the large sums raised today for all kinds of charities. Could it have been that people on those particular circumstances, not knowing what awaited them in the future, were understandably holding on to every penny they had?

The health of the evacuees on board had been good. Seven children had been found to be suffering from rheumatic fever and in each case it had been noted that they had been sleeping continuously in air raid shelters in Gibraltar before embarking. There had been a few very minor accidents but no serious illness. Despite this, with so many elderly people and cripples on board there had been continuous activity in the hospital, and in this respect Austin-Cathie commended the excellent service of Sister Bullock from the Colonial Hospital who had been cheerfully on call day and night. Also commended were the Captain and Officers of the *Neuralia* for their kindness and care throughout the journey.

At Port Royal (20 minutes from Kingston by sea) the members of the Committee who were to manage the Camp where the evacuees were to be housed boarded the ship. Amongst them was the Very Reverend Father Thomas Feeney, in charge of the religious, educational, entertainment and social services of the Camp. He immediately circulated amongst the evacuees, and the sight of this kindly Roman Catholic priest at once put heart into those who had been wondering, speculating and dubious about what they were coming to.

On arrival at Kingston, large buses with a capacity for 35 people each, and many lorries for the heavy baggage quickly transported the evacuees and their luggage to the camp, about seven miles from the port. On arrival some evacuees were interviewed by the Press and there were general expressions of appreciation and gratitude for what was being done for them. On disembarkation they received a warm welcome from the people of Kingston who had gathered on the way from the pier to the Camp; the evacuees responded with cheers. Once in the Camp, many Jesuit priests and Sisters of several orders speedily billetted every one before the impending rain fell.

The arrival of the evacuees from Gibraltar seems to have aroused great interest amongst the Jamaican population. Hundreds of Jamaicans awaited at the water-front, whilst thousands lined the streets through which the buses took the arrivals to Mona Camp and warmly welcomed them in typical Jamaican manner. The Jamaican newspaper, *The Daily Gleaner,* commented:

'History was made in the island as the ship steamed in with its human cargo, for it was the first close up this island has yet received of the devastating European war. Pathetic scenes were witnessed as these haven seekers from Gibraltar, mostly women and children, had their first greedy glimpses of the country, which they will make their home till Hitler is forever crushed . . . Tears trickled down aged faces and young ones too. Many of these people have left behind their sons, their husbands, their fathers, their uncles, their brothers and their sweethearts to defend Gibraltar, who they may never see again. One woman sobbed: "We know that Gibraltar will never fall into enemy hands, but we know that for some of us, too, there will never be a reunion with some of our loved ones." The youngest arrival was a two-day-old baby, born, in Caribbean waters.' *The Gleaner* also reported that the first evacuee to come down the gangplank had been Mrs Carmen Azzopardi, accompanied by her mother-in-law, father, sister-in-law and a little nephew. Right behind her had been Mrs Juaquina Berjaqui, weeping as she spoke of her husband.

Meanwhile, arrangements were being made for the *Thysville,* a Belgian ship, to go to Gibraltar to embark the balance of about 300 Gibraltarian evacuees for Jamaica; the ship left Gibraltar on Thursday, 31st October with 393 evacuees.

With regard to this embarkation, the Secretary of State for the Colonies reported to the Governor of Gibraltar that the *Daily Express* had published on the 1st November a message from Laurence Wilkinson, its representative in Gibraltar, dated the 31st October, stating that on that day a contingent of evacuees had sailed from the Colony. The Secretary of State was much disturbed at the publication of this news coupled with the publication of the arrival of the first contingent of evacuees in Jamaica a week before. This, he pointed out, practically disclosed the ship's movements.

The Governor, in reply, pointed out that it was impossible to conceal an ambarkation of that nature from the enemy as long as 6,000 Spaniards were entering and leaving Gibraltar daily. Furthermore, orders for such evacuations had to be published in advance in the local press. The date of sailing of ships in the anchorage was bound to be known to enemy agents in Spain either at once or at least by dawn after the night of sailing. The Governor, however, conceded that the publication of Jamaica as the destination should have been suppressed.

The *Thysville,* with the second batch of Gibraltar evacuees bound for Jamaica, arrived on the 16th November, 1940. The youngest arrival was a month-old baby, the oldest an 80-year-old woman. Two days out from Gibraltar, one of the evacuees, 45-year-old Julio Peralta suffered a heart-attack and died; he was buried at sea. Included in this party were 34 Spaniards who had sought refuge in Gibraltar during the Spanish Civil War. 'A beautiful trip'; 'it could not have been better.' These were the sort of comments from some of the evacuees on their arrival in Jamaica. Cinema shows and concert and dancing parties had been provided on board during the hazardous sixteen-day journey.

The new arrivals received a tremendous welcome from their fellow evacuees on reaching the Camp. The children jumped on the sides of the buses, as they slowly drove to their stations, and the joy of this reunion of friends and relatives, who could not wait for the doors to be opened, made it somewhat difficult to unload the buses!

Whilst their compatriots were settling in the Caribbean, the evacuees in London continued to endure the realities of war. By the 9th October, the date of *Neuralia's* sailing, London had suffered 28 nights of incessant bombing! On the 11th October there was a direct hit on St Paul's Cathedral.

Some relief came when Her Majesty the Queen visited two of the centres in which Gibraltar evacuees were accommodated, the Royal Palace Hotel and Kensington Palace Mansions, on the 10th October. She spent a considerable time talking to the evacuees who gave her a most enthusiastic reception. She was particularly interested in the arrangements for their medical care and for the welfare of the children. It was also noted that she singled out for a special word some ex-soldiers who were wearing their medals. At the end of her visit Her Majesty was given a tumultuous send off by the evacuees who thronged the hall and windows of the buildings and poured into the street to wave to her as she drove away. Patron later commented that it was extraordinary to see how with a smile and a few kind words she could do more in ten minutes to make the people happy than he and his colleagues had been able to do in two months hard work!

In Gibraltar itself, a Board of District Commissioners was set up. Since this Board included in its powers and duties those of the Evacuation Committee, the latter body held its last meeting on the 21st October, 1940.

After the air raids of the 26th and 28th September, things had been quiet on the Rock. However, at about 8.30 am on Wednesday, 30th October many houses were shaken by a muffled explosion; many people saw a big splash in the harbour entrance. People coming to work from Spain saw a torpedo on the beach.

A communique issued by the Naval Authorities explained that an abortive attempt had been made by Italian Naval Officers to torpedo ships in the harbour with a special device. One torpedo had exploded harmlessly at the harbour entrance and the other had run ashore in Spanish territory. The BBC stated that the Italians had for a long time been known to have a miniature torpedo-boat or sea tank which they had introduced during the last war. The name of this particular submarine, it was disclosed later, was the *Scire,* a 620-ton Mediterranean-type submarine which had been converted into an assault craft transport to carry two-man torpedoes. At 1.30 am on the 30th October, the submarine came to rest on the bottom of Gibraltar Bay after a hazardous passage through the underwater currents of the Strait. At 2.00 am the three crews, astride their torpedoes, set out for the attack on two British battleships at anchor in the harbour. All three machines developed malfunctions and the whole exercise went very wrong!

What of the plans to re-evacuate the Gibraltar evacuees in London to the West Indies? On the 25th October, the War Cabinet was informed by the First Lord of the Admiralty that the present position in the North Western Approaches made the transportation of evacuees out of the question until the Admiralty had tested the results of a new convoy system; since the loss of the *City of Benares* it had been decided not to proceed with the Children's Overseas Reception Scheme. In the circumstances, the Gibraltar evacuees were not too keen to go to the West Indies! The Prime Minister thought that they ought to go and that they should be made to understand that the British Government was determined that they should go. Their attitude, he felt, could be altered by propaganda.

Subsequent to this, the Secretary of State for the Colonies telegraphed the Governor of Gibraltar on the 25th November as follows:

'I greatly regret to have to inform you that circumstances have arisen which now makes it impossible to proceed with plan for re-evacuating Gibraltarians in this country to the West Indies in the near future. I am much disappointed since I am keenly alive to the trouble which the Governments of Jamaica and Trinidad have taken to prepare shortly for the reception of evacuees and am convinced that re-evacuation to the West Indies would be in their best interests. I fear however that reasons are conclusive.

The proposal for re-evacuation is not, however, finally abandoned. The possibility of reviving it will be considered at the beginning of next year in the light of circumstances at that time.'

As a result of this decision, the Gibraltar Advisory Committee was disbanded and superseded by an Inter-Departmental Committee. According to the Minister of Health, in a letter to Patron dated the 19th December, 1940, 'now that the Gibraltarians are to be with us for a considerable period . . . the problems with which we are faced must grow in complexity, and constant and close co-operation must, therefore, be maintained between the various Departments concerned with the welfare of the evacuees.' Major Patron was invited to serve on this Committee and accepted.

And so the Gibraltarians in London had to stay there—at least for the time being. We shall return to them in a later chapter. Meantime, let us look at the lives of those who had made it to the Caribbean.

CHAPTER EIGHT

'Gibraltar Camp'

To prepare for the reception of the evacuees in Jamaica, a special Camp—really a new town—had been constructed. The Public Works Department in Jamaica had been instructed, in the first instance, to provide accommodation for 2,000 people in exactly one month! In that time a great deal had to be done: the selection of the site, the ordering of materials and equipment from abroad, preparation of the plans, the awarding of contracts. The work was completed to schedule. The Water Commission provided the site and laid the water supply, the Materials Board imported materials from abroad, the Hardware Merchants and Jamaican Public Service Company rendered valuable assistance, and above all the Contractors and their staff of workmen spared no pains and effort to complete the work on time. The entire cost was borne by Imperial Government funds.

The Camp itself (called Camp Number One as plans were already laid for the construction of a second Camp) covered an area of some 250 acres in the Mona Estate. It was a good site, gently sloping towards the Lond Mountain, well drained and in pleasant rural surroundings with delightful vistas of near and more distant hills. It was far enough away from the noise and bustle of Kingston and yet not too far from easy access by well graded roads. It was also within range of the City's Water Supply, electric light and power, and telephone services. Some of the access roads had been surfaced with asphalt, and four miles of interior service roads were constructed. This Camp was eventually to house 4,000 people, whilst Camp No. 2 would accommodate a further 3,000. No effort would seem to have been spared to provide for all the care, comfort, entertainment and education of the evacuees.

On entering the Camp Number One from the road to August Town the first buildings encountered were those allotted to Administration. These consisted of an Office Block for the Camp Commandant and his Staff, where all the business of the Camp was conducted. Close by was the Main Store, a large building 412 feet long by 25 feet wide with storage accommodation for the spare equipment and supplies for the whole Camp, and offices for the Commissariat Officer and Stores Staff.

Not far away was the Police Station with barrack accommodation for twenty men and the necessary Mess and Guard Rooms, etc. Close to the Administration Buildings were grouped various miscellaneous structures such as the Motor Transport Garages, carpenter's shop, quarters for cooks and chauffeurs, and a Wood shed with stacks for storing 30 cords of wood, and equipped with an electrically operated wood chopper for the supply of fuel to the kitchens.

What of **the living accommodation?** In Camp Number One, initially, there were thirty-one Units and twenty-four were planned for Camp Number Two. Each unit consisted of two huts, each 150 feet long by 39 feet wide with seven foot wide verandahs on the long sides and a sanitary annexe, 50 feet by 14 feet 6 inches, between the huts.

The huts themselves were of wooden construction, well lighted, and with ample ventilation. They could be subdivided into separate rooms or groups of rooms, or they could be used as dormitories. They were divided by a centre passage lengthwise and another crosswise. There were fourteen rooms on each side of the centre passage, twelve being two-bedded and two three-bedded rooms; i.e. sixty people to a bungalow. Every room opened out on to the verandah mentioned above; thus, by partitioning the verandah, families could be given one-room, two-room, three-room, etc., self-contained flatlets, according to the size of the family, with their private steps leading to the verandah. This system ensured a considerable amount of privacy and also enabled particular groups of people to be billetted under one roof, e.g. the Jewish community numbering 36 had a bungalow to themselves and there was a special bungalow for elderly and invalid people.

In addition, there were twenty small cottages for small family groups, each with a front verandah, three rooms, combination kitchen and pantry, and the necessary sanitary fittings. On the suggestion of Austin-Cathie, the Officer in charge of the evacuees for the journey to Jamaica and for the first weeks of their stay there, none of these three-roomed bungalows were allocated because he was certain that it would revive the very definite jealousies which had been engendered by the preferential accommodation afforded on board the *Neuralia.* This was to bring problems later!

The huts were spaced well apart on fairly generous lines and every tree which could provide shade had been saved.

The furniture in each room comprised the bare necessities: beds, a small table and two chairs, and no wardrobes. The walls were of bare, unpainted wood, and according to one evacuee there was very little privacy since the partitions did not reach the ceiling.

In Camp Number One there were three dining and kitchen blocks; dining room A catered for all mothers with children under five, dining room B was for mothers and children under 14, and dining room C provided all other adults. Such an arrangement went some way towards surmounting problems of overcrowding and diet. A and B dining rooms catered for approximately 1,400 people and the Cafeteria System was soon adopted there. There was a covered way between these dining rooms and the huts of the evacuees. Dining room C was partitioned to accommodate the Administrative staff, Field Staff and Police, with special seating facilities for the Jews and the mothers with very small children. Rations were also issued from C kitchen for those who were confined to their rooms in the huts for medical reasons, or in the Hospital. In Camp Number Two similar blocks were planned, but with the seating accommodation in each increased to 800. (When the proposed re-evacuation of Gibraltarians from the United Kingdom to Jamaica fell through, Camp Number Two remained unoccupied by evacuees).

The kitchens were equipped with eight large stoves using wood fuel, and four large steam kettles or Stock Pots steam heated. Each kitchen had an electrically operated Vegetable Peeler, and the necessary washing up and preparation sinks with hot and cold water laid on. Preparing and serving tables, lockers for cutlery and crockery, and stores for keeping the daily supplies issued from the Main Store, were provided, and perishable foods were stored in an Electric Cold Storage Cabinet.

The Canteen consisted of a dry goods Department where clothes and shoes among many other things were on sale; and a general store which combined a grocery, tobacconist, a stationary shop, a sweet shop and where certain pharmaceutical items were also obtainable. The Canteen opened daily from 9.30 to 12 and from 2 to 4.

Plans were also afoot for the provision of a night Canteen in one of the Recreation Rooms, where hot dogs and soft drinks would be obtainable in the evenings.

At the time of the arrival of the first batch of evacuees a small Cottage **Hospital** had already been constructed in Camp Number One. This was eventually to serve as a six-bed Maternity Unit when a modern hospital to accommodate one hundred patients, with the usual Wards, Operating Theatre, Out-Patients Department, Dental Clinic and other auxiliary buildings, had been completed. Quarters for the Hospital Staff were also to be provided. An Office and quarters for a Sanitary Inspector were also planned.

Three large **Recreation** Halls were erected in Camp One which were used for the recreation and entertainment of the evacuees. Each such hall was 140 feet long by 50 feet wide with a stage at one end, and was available for concerts, cinema shows, dances and other forms of entertainment. One evacuee recalled that the priests and nuns were always present at dances, and that the 11 pm curfew was strictly enforced!

Recreational activities included gymnastics, boxing, table tennis, football, basket-ball, trips and hikes, Girl Guides, Boy Scouts, and band concerts. Amongst the facilities available were table-tennis tables, games tables, Checkers, Chinese Checkers, dominoes, cards and an electric gramaphone, amplifier and a collection of records.

In the theatre, movies were shown twice a week, concerts once a week, and there were other entertainments twice a week. Small projection movie shows were also available, and the capacity was for 500. Footlights, scenery, a new stage and lighting were provided in due course.

There was also a Reading Room with a capacity for 50 to 60. Magazines, books, newspapers were placed at the disposal of the evacuees. Playing fields for football, cricket and tennis were also provided.

The **educational needs** of the children were far from forgotten, The 'Gibraltar Camp School' was started on the 16th January, 1941. School buildings were provided by taking three of the huts which had been prepared as quarters and transforming them into school rooms. These amply provided for the 250 school children found among the evacuees.

The six standards of the elementary school were placed in two of the huts while one was provided for the large infant school. By April, 1941, there were 234 pupils enrolled, 114 boys and 120 girls, but the number was constantly increasing through additional enrolments in the infant department.

The Staff consisted of one head teacher and fourteen assistant teachers. This Staff was composed of five Sisters from the various teaching convents of Kingston, nine lay teachers, all Gibraltarians with the exception of one Jamaican.

The Gibraltar Code (curriculum) had been adopted for the school as it was felt that the school should be considered as still a part of the Gibraltar system of education. On this matter, the Secretary of State for the Colonies commented to the Governor of Jamaica on the 17th June, 1941, that whilst he recognised the propriety of keeping the evacuees educationally in touch with Gibraltar, he was also anxious that the children, as also the adolescent and adult sections of the community, should be brought during their stay in Jamaica as much as possible into contact with British traditions and culture. He added that there was reason to suppose that they would have better opportunities in Jamaica than they had in Gibraltar for acquiring a sound knowledge of the English language and literature, and that, if due advantage was taken of their opportunities, they might be expected to leave Jamaica better equipped educationally for citizenship of the British Empire.

Every facility had been afforded by the authorities for the equipment of the classrooms down to the smallest details. The classrooms themselves were spacious, lighted on both sides, with plenty of blackboard space for each room. In the infant department all the necessary equipment for Kindergarten work had been provided.

Besides the regular studies of the elementary department, there were classes in drill, sewing and singing. The grounds around the school were more than sufficient for recreation and games. Swings had been provided for the lower classes, whilst football for the boys and basket-ball for the girls had been introduced.

The ages of the school children ran from three years of age to fourteen years, but several of the boys and girls of the Camp, who wished to continue their schooling beyond that age had been placed in the Public Secondary Schools of the Island.

Religious requirements were also met. The Roman Catholic church was a spacious and attractive building, centrally situated. Lawns and flower beds surrounded it, and the church bell was to the left of the building. The sanctuary's principal object was a beautiful white altar on a platform and set off by a dark red curtain on the rear wall. There were statues to the right and left of the main altar.

The body of the church had confessionals, some 500 chairs with kneelers and a choir loft with a fine organ. Stations of the Cross adorned the walls. Daily services were held and the Church patronised several societies. There was also a Convent for Roman Catholic Nuns and a hostel for the resident priests.

There was also a small Anglican chapel, equipped with benches and an organ as well as an altar and communion rails.

As there were only 36 Jews in the Camp, they were sent to the Synagogue in a bus. Rabbi Silverman, in charge of the Jewish Community of Jamaica, conferred with the Commandant of the Camp on matters affecting the special diet and observances for the Jews.

The water supply was provided from the Water Commission's Reservoirs at Hope, by a ten inch Supply Main delivery into a steel tank of 131,000 gallon capacity, from which the Camp supply was distributed by four inch Mains. Pillar Hydrants for supplying water for fire-fighting purposes had been installed at convenient points. Both Camps had **electricity** laid on and street lighting had also been installed. Once both Camps had been completed, six million feet of lumber would have been used in their erection!

The Management of the Camp was in the hands of a Committee of four: the COMMANDANT, a CAMP MANAGER (later designated Deputy Commandant), the FOOD CONTROLLER and a ROMAN CATHOLIC PRIEST. When the first batch of evacuees arrived, the Camp Commandant was Major Henry Simms, a silver-haired PWD Director, with burly ex-Mayor Ernest Rae as his deputy. The Reverend Father Thomas Feeney, SJ, who was the Father Superior of the Roman Catholic Church and a member of the Gibraltar Camp Committee, and his brother Father William Feeney, SJ were the Camp Chaplains.

On Thursday, 31st October, 1940, it was announced that the Hon Major Simms had ceased to be Camp Commandant, and that Mr J L Worlledge, Chairman of the Camp Committee and a plump, jovial Englishman (soon to vacate Jamaica's Auditor General's chair), was to be the new Commandant, with Mr Rae as Deputy Commandant. The Food Controller of the Colony was responsible for the Stores of the Camp, and Father Feeney looked after the general spiritual and social welfare of the Camp residents. Four priests of the same Order (Jesuits) resided permanently in the Camp with him, and there were other priests from the Order in Jamaica available to help as required. There were also four permanent Sisters of different Orders in the Camp with many others coming in daily.

The running and organisation of the Camp was covered by **'The Evacuees (Defence) Regulations, 1940.'** Under these regulations, every evacuee was obliged to reside in the Camp. The Commandant could grant a permit to any evacuee to be absent from Camp or to reside elsewhere than in the Camp for a specified period of time. Camp residents were not allowed to work for wages outside the Camp unless granted special permission by the Commandant.

The powers of the Commandant were extensive. He could:

a. hold periodic roll calls of evacuees;

b. lay down the times at which meals would be served;

c. decide on the diet of the evacuees;

d. prohibit or restrict the access to, or egress from, camp of evacuees or other persons;

e. prohibit or restrict the bringing into or taking out of camp by any evacuee or other person of any article;

f. search anyone entering or leaving camp and confiscate any article which contravened camp regulations;

g. enforce periodic medical examination and treatment of evacuees;

h. inspect the quarters of the evacuees and maintain hygiene and sanitation throughout the camp;

i. prevent and punish disorder, insubordination or violence in the camp;

j. provide for the prevention of accident, and for the prevention and control of fire in the camp;

k. arrest any evacuee committing any breach of the Regulations, and detain him, for not more than 24 hours, before handing him over to the police or bringing him before the Commissioner;

l. arrest any person other than an evacuee on similar conditions as (k) above; such an arrest could be made, not only within the precincts of the camp but also within one hundred yards from its boundary.

However, no evacuee could be forced to submit himself to any medical or surgical treatment which was contrary to his religious beliefs, nor could he be required to attend any religious service.

What PENALTIES could the Commandant inflict? He could:

a. cancel or restrict the right of an evacuee to entertain visitors in the camp for a period not exceeding 21 days;

b. cancel or restrict the right of an evacuee to leave camp during the day or any specified portion of the day for a period not exceeding 21 days;

c. restrict or reduce the diet of the evacuees to such extent and for such period not exceeding 21 days as might be approved by a Medical Officer attached to the camp;

d. fine an evacuee a sum of not more than £5;

e. detain the evacuee within the camp for a period not exceeding seven days.

Any person guilty of an offence against camp regulations and every person other than an evacuee guilty of an offence against these regulations could, upon summary conviction before a Resident Magistrate, be liable to a fine not exceeding £25 or be imprisoned for a term not exceeding three months, or both.

The rule that no one could leave the camp without a permit proved irksome in many cases (every evacuee was given a registration number which had to be given on leaving and entering the camp). According to Austin-Cathie in his initial report, the Committee wished the people to settle down thoroughly before they went roaming and passes were initially difficult to obtain, 'principally for the protection of our people themselves.' The whole question of regulations and discipline was to give rise to numerous problems.

Some evacuees stated several years later that there was barbed wire round the camp, and that they had been told that this was for their own protection.

Regarding **employment,** Austin-Cathie also commented on the rule which forbade any person in the Camp from working for wages outside the Camp in competition with Jamaicans. As there was a large staff in the Camp to cook, wash, and generally care for the evacuees, Austin-Cathie observed that there was a good deal of idleness in the initial stages. However, as time went on, every job within the Camp that could be filled by a Gibraltarian was thus filled at the local rates of pay. Bakery (initially in the hands of the Army) and the steam laundry being installed both eventually supplied employment for the evacuees. From the very outset, the Canteen came under the control of a Mrs Dalmedo (who had controlled a chemist business in Gibraltar) and six paid helpers. For those unable to find work there was a dole, a sum of 2/6 a week for adults being suggested.

How good and plentiful was **the food?** The majority view appears to be very favourable. One evacuee reminisced nearly forty years later that the meals were good at first, even including lobster, but that they soon deteriorated. On one occasion, she recalled, sardines were given several days running and people refused to eat them. However, fruit was cheap and plentiful. Another evacuee recalled that food was plentiful: milk, fresh fish, meat, eggs, fruit, etc. However, the food was 'not cooked to our liking', and eventually Gibraltarians took over the cooking.

According to Austin-Cathie, experience had necessitated a few minor changes in the menus, the method of cooking and the manner of serving. A committee of housewives had been specially formed to vet the weekly menus with the caterer and then showed the Camp Cooks how Gibraltarians liked their food cooked and served.

Originally, orderlies drawn from the younger female evacuees had fetched the food from the kitchens and served it, each waiting on twenty people. This had necessitated waiting until everybody was seated, took too long and it was found that the food frequently grew cold. On the advice of two Canadian catering experts (seconded to the Camp from the Canadian Regiment at Jamaica) the 'Cafeteria' system was then tried. Each meal was served over a period of one and a half hours and a person could come at any time during that period and fetch his own meal on a tray direct from the service kitchen.

Austin-Cathie observed that the food itself (augmented with the wonderful native fruits, honey, jellies and jam) was excellent and ample. Fresh iced cow's milk was available all day long for children, invalids and in fact anyone who wanted it. Consumption rose from sixty gallons a day to ninety gallons in the fortnight that Austin-Cathie spent at the Camp.

Austin-Cathie also reported on the **health** of the evacuees. He said that there had been many cases of scabies and head lice taken to the camp, but that the devoted Sisters were soon making great strides in clearing these up. Unfortunately, there had been a small outbreak of pink-eye (a contagious form of inflammation of the eye), principally amongst the children, but this too was soon well in hand.

Before the arrival of the evacuees the authorities in Jamaica had been anxious about the reaction of the Gibraltarians to what was spoken of as **the 'colour problem'.** Practically all the rank and file of the police were black and whilst the evacuees were getting used to this coloured authority the Commissioner of Police very sensibly swore in as Jamaican Special Constables, the three Special Constables who had accompanied the evacuees from Gibraltar, to keep order in the Camp and in case an arrest should be necessary. Austin-Cathie was able to report that in the opening weeks there had been no opposition to this coloured authority and that there had been complete harmony between the police and the evacuees.

Such, then, was 'Gibraltar Camp Number One'. The cancellation of the plans to re-evacuate the Gibraltar evacuees in London to the West Indies meant that Camp Number Two remained unoccupied. On the 30th September, 1942, the Colonial Office in London informed the Governor of Gibraltar that this Camp was urgently desired for barracks for a battalion of local (coloured) militia which was being embodied for full time service. This was part of a general scheme for strengthening local defence forces in the West Indies, which came within the area where the United States was responsible for general defence.

The Governor of Jamaica was not too happy about this proposal on the grounds that Number Two Camp was a continuation of Number One Camp where the Gibraltar evacuees were accommodated. Since amongst these there were a large proportion of adolescent girls, he felt that the quartering of coloured troops in such close proximity was likely to give rise to considerable reactions in Gibraltar.

The Military had proposed to build an unclimbable fence and to make relations with Number One Camp a military offence. However, the Governor of Jamaica did not think that this would solve the problem since Gibraltar women and girls would inevitably be using the same approach or access roads. The Father Superior of the Roman Catholic Church in Jamaica, who as we have seen was a member of the Gibraltar Camp Committee (Father Feeney) had written to the Governor of Jamaica expressing deep apprehension at the proposal.

The Military authorities had pointed out that if Number Two Camp could not be used for the troops it would be necessary to build a hut camp at an estimated cost of £50,000 and that no accommodation other than tents would be available during its construction. Notwithstanding such arguments, the Governor of Gibraltar was strongly opposed to the proposal because he felt that the effect on morale in Gibraltar would be deplorable. As a result, the decision was then taken not to use Number Two Camp for this purpose.

Some four months later, on the 20th January, 1943, another opportunity arose of making use of Number Two Camp, this time to house internees and refugees of various nationalities. The conversion of part of this camp at the northern end for this purpose, it was estimated, would cost something in the region of £30,000. Not surprisingly, the Director of Public Works in Jamaica favoured the former proposal!

Once again, the Gibraltar Camp Committee came out in strong opposition to the proposal since they felt that the psychological effects on the Gibraltarians of the establishment of an internment camp within the precincts of the camp would be serious.

The Jamaica authorities, whilst not seeing any force in the Gibraltarians' objections, nonetheless realised that their 'baseless complaints' could well embarass the Governor of Gibraltar. However, if the second, and considerably more expensive, proposal was adopted Jamaica would require some financial assistance to carry it out. Gibraltar's response to this was that they had no surplus funds for such a project!

By April, 1943, the British Government had decided to approve the use of Camp Number Two to house internees, following an assurance from the Governor of Jamaica that the proposed camp would be separated by an appreciable distance (about 200 yards) from that occupied by the Gibraltarians, although not out of sight being overlooked from Number One Camp which was on higher ground.

We now look at how the evacuees from Gibraltar adapted to their new environment.

CHAPTER NINE

Life in Camp Gibraltar

On the whole, life for the evacuees in 'Gibraltar Camp' appears to have been good, and the large majority were as happy as it was possible for any people to be, separated as they were from their homes and families. Those responsible for looking after them during their enforced exile did their best to make their lives comfortable, witness the many facilities provided and already described in the previous chapter. Inevitably, some were discontented and occasionally things went wrong.

At the very outset there were problems with the allocation of accommodation. As we have seen, none of the three-roomed bungalows were allocated for fear of arousing jealousies amongst the evacuees. This led to one individual expressing himself in public so freely on the second day of arrival, using the word 'revolution', which was anathema in Jamaica, that he was called before the Commandant and nearly put into prison.

Nevertheless, the first month went well and the evacuees seemed to be settling down to the strange conditions. One Jamaican journal 'Spotlight', put it thus: 'Jamaica's wartime guests gradually metamorphosed from a home-sick crowd to a more or less happy family.'

Communal life centred round the dining sheds where the evacuees gathered three times a day for their meals and in the evenings for entertainment. There was a daily routine, everyone at the Camp awakening at around 6 am with the first call for breakfast at 7 am, and the second batch following an hour later. This meal would consist of perhaps bacon, tomatoes, bread and butter, jam and coffee. Lunch was served at 12 noon and 1 pm and supper at 5 pm and 6 pm. Fresh milk was served after supper.

A broadcasting system had been installed and over it announcers kept things going smoothly by giving general directions; the system was also used to broadcast music. In the evenings the evacuees amused themselves with amateur theatricals, songs and dances. With Mr Nemesio Mosquera, well-known Gibraltarian comedian, there, as well as the Valverde family, one can imagine that some good times were had!

Of course, all was not smooth sailing, and early in November, 1940, the Jamaica newspaper, *The Daily Gleaner,* pointed out some potential dangers: '. . . everything seems to have been provided for our evacuee visitors . . . except something to do . . . A human being, particularly a female human being, must have some occupation in order to keep his or her mind in a state of normal health; and yet the very daily occupations which form the background of a woman's existence, housekeeping, washing, cooking, have been taken away from our visitors, who have highly qualified chefs . . . to cook for them; a scientific (and expensive) laundry to wash for them. All they really need now is a valet service to dress them . . . One of the worst hardships you could place these people under would be to leave them with nothing to do, no interest in their daily lives.'

The Governor of Jamaica, Sir Arthur Richards, paid the Camp an unexpected visit on the 4th November. His visit coincided with the opening of musical entertainment as the Military Band played there for the first time. It was announced that similar performances would henceforth be held every Monday and Friday from 4 to 5 pm.

There was a gradual growth of amenities and an increasing involvement by the evacuees in the running of the Camp. Within a couple of weeks of the arrival of the first contingent a post office with savings bank, a telegraph office, and a canteen where such items as postcards, sandwiches, sweets and cigarettes could be purchased, had been set up. Also installed was an information office. The elder children were soon helping to unload and store the thousands of loaves of bread delivered each morning, while the elder girls and young women served as dining room orderlies, taking meals from the kitchens to the tables. The Jamaican cooks were doing their best to produce typical Gibraltarian dishes to make the evacuees feel as much at home as possible. A local radio programme even had a song composed entitled 'Welcome Gibraltar.' Lady Richards, wife of the Governor of Jamaica, visited the Camp on the 7th November, and was entertained by a troupe of twenty children who put on a fine show consisting mainly of choral selections.

Leisure activities were soon being organised, parties of evacuees being taken to visit Hope Botanical Gardens. These parties consisted mainly of young ladies who had been working hard in the Camp, assisting with the serving of meals and other domestic duties. The outing was in the nature of a reward and a rest. Though greatly admiring the gardens, some evacuees commented that it did not surpass their own Alameda Gardens at home! Memories of Gibraltar were clearly strong in their minds! Plans for the making of a film about Gibraltar Camp were also afoot; this was completed by the 23rd January, 1941, after two months work, and was entitled 'Gates of Gibraltar.' The film depicted every phase of life at the Camp.

Breaches of rules, mainly by outsiders, almost inevitably occurred. (The Governor had published the Camp Regulations on the 18th October, and Commandant Worlledge had drawn up strict rules under these regulations.) Among the rules insisted upon was that forbidding anyone but Camp residents from entering without a pass signed by either the Commandant or his Deputy. The main reason for this rule, claimed the local press, was to prevent the evacuees and the workers from getting too sociable with each other. Five persons were fined for 'gate crashing' (i.e. entering the Camp without permission) in late November, the Magistrate at the Half-Way Tree Court warning that while these cases, as the first brought before him, were leniently dealt with, there would be an increase of penalty in future cases. One fruit-seller was charged with unlawfully selling fruits to residents of the Camp within a distance of 100 yards (in fact, 4 feet) from the Camp boundary. During the hearing, Sergeant Major Shand, in charge of the police station at Gibraltar Camp, informed the court that a great deal of trouble was being caused by persons who tried to sell fruit to the evacuees, sometimes at exorbitant prices.

Further breaches followed. One person was charged on December 1st with having exhibited for sale, bread, ham and butter to persons within the Gibraltar Camp. Two others were charged with entering the Camp without previously obtaining written permission from the Camp Commandant. Employees engaged in work in the Camp but who happened to enter it without their passes, and employees found on the Camp after 6 pm without being in pursuit of their employment or with the written permission of the Camp Commandant were also charged. The rules were being strictly enforced!

Commenting on the question of discipline on the 23rd November, 1940, *The Jamaica Times* referred to the task facing Mr Worlledge and Mr Rae, Commandant and Manager of Gibraltar Camp, in sympathetic terms: 'We wonder how many people comprehend the great difficulty of the job that these gentlemen have undertaken. The evacuees are decent, self-respecting persons who are in no sense of the word under any kind of stigma; yet it is clear that hundreds of persons, moved bodily into a new country, under strange conditions and in what is really a foreign environment, must for their own protection be subjected to a certain amount of benevolent discipline. To keep order among a large population, to inspire contentment and satisfaction among people removed from their normal surroundings, to feed, to cater for the bodily, mental and spiritual needs of such a body, is no easy task. If the public understand the problem, we feel sure that they will extend that co-operation which is so necessary if the right spirit is to be created. Our visitors are welcome guests, who have been brought to a place of safety, where all possible is being done for their welfare. We feel sure that the two officers responsible for ensuring it will be equal to the task.' Not all subsequent press reports were to be so understanding!

Broadcasting on the 28th November, 1940, the Commandant, Mr J. L. Worlledge, stated that the evacuees 'seemed settled down . . . to their new and undoubtedly strange surroundings and have never ceased to show their willingness to co-operate with the staff in all matters.' Mr Worlledge also stated that two football matches had already been played against outside opposition, the evacuees winning one and losing one. The first cinema show and Vaudeville had also been given and the local music and dancing had been highly appreciated by the audience.

A Choir had soon been formed at the Camp, and on Sunday, 15th December, 1940, it gave a musical programme at the evening service in the Holy Trinity Cathedral. There were 38 voices in the choir, and Miss Valverde, who played the organ for the major portion of the service, gave a very good impression.

In December, too, building activity suddenly ceased at Camp No. 2. Workers trooped out, leaving but a few to finish up the laying out of lawns, paths, etc.

And so came the first Christmas at Gibraltar Camp! It was bound to be a difficult time for the evacuees, memories of families left behind being particularly strong at such a time. Nonetheless, evacuees and the authorities in charge of them seem to have made a brave effort to overcome such problems. At eight o'clock on Christmas Eve, presents, which had been neatly parcelled, were brought down from the Nuns' quarters and distributed in the huts to every evacuee. On each was written the name of the recipient, and the sisters themselves did the distributing. The Commandant, his deputy and Father Thomas Feeney visited nearly all the houses.

According to rumour, a touch of humour laced the distribution of presents. In one of the parcels was included a tube of toothpaste among other articles. The recipient, after examining some of the other items, took up the tube, glanced at it, for a moment looked puzzled, and then with a broad smile displayed his toothless gums to the amusement of everyone including himself.

The big tree in the camp had been decorated with lights with five different coloured lights and a big diamond-shaped star perched on the top. The Christmas Eve celebrations culminated with Midnight Mass, though there was little sleep in the camp for the remainder of the night.

At 9.30 am on Christmas morning the full Cathedral choir arrived and sang at Mass. Shortly afterwards, an historic occasion took place—the Gibraltar flag was hoisted amidst tears and sighs. This flag, designed by one of the evacuees, was red and white with a castle neatly worked in the centre in gold with a golden key suspended from the castle. As the evacuees looked on, two members of the Jamaica Constabularly raised the flag and 'God Save the King' was sung, followed by the Gibraltar anthem, in which a little boy led off and was then accompanied by his fellow countrymen. Carols were then sung at the Camp Hospital by the Cathedral choir and the entire gathering. The rest of the day was given over to games and at night there was a concert which the evacuees themselves had arranged. The flag remained proudly flying at the eastern end of the Administration buildings—probably the first time a Gibraltar flag had flown anywhere!

Football continued to increase in popularity amongst the evacuees. On the 27th December, 1940, *the Gleaner* commented:

'We are reliably informed that there are times when the Very Reverend Father T. Feeney, Father Superior of the Roman Catholic Mission, and a member of the managing committee of Camp Gibraltar, cannot look Mr J. L. Worlledge, Auditor General and Acting Commandant, in the eye.

The position is this. The Very Reverend Father decided from early after the arrival of the evacuees from Gibraltar to show them how football is played. He therefore went to the trouble of getting a team of tots up at the camp; but they were badly beaten by the Gibraltarians. Profiting from experience, he brought a second and bigger team; but they too were defeated. Much disillusioned, the Father Superior still had up more teams; but on Saturday last, his latest team met with a four-nil defeat. This team consisted of big, hefty fellows, sporting the famous light blue of the Dragons.

Frankly, these evacuees play a very fair brand of football. They use the short passing tactics—so reminiscent of the old 'Christians'—with effect, have fine ball control and should give our Manning teams considerable trouble.

We suggest that the JFA come to the aid of the Reverend Father Superior and arrange a match, say, first of all against the Alpha Boys, the Aguilar Cup champions, and then ask either St George's or KC to finish the lesson—if they can!'

The good relations between the Camp Authorities and the local press, and in particular *The Gleaner,* went suddenly sour early in the new year. One cannot help but feel, from some of the exchanges which followed, that local politics became mixed up with the whole affair! Early in January, 1941, *The Gleaner* sent their News Editor to the Camp to put some questions to the Commandant. According to 'Spotlight', 'probably relying on newsmen's resourcefulness and long friendship with Rae to get him inside, the News Editor made one fatal omission; arriving at the Gate of Gibraltar without a pass.'

The News Editor did not get in, and *the Gleaner* took umbrage at this rebuff. From his colum *Today* columnist Gordon Scotter fired 'a salvo which swelled to a blistering broadside against Rae, from whom the snub allegedly came.' (*Spotlight*)

'This crop of 2 × 4 dictators . . . sprung to like fungi since the war started . . . now we have our "little" Ernest Rae of "Gibraltar", complete with sports model concentration camp, scuttle helmet, and off-with-his-head manners.' Scotter played on the rebuff to the paper's busy News Editor who had 'something rather important' to ask Deputy Commandant Rae, who arrived at 'the frowning portals of Gibraltar' to be informed in curt Berchtesgaden style: 'The Deputy Commandant does not wish to see *The Gleaner.*'

The article continued: 'These things undoubtedly have their funny side . . . (but) free British subjects are getting thoroughly disgusted with this dictatorial attitude taken up today by so many of our officials . . .'

This report elicited the following letter from 'One of the Evacuees' on the 18th January, 1941 (and published in *The Gleaner*):

'I read in yesterday's issue of your paper that your News Editor was recently refused entry to Gibraltar Camp by order of our local dictator. Of course, he was refused entry through the 'gloomy portals' (by the way we always refer to the prison gates as 'gloomy portals').

His visit might have coincided with a mealtime. He would then have seen the bad catering and indifferent cooking to which we are treated and the unpleasant conditions under which it is served to us. The founder of the Camp has unfortunately sailed for his home at Gibraltar, satisfied that he has left us in safe and happy conditions until the war, which has deprived us of our homes and livelihood, is over. (The reference is obscure!—author). It is the greatest wish of all of us that he could see how the people he has entrusted us to have developed into dictators, small in their way but definitely to be felt. Whole families in the Camp who have been sufficiently lucky to catch the dictator's approval are employed at 10/- and 15/- a week, each member, in spite of the fact that the head of the family is drawing a government pension. For the unlucky (or untactful) ones amongst whom there are many capable professional and reliable workers, they must eat their hearts out for work, and a little wage to supplement the poor food and the little money they have managed to bring with them. What is to happen when their small savings are exhausted no one can foretell. But all this is of no interest to our own particular dictators. I can give you the name of an ex-Serviceman, a member of the British Legion, who has received no pension since he came to the Camp, and has not yet obtained the necessary interview with the Camp authorities. He is still trying to break through the bodyguard.

I quite realise that owing to the war there is intense suffering throughout the world, but that does not excuse unpleasant conditions that could be avoided. We all like Jamaica and we deeply appreciate the great kindness and sympathy we are receiving from outside the Camp, but we do feel that having been brought here under military exigencies, thereby depriving us of homes and means of livelihood, we should be treated as responsible human beings, and not mere nuisances to provide a living for a few petty officials. I am enclosing my full name and address, but not for publication. If my name is published, the writing of this letter might be termed insubordination, and dire punishment for that, as you would see in the printed rules if you were permitted to see them, is deprivation of food which, bad as it is, would be unpleasant for me as I am one of the unfortunates in the Camp who at present have no visible means of support . . .'

Spotlight, which described this letter as 'scathing' and 'too well-written', followed up the case. A telephone call to Deputy Commandant Rae immediately achieved an appointment for the following morning. Indeed, *Spotlight's* news-hound found that the Papine-Camp motor bus driver had been instructed to give him a lift in, that a pass signed by Rae had been left at the gate, and that Rae himself was waiting to lead the way to the Commandant's sanctum.

Commenting on the letter, Commandant Worlledge said that it had caused great consternation in the Camp, and that Mr Rae had been approached by several evacuees who were very upset by the letter. The Commandant said that the statements contained in the letter were obviously untrue, and that the administration of the Camp as individuals were friendly to the evacuees. 'We are all very happy. This interference annoys me very intensely', he continued. Regarding the refusal to admit *The Gleaner's* News Editor, Mr Worlledge explained: 'that was a misunderstanding caused by not following the proper procedure, which they at *The Gleaner* know well . . . We have always given every facility to the Press.' Deputy Rae chimed in: 'It isn't true that I said I didn't want to see *The Gleaner.*'

The Commandant then proceeded to take the allegations one by one: on the reference to 'gloomy portals'—'as you can see for yourself, the location of the Camp is quite sunny.' (Such comment clearly ignored the metaphorical nature of the remark!). 'There is complete freedom of movement among the evacuees. Each one has a permanent identification book and does not need a pass to go out or come in. All he has to do is to show his book to the man at the gate so that the number can be registered.'

On the reference to 'bad catering and indifferent cooking', the Commandant said that this was entirely untrue, 'and you can go to the kitchen and see for yourself at mealtime. You might get one per cent grumblers, but *I know the food is good*—extraordinarily good.'

The reference to 'Dictators', the Commandant dismissed as 'pathetic.' As to the implication of favouritism in the provision of employment ('whole families . . . employed'), Mr Worlledge said that there were many families with the same name and the authorities did not know who was who. Practically everyone who could work would be given employment. Already, 400 evacuees were employed in the kitchen, the pantry, as carpenters, tinsmiths, sign-writers, labourers, shoe-makers, etc. 'We have 1,500 people here and if we get only one per cent grouses I think we are doing very well.'

The *Spotlight* reporter then visited the kitchen, where lunch was being prepared under the direction of 'big, brown-skinned Master Chef David Thomas. Gibraltarian women were singing while cleaning potatoes from an automatic peeler; on a big table, large flat cakes were being cut into diamond-shaped titbits for dessert by uniformed cooks. The main dish being prepared consisted of mixed meat and sliced potatoes.

The furore raised by this affair necessitated the Governor of Jamaica to cable Gibraltar as follows: 'It would appear that false rumours are being spread in Gibraltar concerning sanitation and health at Evacuation Camp here. No truth whatever in the rumours. Health and sanitation of the best.'

An official denial of the charges was also published in *The Gleaner* on the 27th January, 1941. This stated that everything compatible with discipline was being done to make the evacuees feel at home. Their liberty was not curtailed; they often left the camp at eight o'clock in the morning and could remain out as late as 10 pm.

There was no attempt at dictatorship; the most pleasant relations existed between the authorities and the evacuees and neither the Commandant nor his deputy was inaccessible. Over 400 evacuees were already employed in different tasks in the Camp, and there was no discrimination when these people were being employed.

An ex-serviceman had been appointed as chief of the Special Police which consisted wholly of Gibraltarians. He was a most efficient man with 28 years' service in the Gibraltar Police. The delay in the paying over of pensions to some of the pensioners from Gibraltar was not the fault of the local authorities and steps had been taken to adjust matters with the Gibraltar Government.

Things quietened down—though not for long! Meantime, the evacuees got on with their lives. Following upon the success of some of the males on the football field, some of the girls took to netball with fair success. Plans for beautifying the Camp by laying out flower gardens and for providing plots of land for growing vegetables were being mooted. Some families set about improving upon their accommodation: one family, housed together in adjoining rooms, had, by a system of sharing bedrooms managed to achieve a dining-room and a sitting-room. All the rooms were charming; curtains of blue silk screened windows, shelves and home-made wardrobes; the beds were covered with attractive bedspreads whilst photographs and the usual Catholic symbols adorned the walls. The Camp School opened and soon the registered attendance numbered 230.

On February 6th, 1941, it was announced that Mr Worlledge had been promoted Deputy to the Director of the Colonial Audit Department in London, and would leave Jamaica in April. The forecast was being made that Mr E A Rae would succeed him as Commandant.

Towards the end of February, 1941, the regulations at Camp Gibraltar made the news again! The fining of two men in the Half Way Tree Police Court for having entered the Camp without passes drew a strong attack on the principle underlying the issue from a well-known speaker on political matters. Mr John Soulette, a former alderman of the Kingston and St Andrew Corporation, was strongly critical of the increasing restrictions generally being encountered on the island.

Dealing specifically with Gibraltar Camp, he argued that the way in which the Gibraltarians were roped in was in direct opposition to the principles preached and hitherto practised by the English people. Soulette questioned the motives behind such restrictions at the Camp. 'Is it that the authorities do not want them (the Gibraltarians) to mix with the natives?', he asked. He reckoned that the evacuees deserved a better fate than that of semi-internees.

The real motive behind Soulette's remarks then emerges: 'All this comes from the little brief authority enjoyed by certain men sent to this island who call themselves Englshmen, but do not know English principles . . . Our freedom is assailed on all sides.' Could the reason for this, continued the argument, be that the Government did not wish the people to see how their monies were being spent? He also blamed the Elected members for so lowering their dignity by taking money for their services. Clearly, Gibraltar Camp was being dragged into local political issues!

In early March, 1941, two Gibraltarians, Mr F Alecio and Mr M Mena, arrived at Camp Gibraltar from New York. Both were members of the Gibraltar Evacuees Fund Committee of New York, and both had mothers in the Camp. The object of the visit was to see for themselves and their committee the treatment being meted out to their fellow 'exiles', and the men stayed at the Camp for three weeks before returning to the States. They subsequently submitted very favourable reports, giving glowing descriptions of the food served, the housing arrangements, the care taken of the sick and the education facilities afforded the children.

A little later, another Gibraltarian, Mr Matias Reyes, arrived at the Camp from Gibraltar, apparently sent by members of the families of some of the evacuees to see how the latter were getting on. Mr Reyes had his wife and son in the Camp. On his return to Gibraltar he sent a letter to the authorities in Jamaica thanking them on behalf of himself and his friends for the splendid treatment he had received and he assured the authoritites how satisfied all were after having heard what he had to tell them about conditions at Mona.

In mid-March, 1941, the retiring Commandant was honoured at the Camp, and a few days later it was announced that Mr Rae had been appointed Acting Commandant. Another Jamaican, Mr G Phillpotts Brown of Montego Bay, formerly Commissary Manager of the Camp, was promoted to act as Deputy Commandant.

Efforts to add to the diversions of the evacuees continued. At the beginning of April, 1941, the first troop of Girl Guides was enrolled at the Camp, a Boy Scouts Troop being invested in June. The occasional concert was held in the Camp theatre at which local artistes displayed their varied talents. Occasions such as Empire Day and Corpus Christi were celebrated with parades, processions, songs, etc. Outings continued to be organised. Things seemed to be going well as everyone made the best of a difficult situation, but some would not leave well alone!

On the 17th July, 1941, the following letter appeared in *The Daily Gleaner:*

The Editor:

'Sir—It may surprise you to hear that I was told by an evacuee yesterday that the Germans in Camp are being better treated than these simple folk from Gibraltar. Things are not going too well up there. They are all disgusted with the restrictions that seem to be growing daily and yet another sign board has been put up until the state of complete encirclement seems to be near at hand.

Now, I have made some friends among these people, and I am not guessing at what I am writing, as I was given it straight from the shoulder by one of them.

These people are neither refugees nor are they prisoners of war, they are British Subjects sent here by the British Government. They have left their loved ones far from these shores, some are in England and in London, subject to the bombing of that City. It is therefore only common decency and simple kindness to see to it that we, Jamaicans, treat these people properly, and not as if they were prisoners of war.

I am quite sure that in England these people do not get this kind of dictatorial and wire fence treatment. My experience with them proves them to be very loving and kind. Why should they be so treated? I hope His Excellency the Governor sees to it that an inspection be made of existing conditions there, which will result in these evacuees being made happier and given less of this sign post stuff which makes them feel that they are not in a British Colony. The people there appear to live in constant state of fear and intimidation.'

(Sgd.) 'Ashamed of it all'

The letter is not very convincing and clearly the work of someone with limited education! What could possibly have motivated it? The Colonial Secretary of Gibraltar thought that the whole thing was a canard put up to foment discontent in Jamaica with a view to undermining the authority of the Governor and his Administration. A Camp spokesman suggested that such rumours were being spread by young Jamaican 'Romeos' who had their eyes on some of the many 'Juliets' in the Camp! The charges made in the letter were emphatically denied.

Esther Chapman, Editor of the *West Indian Review* and *Jamaica* went to print in defence of the authorities:

'It is a pity that publicity has again been given in your columns to an anonymous attack upon the administration of Gibraltar Camp.

I have had what are perhaps unique opportunities of judging the attitude of the evacuees, both during Mr Worlledge's time and under the present regime. The spontaneous tributes paid to Mr Worlledge before his departure were signs of an appreciation that amounted to affection. I have not noticed a lessening of this appreciation under Mr Rae's direction.

I was invited by the bridegroom to this morning's Camp wedding. The mass of evacuees who attended were fit and contented. I questioned some of them and found only indignation at the attack in this morning's *Gleaner*.

The evacuees naturally are nostalgic for their own homes, and sad to find themselves exiled. They have to endure the restrictions, however merciful, inseparable from camp life. But I have never yet in my considerable experience of the evacuees, heard a single complaint. Instead, I have been told again and again how fully they realise what efforts are continually being made so that they may be as happy as possible.

No doubt there are minor grievances, as there must be in every institution, from a boys' preparatory school right up to heaven; but I have not heard them. The very reverse is the fact at Gibraltar Camp.'

Esther Chapman,
21st July, 1941

These contratemps aside, life went on at the Camp! The first Camp wedding, referred to in the above letter, took place on the 21st July, 1941, the happy couple being Mr Alfonso Manito and Miss Aurelia Fernandez. A week later, five male evacuees from Gibraltar joined the Camp, and in a colourful ceremony the Scout Troop were presented with a new flag. The flag was the work of Mr Benyunes, a noted Gibraltarian artist, with the assistance of his wife.

On Saturday, 30th August, 1941, a new Sports Ground, situated in No. 2 Camp, was opened. The area of four acres was spacious enough to accommodate two football grounds, a cricket pitch and two tennis courts. Most of Gibraltar Camp's 1,600 evacuee population and their guests and friends took part in the ceremony, and it was one of the rare occasions when the public generally was admitted into the Camp.

The Alpha Industrial School Band led a parade of Gibraltar Girl Guides and Boy Scouts, and Commander Hawkins of the Fleet Air Arm officially opened the ground by hoisting the Union Jack in front of the pavilion, while the big crowd cheered, clapped wildly and sang. The Commander was assisted by Mr Rae, Acting Camp Commandant. The ceremony was followed by a football match in which the evacuees' team beat Fleet Air Arm 2-0. This was followed by a decision to enter the team in the local Senior League.

A great deal of publicity was given in the local press to this move, and the potentiality of the Camp side was highlighted. Results were not to bear out the favourable forecasts made! Five of the opening games were lost, and then disaster! In a match against Kingston at Mona Camp, the Gibraltar players lost their heads, four of them assaulted the referee, the game had to be abandoned, and the Camp authorities withdrew the team from the competition!

Concerts and parties continued to be held. On the 4th September, 1941, 'in appreciation of the hospitality and kindness shown them since their arrival in Jamaica', evacuee artistes gave a concert party in the Mulry Hall before a capacity crowd. The proceeds went to the St Vincent de Paul Society.

With a second Christmas approaching, and the Camp population increased by nearly one hundred Jamaica-born babies, a big pre-Christmas Garden party was organised at the Camp's recreation ground in the presence of Lady Richards. This was followed in the evening by a Concert at the Ward Theatre in aid of War funds. The Show was called 'Gibraltar Comes to Town' and contained great variety. It was directed and stage-managed by Mr Nemesio Mosquera, who also contributed a number of comic items.

Thus another Christmas came and went, and the prospects of an early return home dissipated. The incident which seems to have attracted the most publicity and created the greatest problems was the so-called 'dining-room incident' of the 19th May, 1942. The whole affair was sparked off by a decision of the Camp Management to prohibit the taking of food out of the dining room (apparently, some evacuees were taking more than their faire share!), and this necessitated the closing of all the dining room doors during part of the meal. This move aroused resentment amongst some of the evacuees, who objected to being thus locked in.

On the 19th May, 1942, in Dining Room A, some evacuees took the law into their own hands, broke open one of the exit doors, and behaved in a disorderly manner. The leader of the demonstration, a man, was requested by a Special Constable to report to the Police Station after his meal. He was followed to the Station by a large crowd, mainly women, who had to be dispersed by the Police. The man resisted arrest and he was later sentenced to seven days detention for damage to camp property. One woman was fined £5 and admonished on the same charge, and eleven others were charged with breaches of Camp Regulations, eight being fined 5/- each, one being admonished, one bound over, and one reprimanded. Those involved in the incident were restricted to camp for several days. One evacuee recalled many years later that the leader of this fracas had been a half-witted individual and that the whole affair had been a storm in a teacup.

Nonetheless, the incident had serious repurcussions in Gibraltar. On the 3rd June, 1942, Chief Inspector Brown reported to the Colonial Secretary that a slip of paper was allegedly being passed from hand to hand in the streets and cafes frequented by Gibraltar men; 'and as I had this from a soldier of the GDF who came to ask me whether I thought it was true, evidently amongst them too.'

The slip read:

CITIZENS

'In Jamaica for a simple protest brought about by the bad food provided, they order the Black force of Jamaica to charge pistol in hand against our families, undefended women; they beat them and take them to prison making them undergo dishonourable humiliations in prison

and

What is being done in the meantime by those who are supposed to look after them?'

On the following day, the Chief Censor in Gibraltar informed the Colonial Secretary that 'for some time past examination of mails received from Jamaica tend to show that conditions of Gibraltarian evacuees over there are not entirely satifactory.' He enclosed examples of such letters, one correspondent referring to harsh measures taken by a 'nigger inspector'.

One letter, translated from Spanish, went as follows:

'I am going to tell you what happened. To reach the dining hall we go through a certain door, to leave, we come out by another. If the food is good, we take it along with us, if not, we take the bread. An order came out that the exit doors should be closed. You can imagine mothers with their children's food unable to leave the dining hall until after twenty minutes. One day the men and women between them pushed open an exit door, it resulted in . . . getting sentenced to fourteen days in jail, the women were also locked in for a few hours. The next day they had to pay fines, some were fined only five pence, others five pounds . . . It was scandalous, the Commandant gave orders to the police to use their truncheons, you should have seen women being knocked down. I tell you it was awful. Afterwards a crowd went to the church to protest. The Father Superior managed to calm them down, and told them that the matter would be seen to.

But up to now nothing has been done. They closed the Camp gates so that nobody could leave the Camp. They have now opened them again . . . was cautioned for opening the Camp gates and letting some women through. We will see how it all ends. I will let you know that when we saw how things were we shut ourselves in our room. Don't be alarmed as it is all over now.

There is a double war here, the best thing to do is to lie quiet, or we won't be able to live peacefully. Let the families hear about this. I tell you it makes one lose one's head. I repeat don't be worried for although we had a good fright, nobody interfered with us.'

Another correspondent stated that the Commandant had 'ordered out the Negro police and other policemen with truncheons and revolvers with orders to arrest everyone.' The leader of the demonstration had been 'handcuffed and put in a cell which was so small that I wonder how he could even breathe. It was frightful to see how the police were acting. They arrested a woman who then fainted away, but even in this condition she was taken to prison . . .'

Yet another writer stated 'that God alone could give her the strength to put up with all the suffereings she was going through.' She also stated that the food was so bad that she had to get all the money she could to buy it outside, and that to this end she had to borrow money from a neighbour and repay it when she got it from her husband. The cooks, she continued, 'all niggers', although getting high wages spent most of their time playing dominoes and the food was so badly cooked that no-one could eat it.

Another writer stated that children under thirteen years of age had been arrested, that one girl had been left in prison with nothing but knickers and brassiere. Because the evacuees were kept within the Camp no telegrams could be sent. The letter ended by complaining that the Commandant only protected the people of Jamaica.

One evacuee likened the Camp to a concentration camp, another said that it would have been preferable to have been sent to the United Kingdom, even with the bombings going on there than to endure the conditions in Jamaica.

Such statements, as will be imagined, caused great disquietude amongst husbands and relatives in Gibraltar. On the 10th June, 1942, a petition signed by about 500 was handed in to the Colonial Secretary in Gibraltar:

'We the undersigned, citizens of Gibraltar, most urgently request the immediate amelioration of the precarious condition of the evacuees at Gibraltar Camp, Jamaica, owing to their unmerited sufferings and constant ill-treatment at the hands of the Camp Commandant.

'It is a great pity that after the invaluable propaganda which is continually broadcast with the approval of HM Government, the above mentioned gentleman owing to his incapacity and ruthless lack of concern, acts in such a manner that the place is likely to be mistaken for a Nazi Concentration Camp instead of a place in the British Commonwealth of Nations.

Our suggestion is that the inhuman conduct of the Commandant is sufficient justification for his removal.

We should be more than pleased if you give your fullest attention to our petition and beg you to make appropriate representations to those whom the case may concern.'

The Colonial Secretary wrote to his counterpart in Jamaica on the 19th June, 1942, explaining that husbands and relatives of evacuees in Gibraltar Camp were getting greatly worked up 'which was very natural in view of the lurid descriptions contained in some of the letters (being received). Living, as we all are here, away from our wives and families, we are apt to become worried and upset even by complaints which if they were made by word of mouth we would treat as being of little consequence.'

The investigations which followed in Jamaica revealed that the statements quoted above were gross exaggerations and misrepresented the facts. *No* force had been used by the police nor had they been armed with revolvers, truncheons or other weapons, and no-one had been injured. One special constable, a Gibraltarian, had been threatened by the crowd and on patrol later in the day wore an *empty* revolver holster. Two hours after the incident calm had been completely restored and had so continued. For three days permission to leave the camp had been refused to all concerned in the incident.

On the 17th August, 1942, the Chairman of the Gibraltar Camp Committee, a Mr Mortimore, reported to the Colonial Secretary in Gibraltar. It was his 'considered opinion that the evacuees had no real ground for complaint concerning either the quantity or quality of the food they are given in Camp, or concerning their treatment by the Camp Commandant and the Special Constables.'

He continued: 'In regard to the Commandant, my experience has been that as far as I have seen, he endeavours to give the fullest consideration to the evacuees and refugees under his control. It will be appreciated that at times it is very necessary to maintain discipline and that any disciplinary action will probably bring forth exaggerated reports in correspondence to Gibraltar. In my opinion, however, he has always been fair and just, and I believe him to be generally well liked by the majority of the evacuees.' Furthermore, 'the writers of the letters were . . . in most cases, people of not very satisfactory character.'

At the same time, the Commandant submitted his own Report on the incident, which included statements by those involved. The girl who was allegedly imprisoned in a semi-nude state testified that her clothing had in no way been disturbed by anyone, and that she was properly dressed: ('The Police took away my chain, wrist watch, bracelet and shoe laces, but no one troubled my clothing and I was properly dressed otherwise, excepting that I was searched by a female sent by the Police.') This same girl was also alleged by the Commandant to have assaulted an old lady who had refused to co-operate in the demonstration.

The writer who had stated that the leader of the demonstration had been handcuffed now admitted that her statement had been based on rumour and that she had not actually seen the handcuffs. She also denied that she had said that a woman had been put into prison in a faint condition. The Commandant stated quite categorically that no-one had been handcuffed during the incident.

The Commandant was also of the opinion that the statements about the food, made by one of the evacuees, were nothing but an attempt to get relatives to send her money. It was admitted on all sides that the food was good, though it was natural that there would always be a few people who would find certain dishes not to their taste.

The writer who had complained of the ill-treatment of children was described as 'a horrid type of woman who has given a great deal of trouble at different times.' She had 'even insulted the Chaplain with regard to the education of her children.' It seems that the Chaplain's choir had also been broken up because the other evacuees had refused to associate with her, and that it had been reorganised without her. The statement that no telegrams could be sent once those involved in the incident had been restricted to camp was false since the Post Office Telegraph Station was in the camp itself!

The evacuee who had likened the camp to a Concentration Camp now stated that he had not intended his statement to be taken literally ('I do not find it like a Concentration Camp because I can go out and come in at any time I like.')

Another of the writers was described as 'mischievous and unreliable.' The Commandant reported that this person received remittances, sometimes of rather large amounts. 'By an error of judgement he was temporarily employed in the Fire Brigade but after a few days was laid off and the position given to another evacuee who was in poor circumstances, and for this reason he was 'aggrieved.' This man's statement would seem to support the Commandant's views: '. . . what I wrote refers to my individual condition. If I had a job I would not feel as I do . . . Apart from being withdrawn from the Fire Brigade I have never had any trouble.'

Such, then, is the full story of 'the Dining Room incident.' Readers can draw their own conclusions!

CHAPTER TEN

The Evacuees in London

The decision to evacuate the bulk of Gibraltar's civilian population to London has come under some criticism. Was it not incomprehensively stupid to transfer these civilians from a spot which hardly felt the horror of war to one which endured so much of it? Quite apart from the fact already made clear in earlier chapters of this book that the British Government strongly resisted the move of Gibraltar evacuees to the United Kingdom, and that once there every effort was made to re-evacuate them to the West Indies, such a view can be charged with 'reading history backwards.'

In 1940, there were good reasons to believe that the Fortress of Gibraltar would be in the forefront of the battle. The entry of Italy into the war seemed likely to make the Mediterranean area one of the centre spots of the war, and there was always doubt regarding the position of Spain, given her many flirtations with the Fascist colleagues. Spain harboured tens of thousands of German agents, Hitler was planning his 'Operation Felix', and Mussolini was banking on Franco's assistance in the projected attack on Gibraltar. If such an attack had materialised upon such a small area, the civilian population would almost certainly have been decimated. That it did not occur is no reason to accuse those who logically anticipated it of crass stupidity! Gibraltar had to be stripped and prepared for action. In those circumstances, there was no room for non-essential civilians, 'useless mouths' or not!

The question still remains: why London? Why there at a time when British children were being sent from the capital to the country? The official answer to this was that London was the only place in the United Kingdom where suitable accommodation could be found at such short notice for so many people. It was also the place where a regular and constant food supply could best be relied upon, and another deciding factor was the question of health. The change of climate, alteration of diet, and general mode of living, with a possible adverse effect on physical fitness, made it imperative that all the most up-to-date in medical service should be right on the spot.

So much for the decision to send the Gibraltarians to London. Once the project to move them on to the West Indies had been abandoned, they had to settle down as best they could in their new environment with little prospect of an early release. How did they fare?

In the initial stages of their exile, their nerves, somewhat frayed by their prolonged and often uncomfortable sea voyages, were not helped by the several months of almost nightly bombing raids which they had to endure. For some time, many of them dared not wander far from their Centres, even in the daytime. There was also ever-present a mental anguish born of the fact that while their bodies were in England, their hearts and minds, and all they held most sacred, were in Gibraltar, which was expected to be attacked at any moment.

Such inhibitions were gradually broken down as the months went by. Shopping had to be done, particularly for clothing, and once the evacuees had discovered the attractive shop windows of London and seen the unconcern with which the Londoner went about his, or her, business, they gained in confidence. The entry of children into various schools meant going out twice daily, and some of the evacuees also found employment. Gradually, then, the Gibraltarians settled down to some form of routine and made the best of their situation.

In November, 1940, the Ministry of Health established a committee to organise a systematic arrangement for the education of the evacuee children, some 2,880 boys and girls between the ages of five and sixteen. (The hope of enlisting the aid of the Christian Brothers never materialised).

The provision of accommodation and staff took some time and buildings such as the Victoria and Albert Museum had to be adapted to school purposes. In due course, school facilities were provided within two miles of each evacuation centre. Given the large majority of Roman Catholics amongst the evacuees, the co-operation of the Roman Catholic authorities was sought. Although accommodation had been provided only in one Roman Catholic school, in the others the London County Council had selected Roman Catholic teachers for the work. In addition, nineteen lay teachers from among the evacuees were employed.

Since many of the teachers did not speak Spanish, there were some difficulties, particularly with the lower stages. In the long-term this association of the younger generation with the English language and this exposure to a different way of life was to have profound effects upon the future of the civilian population of Gibraltar. The Gibraltar Government and the Secretary of State for the Colonies attached great importance, not only to progress in the English language, but also to the acquisition of English atmosphere and traditions.

Enrolment of children and regular attendance also presented problems. There were those mothers who refused to send their children to school for fear of exposing them to wartime London, and these had to be reminded of their legal liability and possible penalties!

Pupils between the ages of twelve and sixteen who had qualified by their attainments were admitted to approved secondary, central or junior technical schools. By the spring of 1941 some 80 pupils were receiving post-primary instruction. The London County Council had also opened 24 classes for the teaching of English, commercial subjects, music and other subjects for adolescents who wished to continue their studies, whilst some women evacuees were attending a secretarial training school under private management.

The WVS, with the aid of the Boy Scouts, Girl Guides and the Red Cross Victoria League, had organised community and welfare work, and educational facilities included classes for French, dress-making and physical training.

Reporting nearly two years later, in April 1943, Patron stated that the arrangements for Secondary Education had not been too good, and that a proportion of the parents had made arrangements for their children privately. Due to the work of the British Council an appreciable number of scholarships had been given to the most promising boys to take up Secondary Education, but there remained considerable scope for more to be done in this direction. Patron felt that it was essential that such education should be of a practical nature, and should be so organised as to be useful to the boys on their return to Gibraltar. By this he meant commercial and technical education which would fit them for such employment as was likely to be available for them.

In consequence, Patron was trying to arrange with Pitman's College to have classes for Gibraltarian boys, on the basis that the boys would be selected by recommendation and that the parents would be asked to pay part of the expenses in proportion to their means. Such classes would be of a strictly practical nature and would be restricted to English, Accountancy and Book-keeping, typewriting, shorthand, and some technical subjects.

Many efforts were made, often by the evacuees themselves, to provide leisure activities. On the 19th July, 1941, a gala dance was held at the Empire Pool Evacuee Centre in Wembley to raise money for a memorial fund on behalf of HMS Hood, which had been sunk on the 24th May, 1941. HMS Hood had been on the Gibraltar station and her crew had made many friends among the inhabitants of the Rock. The news of the loss of the ship had decided the evacuees in London to start a 'Hood Memorial Fund' on behalf of the dependents of men lost in the ship.

At the gala dance there was an attendance of 1,500, including the Mayor and Mayoress of Wembley and many well-known local personalities. Youthful Gibraltar cadets, led by Sgt Orciel, paraded during the evening, bearing Allied flags, and finally formed a 'V'. At the apex was little Anthony Cefai, in naval uniform, who presented a bouquet to the Mayoress, and placed the first coin in the collecting box.

The President of the House Committee, Mr J Silva, thanked the Mayor and the visitors for their attendance, and the Deputy Mayor addressed the evacuees in Spanish, amusing them by saying that, beautiful as the decorations were, the young ladies who graced the floor with their presence were more beautiful still! Dances became a fairly regular feature at most of the Centres.

Film shows were introduced and excursions by motor-bus arranged. Thus, in the summer of 1941 over one hundred evacuees were taken to Hampton Court to sample the delights of this beautiful building and its gardens. The outing was provided, including tea, for the small charge of 1/3 per head, thanks to the generosity of the British Council. Another trip was arranged to Windsor Castle, the country residence of the King and Queen.

On yet another occasion all the womenfolk over 60 years of age were taken round London and were shown the havoc caused by German bombs to St Paul's Cathedral. They were also shown Westminster Abbey, the Victoria Embankment, Somerset House, the Houses of Parliament, Whitehall, Hyde Park, Kensington Palace and Gardens.

Many of the Gibraltarian women also helped to while away the hours with needlework. In the summer of 1941 an exhibition of such work done at the different Centres was arranged by the WVS, and Lady Smith-Dorrien, who judged the work, commented that it was of an exceptionally high standard and that she had found it extremely hard to select the prize winners.

The evacuees also formed their own orchestra, the instruments being provided by Major Patron. In August, 1942, Mr Teuma of 'the Music Store', Main Street, presented them with orchestrated Spanish music.

For the younger children under school age, special rooms were allocated for use as nurseries and they were looked after by specially trained child-care reserve workers. Boy Scout Troops were soon started in several of the centres. By early 1941, the National Hotel had Rover Scouts, Sea Scouts, Boy Scouts and Cubs, and so many boys wanted to join that the Holborn Commissioner decided to start a new Troop for them, as well as for the boys from the Thackaray Hotel. Girl Guides were started at the Royal Palace Hotel, where they had their own Company, and girls from the National Hotel joined with the Holborn Company. Brownie Packs were also being started in several centres.

All the Centres were soon provided with wireless sets and several were also provided with pianos. At many of the centres concert parties were held once a week. Obviously, conditions varied in the different Centres: according to Patron, much depended on the officer in charge and the enterprise, energy and communal spirit of the people in them. Thus, one Centre soon had a well equipped Club with a library and a billiard table, as well as a fully-equipped football team, who looked very business-like in red and white jerseys.

Sport proved a valuable recreation. According to the *London Evening Standard,* reporting in May 1942, there were among the evacuees from Gibraltar in London many footballers. Junior and senior league and cup competitions were arranged for them by the London Gibraltarian Football Association, and the finals of the cup competitions were played on the Queens Park Rangers ground at Shepherd's Bush on the 9th May, 1942. In May,

1944, the *Gibraltar Chronicle* reported that a team of young Gibraltarian evacuees in London had won another silver cup in the final of a special soccer competition organised by the British Red Cross. Teams representing Britain, Spain and Free Austria had participated, and the Gibraltar boys had won two of their games by the considerable margins of 7-1 and 5-1. The team played in the well-known colours of Gibraltar in red and white, and every evening in any sort of weather the team could be seen practising in London's famous Kensington Gardens.

In November, 1942, the evacuees living at Courtlands in Richmond took part in an enjoyable sports meeting at the Surrey CC county school ground.

How did the evacuees behave? Inevitably, with such an assortment of people from all social groups, behaviour patterns differed widely. Many of the evacuees displayed dignity and a sense of responsibility; others gave Gibraltar a bad name.

Some of the Centres to which the evacuees had been sent were situated in the better residential districts of London. Kensington Palace Mansions in South Kensington, for example, were blocks of suites with views over Kensington Gardens, where rents of one hundred guineas a week had not been unknown before the war. The Royal Palace Hotel also in Kensington, was a luxury hotel, and those evacuees sent there found themselves in a place previously frequented by more affluent visitors. As one evacuee remarked many years later, the place was 'ready as if to receive tourists.' But, she added, 'the people spoiled it.' Fittings were damaged and in some cases stolen when some evacuees moved on to another Centre or left the Scheme for private accommodation. Undisciplined children were allowed to be destructive, and what had been a spotlessly clean hotel with top-class facilities soon degenerated into a semi-slum!

The problem of discipline was highlighted by Patron in a letter published in the *Gibraltar Chronicle* on the 20th August, 1941.

'There is one very important point on which I would like to ask the assistance of all left in Gibraltar who have children here. It is often very difficult for the mothers to enforce sufficient discipline on the older boys who have been away from their fathers for a long period.

These long days they have many hours at the Centres on their return from school. Some of the Centres are far away from parks and open spaces and the result is that the boys are destructive in the Centres and do a great deal of damage to property and are noisy in the streets.

Therefore, I am sure that any father who keeps impressing on his family the need for stricter discipline, both for their own sakes and that of the community generally, will be doing good work.

We should remember that our people are living in some of the best residential districts of London amongst influential people; that they are, naturally, judged by the way they behave and that this will affect their neighbours' opinion of them and their attitude towards them.

If we take advantage of the opportunities given us, much good may come out of evil and not only can our young generation learn much from their stay here, but their behaviour can win much sympathy for our little town, and I am certain we should not like the good citizens of Kensington to look forward to the departure of the Gibraltarians from their midst as one of the blessings that Victory will bring them.'

In an effort to divert such youthful energies along less destructive channels ('away from the usual snares which beset young people in London', as a Colonial Office official put it) the idea of a Club for Boys, which would be purely a Gibraltarian Institution outside the Centres was mooted. According to Patron, such a Club would have the dual advantage of bringing the boys under proper influence and leadership whilst leaving more room in the Centres to organise social activities for the girls.

Patron interested himself in the project from the outset, and he was responsible for finding the necessary premises at 48 Lancaster Gate, a house with five floors and a basement which had been unoccupied since the outbreak of the war; there were 24 rooms all told, as well as bathrooms, kitchen and scullery. Clearly, before occupying these premises certain adaptations and redecorations would have to be carried out: damp had affected some parts, there were broken panes to be restored, and wallpaper to be replaced. The electricity and water supplies would also have to be checked. The cost of such work was estimated by a Ministry of Health architect on the 2nd October, 1942, at around £500.

The proposals were clarified by Patron at a meeting of the Inter-departmental Committee on the 9th October. The idea was to provide an establishment for cultural and social activities for youths aged between 14 and 25. All sorts of indoor games would be available, as well as a library and facilities for study, music, and educational classes. The Club would open from 6.30 to 10 pm daily and for longer hours over the weekend. Outdoor sports and other activities would also be catered for, and it was hoped to attract a membership of about one hundred.

Apart from the initial outlay of £500, it was estimated that the recurrent cost of such a Club was likely to amount to about £500 a year. Patron had undertaken to find the money for furniture and equipment from his 'comforts fund'. The Colonial Office felt that the Gibraltar Government might be glad to take the opportunity thus offered to reaffirm its close interest in the Gibraltarians in London by finding the relatively small sums required and lending its name and prestige to the proposed Club, which would be an amenity provided in London by Gibraltar for its own people. It was also felt within Government circles in London that everything possible should be done to maintain the ties between the evacuees and their home Colony, from which they had now been absent for two years. The Gibraltar Government readily agreed to such a proposal.

The Club, named the Calpe Institute, eventually opened in early June, 1943, at which occasion the Governor of Gibraltar, General Mason MacFarlane, sent the following cabled message:

'At inauguration of Club for Gibraltar Boys I wish it all possible success and send greetings from all of us here to its members. We shall watch its future with great interest.'

The large number of visitors to the institute every evening is ample evidence of its popularity.

The Club, having been thus established, was to have a very short life—about a year in fact! By the summer of 1944, the great majority of the evacuees had been moved to Northern Ireland, and Patron consequently saw no further need for the London Club.

There were, however, some interesting sequels to this venture. In November, 1944, the authorities in Gibraltar were planning to open a Gibraltar Society. It was decided to adopt the name 'Calpe Institute' for the building in which this Society was to be housed, some of the furniture of the London Club was put at the disposal of the Gibraltar Society, and it was proposed to make possession of the badge of the London Club an entitlement to membership of the new Society. Some of the London Club's furniture was eventually used in Gibraltar schools.

The hazards of war, of course, were never far away. The intensive bombing of the 'Battle of Britain' might have ceased after September 1940, but air raids continued, and alarms and rushes to the shelters were part and parcel of life for the Gibraltar evacuees in London. On the whole, luck favoured them—residents of London said that they liked living near the Evacuation Centres as they felt safer there! Sometimes, however, that luck ran out.

In April, 1941, for instance, the Germans carried out heavy air-raids over Britain in relatiation for the Royal Air Force's pounding of Berlin. On Friday, 18th, during a severe air-raid, three Evacuee Centres (the Dean Hotel, the Harewood Hotel and the British Empire Hotel) were badly damaged. As a result, Henry Balestrino Sr died of injuries received. There were five other casualties, but these were all minor. According to a telegram from the Secretary of State, 'the behaviour of the evacuees was admirable and their help where required during the raid was readily given.'

Many years later, an evacuee recalled: 'A bomb fell on Dean Hotel where my mother and sister resided. My sister escaped unhurt, but my mother, an old person of 76 years, was trampled on by the other residents trying to escape from the hotel whose structure was collapsing . . . she died shortly afterwards. When the air-raid siren was sounded we took shelter in the underground, where we sometimes spent the night sleeping with our mattresses on the floor. We once saw the German fighters machine gunning civilians in the streets of London.'

Another evacuee recalled: 'We were bombarded when we were at the Empress Hall. Two bombs were dropped on the roof of the shelter and as it was a car park it had no walls. Beside us there was a railway coal junction, bombs also fell there, and fumes entered the shelter and somebody cried out that it was poison gas. Everybody panicked. Jewish families sheltered in another place and when they came they thought we would be dead. Nothing happened to anyone.'

Other recollections include the evacuee who said that 'due to the bombs I lost a brother and my mother was very ill and died a few months after her return to Gibraltar in 1945. I remember that we had to run away many times to the shelter and seeing many houses on fire because of the bombing.' Yet another remembered being bombed out of the Royal Stuart Hotel. But perhaps the worst was to come when the Germans launched their V1 and V2 rockets in the summer of 1944.

The medical arrangements were good and gave rise to few criticisms. There were doctors and nurses in attendance at the Centres and in each Centre there was a sick bay open day and night. Cod liver oil, malt, and preparations of vitamins B and C were supplied free in all the Centres. The health of the evacuees, too, appears to have been generally good and they would seem to have adapted well to the cold damp winter climate of London. Apart from measles, which caused a good deal of sickness amongst children in the early stages of their stay in London, the incidence of children's ailments and infectious diseases was noticeably low, and, according to Patron, writing in the *Chronicle* in May 1941, the children looked fit, healthy and happy. Patron was of the opinion that the great majority of the children had benefited by the change of climate. Amongst the other evacuees, too, the incidence of sickness had been very low, and according to Doctor Durante compared very favourably with the normal incidence in Gibraltar. The doctor also commented that he had watched the children playing football in the gardens and that a fitter and happier looking crowd of children could not be desired.

All this despite the fact that the winter of 1940/1941 witnessed severe conditions throughout Europe (the worst for fifty years) and that the winter of 1941/1942 was also a very bad one. In Britain an icy spell began on January 6th, 1942, which lasted until February 21st—the longest icy spell of the century! The average temperature in London was only three degrees above freezing point, and on only twelve of the 47 days was no frost registered.

The provision of food for the evacuees, as we have seen, had posed problems in the early stages. In April, 1941, Patron reported in the *Chronicle* that this continued to be a problem due to the difficulties of obtaining the classes of food the people were accustomed to, and a Food Advisory

Committee had been formed which had done a good deal of very useful work. Such dishes as 'bacalao' (cod), 'albondigas' (meat balls in a tomato sauce) and 'rosto' (pasta with tomato sauce and carrots) had been tried out and had proved very popular. The 'bacalao' was especially successful, and the staff at one of the Centres, who, never having seen it before and disliking the smell, had to be coaxed into trying it, all finished by having a second helping. An attempt at 'olla de coles' (cabbage stew) had not been successful, but, wrote Patron, these efforts to vary the diet and to give the evacuees the type of food to which they were accustomed were very much appreciated.

By the summer of 1941 Patron was reporting that the Food Committee had been doing excellent work, and he supplied details of four days' menus for the week beginning 27th July:

FIRST DAY

Breakfast — Savoury Pasty.
Lunch — Goulash of veal; cabbage; pineapple and custard pie.
Tea — two sardines and lettuce; rock cake.

SECOND DAY

Breakfast — boiled egg.
Lunch — bacon pie, cauliflower, custard trifle.
Tea — noodles au gratin; jam.

THIRD DAY

Breakfast — Meat Rissole.
Lunch — Bacalao estilo viscaina; cabbage; apricot tart.
Tea — bacon rissole and mashed potato.

FOURTH DAY

Breakfast — two sausages.
Lunch — albondigas de carne; rice pudding.
Tea — ½ veal and ham pie and pickles; ginger cake.

For supper each night there was cocoa, coffee was served with breakfast, tea at teatime, with margarine at both meals. Bread formed a part of each meal, and there were always potatoes for lunch.

Reporting in September, 1942 the *Daily Express* commented that the evacuees were 'beginning to like the English food and as far as possible it is cooked the way they prefer.' Two months later, the same periodical added that the evacuees were even eating porridge and liking it! However, there were those who yearned for more garlic-flavoured dishes!

Despite the alleged improvements made in the food provided and its presentation, there is evidence that most of the evacuees considered it necessary to spend a large proportion of their income supplementing the food provided in the Centres. And notwithstanding Patron's assurances, the question of food continued to pose serious problems, as will be seen in the next chapter.

From time to time, the British Press focussed its attentions on the evacuees from Gibraltar, and some of these are offered here at the close of yet another chapter.

In November, 1942, Norman Smart of *the Daily Express* wrote as follows:

THE ROCK, KENSINGTON W.8
A VISIT TO GIBRALTAR EVACUEES IN THEIR LONDON HOMES

'Mr Howell E Jones, Chief General Inspector of the Ministry of Health, threw open a door in a gloomy basement of the Ministry of Health building in Tothill-street, Westminster, saying, "And here are the toys." The electric light flashed on brightly coloured rocking horses, see-saws, bagatelle boards.

Civil servants get curious jobs to do in wartime . . . With about a dozen other civil servants he administers what is virtually a "Crown Colony" in England—the 12,000 people evacuated from Gibraltar in August and September, 1940. You cannot have a "Crown Colony" without children—hence the civil servant as an undisguised Santa Clause.

This group of civil servants have had one of the most ticklish jobs of the war. They have taken a small town of people, most of whom have never strayed far from Gibraltar—three miles long by one mile wide—and introduced them, slowly, gently, into the coldness of the great big world which is London.

GAY AND NOISY

I know our British subjects from Gibraltar. They are gay, noisy, happy people, living their comfortable lives in the sunshine of the Mediterranean. The people who arrived in this country from Gibraltar two years ago were not gay. They were British who, climatically and temperamentally, felt foreigners when they came to the home country. It wasn't an easy job to deal with these exotic, olive-skinned people who were proud to be British, but rather frightened to be in England—at first.

TOY DEMOCRACY

They do not claim to have made a great success, but they have worked like slaves for whatever success they have achieved. When they have finished their day's work at the office they go out in the evening to sit on food advisory committees and sports committees. They give guidance in organising Scout and Guide rallies and concerts. They are the spirit behind this toy democracy—leaving the Gibraltarians to run the show themselves as much as possible.

I went along to see how this two-year scheme is working out. The evacuees are housed in thirty centres all over London. Each is, as far as possible, a self-governing little community linked with the whole. . . .

BILINGUAL PRATTLE

With a civil servant I toured one of these centres; Kensington Palace Mansions, South Kensington . . . The 'under-five' children in the nursery grouped themselves and shrilled 'Baa, Baa, Black Sheep' for my benefit. Two years ago they knew no word of English; now they prattle bilingually. The English climate has toughened them. They are beautiful children.

Among the 'over-fives' they played an amusing game of asking each other questions in newly-learned and almost faultless English. During this, most children announced gravely that they wanted to be soldiers, sailors or airmen.

It looks like a peacetime Sunday in Main Street, Gibraltar, when the women come to Mass in the converted chapel, wearing their elegant black lace mantillas . . . one evacuee sat in her room with sunlight streaming on her glossy black hair. "Just like Gib?" I suggested. She shook her head and looked sadly nostalgic. To her mind British sunshine, pale and cool, doesn't resemble the Mediterranean sun in the slightest degree.

NEWS FROM HOME

When I told some of them that I had just returned from the Rock they chattered so enthusiastically about their homes, looking at me with wonder, that I felt a bit like Father Christmas.

The escorting civil servant, a man who has spent most of his spare time in the last two years assisting in the scheme, looked on with pride. He is one of the men who are going to miss the colourful slices of Mediterranean life in London when the war is over and the toy democracy is disbanded.'

Also in November, 1942, the London *Daily Sketch* reported on the Gibraltar evacuees.

'Yesterday I visited one of the most amazing communities in the world, and it is in England. It is the city of Gibraltarian evacuees who came here in 1940. Among them is Mrs Yeo, aged 94, who, until two years ago, had never been away from the Rock. She is now busy learning English, and is quite undaunted by the intricacies of our not too easy language.

FIVE GENERATIONS

At the other end of the Yeo family is two-year-old Charlie Dempsey, Mrs Yeo's great-great-grandson. He was born only seventeen days after his mother's arrival in England. He has never seen his father, who is still in Gibraltar. Under one roof, there are five generations of the Yeo family—surely a record.

Though the evacuees are not liable for call-up, some of the young men have volunteered. Typical was Peter Buttigieg, who, after four months in England, joined the RAF. He was shot down recently, and is now a prisoner. His sister, who told me this, is working in a factory, as are over ninety per cent of able-bodied Gibraltarians.

One of the residents said he was surprised by the modern facilities provided for them, ''although there's no place like home.'' He remarked: ''there will be a lot of changes to be made in Gibraltar when we go back.'' '

CHAPTER ELEVEN

The Marlborough Court Incident

The problem of food was to prove the catalyst which triggered off a chain of reactions destined to upset the administration of the Evacuee Centres in London. What began as an apparently straightforward disagreement about the quality of the food provided, developed into much wider issues including the rights of the evacuees, the powers of the Ministry of Health, and the position of Major Patron as Evacuation Commissioner. Dragged into the whole affair were the Law Courts and *The Times* newspaper. It also gave the recently formed Association for the Advancement of Civil Rights in Gibraltar an opportunity to set in motion the campaign for the gradual replacement of nominated officials and committees by democratically elected ones.

Some evacuees, possibly tired of communal feeding, the quality of the food provided and the manner of its preparation, began the practice of taking the food to their rooms, there to re-cook it in such a way as to make it more palatable and to supplement it with food purchased outside the Centres. The Ministry of Health objected to this practice on the grounds that there had been many cases of fire and that it was an encouragement to Black Market activities. They therefore issued regulations to stop all food being taken to individual rooms.

In most Centres the officers in charge realised the impossibility of stopping food being taken into the rooms and, so long as the practice was kept within reasonable bounds, they tolerated it. However, at Marlborough Court Centre in Earls Court, the regulations were strictly enforced. In June, 1943, a new system was introduced by which, in order to prevent any leakage of food, the evacuees were given cards which they had to present to obtain their meals.

At Marlborough Court resided an evacuee named Gustav Bellotti, who had been a member of the first City Council of Gibraltar to have Councillors elected by popular vote, and who had served three times, from 1921 to 1930, sponsored by the Transport and General Workers Union. Bellotti had held the position of Chairman of the House Committee at the Centre, but he had resigned that post because of differences with the Liaison Committee (which acted as an intermediary between the evacuees and the Inter-Departmental Committee responsible for their welfare) and in particular with its Chairman, Agustin Huart. Now, on the issue of the cards a meeting was held at Marlborough Court at which Bellotti was elected Chairman and a Salvador Holliday Secretary.

According to Patron, Bellotti was one of those people who thought nothing could be obtained except through legal action and pressure, and who had not co-operated with any organisation set up. Patron complained that three years previously, after attending a meeting at which it had been agreed to send a deputation to see Mr Malcolm MacDonald, the Minister of Health, Bellotti had taken action on his own, without consulting others, and sent a solicitor's letter to the Ministry.

On the evening of Tuesday, 25th May, 1943, 'the Bellotti Committee' informed the Officer in Charge of the Gibraltar Evacuation Centre at Marlborough Court that the evacuees intended to take their food out of the dining room into their quarters in defiance of the Ministry's rule. The Officer in Charge reported to the Ministry of Health and was told that the rule must be adhered to.

Despite this, beginning on the 27th May nearly all the evacuees proceeded to take their food out of the dining room, and continued to do so although Notices were posted in the Centre advising the people of the Ministry's rule.

The Liaison Committee resigned on the 3rd June, having taken the line that although they were in complete sympathy with Patron's attitude they did not wish to take any active part at this stage. Three days later, Bellotti, Holliday and three other evacuees were seen at the Ministry. When asked by the Officer in Charge whether they were prepared to carry out the Ministry's rule, Holliday said that he was not, whilst the others refused to answer. At the interview, Bellotti told the Ministry that 'our solicitor Dr Wright' would be prepared to discuss the matter.

Dr H Newcome Wright, a solicitor living in Holland Park, was to feature large in the events of the next few months. Patron took an instant dislike to the man, which is hardly surprising given that his methods of litigation and agitation were anathema to an 'establishment' man like the Major! Writing to the Colonial Secretary on the 5th July, 1943, Patron commented on Newcome Wright: 'I do not know whether his action in this matter has been brought about by a genuine desire to help the evacuees or for publicity or other reasons of his own. His actions have been such as to leave considerable doubt in my mind as to his motives.'

It was not the first time that Dr Wright had involved himself in matters relating to the Gibraltar evacuees. In November, 1940, he had sent letters to the Minister of Health and the Secretary of State for the Colonies alleging inadequacy of food provided in the Centres, overcrowding and mixing of the sexes, and victimisation of persons who complained. He had threatened to circulate similar letters to Members of Parliament if the Ministry would not reverse its policy towards the evacuee whom he was representing. A Miss Daphne Foster, believed to be his clerk, had visited the Centre at that time and urged the evacuee concerned to resist eviction. In November, 1942, he had acted as the representative of an evacuee who was under notice to leave because of her misconduct. At that time he had contended that the Ministry of Health had no legal right to evict an evacuee but he had not maintained his argument after receiving a letter from the Ministry's solicitor. He had later sent information about overcrowding and inadequacy of food to the *Evening News* who refused to publish it. In May, 1943, he had represented an evacuee who had been charged by the Ministry of Food with wasting food. On the 2nd May, 1943, Miss Foster, signing herself as 'Hon. Secretary, Petitioners Committee' had addressed a petition of 879 evacuees to the Secretary of State for the Colonies requesting that they be issued with ration books. On the 3rd June, 1943, Dr Wright had written to Mr Howell James, Chief General Inspector of the Ministry of Health, informing that a Petition of Right was to be presented to the Courts shortly in respect of various matters arising out of the steps taken by the Ministry under its circular to instruct Officers in Charge to prevent cooking in rooms and in respect of the storage of goods at Alexandra Palace. Regarding the latter, the Ministry of Health had presumed that Dr Wright was acting for evacuees who wanted compensation for luggage lost in transit from Gibraltar or while in store in Britain. He later asked why 'Inducement Workers' were not insured under the National Insurance and Workmens Compensation Acts. Thus, even before 'the Marlborough Court incident', Newcome-Wright had proved to be quite a thorn in the side of those authorities responsible for the Gibraltar evacuees in London!

But to return to 'the incident.' Since Bellotti and Holliday had refused to assure the Ministry of Health that they would in the future obey the rule which forbade the taking of food out of the dining room, the Minister gave them a week's notice, on the 8th June 1943, to leave the Centre together with their dependents taking all their possessions with them. When they refused to comply with this order, an attempt was made, on the 16th June, to eject them with the help of the police. What followed was a total fiasco! Many of the women evacuees lay down in the corridors to obstruct the passage of the authorities, Bellotti resisted eviction and four porters attempted to drag him out, and Holliday and his family locked themselves inside their flat. The police inspector present then gave up the attempt since he considered that the eviction could not be carried out without making a number of arrests.

According to the Ministry of Health, Dr Wright had advised the evacuees, chiefly the women, to adopt passive resistance when the eviction was to be carried out. On the day following these events, the 17th June 1943, Dr Wright advised the Ministry that he was acting for Bellotti and Holliday, and on the 20th June he wrote accusing the Ministry of Health of tactics of intimidation. He followed this up with an extensive campaign which included calling at the *Daily Herald's* Office and inviting them to send a representative to Marlborough Court, writing to the Conservative member for Kensington pleading for his support and warning him that the Gibraltarians' grievances might be taken up by papers of the Left, writing to a number of Members of Parliament and to *The Times*. This agitation was clearly directed at English readers and made great play on the non-segregation of sexes in some of the Centres, though the Ministry pointed out that this was a matter where it had been very difficult to persuade evacuees to accept the standards advocated by Dr Wright. Meanwhile, Dr Wright's clerk had been visiting the Centres whilst he himself had been holding meetings of Gibraltarians at his flat. To them, claimed the Ministry, he had been using other arguments, chiefly playing on their grievances on the matter of food.

On the 29th June, the secretary of the Association for the Advancement of Civil Rights in Gibraltar cabled Dr Wright as follows:

'AACR support your efforts check unjust treatment and improve unfortunate condition Gibraltar evacuees London. Please confirm TIMES published your letter 21 June.' (The Colonial Secretary, Miles Clifford, felt that it would have been prudent for the AACR to have awaited receipt of the official report before becoming thus involved). The AACR also cabled Major Patron: 'Request you investigate incidents to Bellotti and others at Marlborough Court and telegraph result. Great resentment amongst civilian community here.' Patron replied: 'Am in contact with position. Will be sending Colonial Secretary a report. Suggest you wait till you have full facts before forming an opinion on the matter.'

At the same time, a spate of telegrams arrived at the offices of the AACR in Gibraltar. These asked the Association to make representations to the Colonial Secretary in Gibraltar with a view to getting democratically elected Committees in London. One of these telegrams came from Gustav Bellotti and was received on the 8th July, 1943. It read: 'It is the earnest wish of all, that all the other posts apart from that of Commissioner already appointed to look after our welfare in this country be left to us for nomination.' Similar telegrams were received on the 10th and 11th July from Bruzon and Garcia (delegates for North End House), C J Grech and A Caruana (King's College), Obdulio Sanchez and Joseph Bugeya (Marlborough Court) and Mrs Harrison and Albert Bellotti (St Stephen's Close). The AACR followed this matter up by approaching the Colonial Secretary and requesting that the posts previously filled by selection should now be filled by popular election. This, the Association argued, would place the election of the posts on a democratic footing and would be much more helpful in its smooth working, as those elected would be the genuine representatives of the evacuees to whom they would be responsible.

According to the Ministry of Health report on the matter, an attempt was now made to resolve the difficulties by negotiation. Now, that word 'negotiation' implies a certain amount of 'give and take'. Readers can judge for themselves whether what follows comes under that category! On the 23rd June, Major Patron prepared a notice, in English and in Spanish, which was displayed in all the Centres. In it he announced his appointment as Commissioner for the Gibraltar Evacuees in the United Kingdom, spoke of his work for the evacuees, and said that Mr Huart had offered to work as his Deputy if the general body of the evacuees desired him to do so. He explained that his new organisation would be a new means of approach to the Ministry of Health. He also said that *the Ministry of Health had allowed him to tell the evacuees* (an unfortunate turn of phrase taken up by his adversaries!) that:

'(a) although in the interest of the majority of the Evacuees it is not possible to permit separate cooking by individuals, and that, as in boarding houses and hostels ordered arrangements for feeding are essential, they will carefully consider suggestions made to them to meet the wishes of the Evacuees in the question of food.

(b) as in the past, every case of eviction will be carefully studied, but in addition a fellow Gibraltarian will be able to give their case before the eviction is proceeded with.'

Patron added: 'It is to be clearly understood that the administration of the Scheme will continue entirely in the hands of the Ministry of Health and that our function will be purely of an advisory character, and that we cannot in any way intervene in the Administration of the Centres.' Therein lay the basic difference between Patron and those who wanted a more democratic arrangement!

On the following day, the 24th June 1943, Patron wrote to Bellotti and Holliday as follows:

'As you are aware, I very much regret the action taken, and though you have not thought fit to approach me in the matter, I have considered it advisable, in the general interest of the evacuees, to take up the matter with the Ministry of Health.

A Notice from me explaining the steps that have been agreed upon, following my recent visit to Gibraltar, will be posted shortly in the Centres.

I am pleased to inform you that the Ministry have authorised me to tell you that if they receive an undertaking from you within seven days that you will, in future, refrain from taking any direct action in regard to rules and regulations that they may find necessary for the general welfare of the evacuees in the Centres, and that you will co-operate with the new arrangements being made, they will withdraw their Notice of Eviction and will, in the meantime, take no action in the matter.'

The Ministry of Health also sent letters to Bellotti and Holliday confirming Patron's. One may well imagine the reactions of Bellotti, Holliday and Dr Wright to these 'offers'! The only reply came from Dr Wright who wrote to Patron that the Petition of Right was being prepared and that it would be as well if they discussed the matter.

Such a discussion never took place because Dr Wright declined to go and see Patron who was to be attended by a solicitor, after Patron refused to agree in a telephone conversation to bring pressure to bear on the Ministry. In any case, Dr Wright did not wish to discuss the particular cases of Bellotti and Holliday.

On the 3rd July, 1943, Patron, assisted by Huart, held a meeting of representatives of the Centres at which he threatened to resign his new position of Commissioner unless he was accorded a vote of confidence—which he received unanimously.

Meantime, Bellotti and Holiday continued to reside at Marlborough Court, considered as trespassers by the Ministry and Patron. Their meal-tickets had been withdrawn, though, on the application of Dr Wright, ordinary ration cards had been issued to them by the Ministry of Food.

What was the Ministry of Health to do now? It seems that counsels there were divided and that there was a reluctance to take the matter further, partly perhaps because it was felt that some of the things which the agitators were urging were sensible and ought to be done, partly because of uncertainty about their legal powers. The Ministry's own assessment of the situation was that the source of difficulty was the food provided in the Centres, and that the other complaints were minor and had been produced more to impress the outside public than because they were looked upon as injustices. As their report on the incident observed:

'The food is not popular, it is not the food to which the Gibraltarians are used. The cooking is not perhaps all that might be desired . . . The existence of the problem is known to the Ministry and further measures to overcome it are under consideration.'

The one flaw in this statement was that by the time it was made (in July 1943), the whole affair had gone well beyond a dispute about food. Some of the evacuees had already formed themselves into a so-called Provisional Executive Committee, which was to call into question the right of the Ministry to administer the Centres without consulting the evacuees and which was to launch a vicious campaign against Major Patron.

Whilst the Ministry hesitated, Patron was quite adamant that no improvements ought to be brought into effect, which the agitators were supporting, until the agitators had been put in their place, since to give way to their demands on some issues would merely strengthen their hands in the conduct of the general campaign, which was undoubtedly directed towards undermining the whole authority of the Ministry. Patron felt that the first thing to do was to establish in the Courts the power of the Ministry to expel Bellotti and Holliday: this would burst the bubble, and the Ministry could then proceed with magnanimity and without loss of prestige to introduce as many reforms as they liked.

The Ministry disliked the idea of prosecution, and there was a long interval before proceedings were instituted. In the meantime they did not seem able to make up their minds what to do. An attempt was made to get new House

Committees elected. In a Notice circulated to the Centres in September, 1943, it was claimed that the Minister of Health had always encouraged the establishment of Committees representative of the Gibraltar Evacuees, to make known their views and to co-operate in the administration of the Scheme. Such Committees, the Notice continued, could do much to promote the welfare of the evacuees, and to accept a share of the responsibility for the maintenance of good order in the Centres. The Minister noted with regret that since the resignation of the Liaison Committee on the 3rd June, no duly elected body had taken its place (a deliberate snub at the Provisional Executive Committee?) Detailed proposals followed for the election of such bodies.

In a letter to Patron, dated the 21st September, 1943, the Ministry referred to this attempt at securing representative committees of the evacuees, and also outlined further proposed improvements:

(a) The system of 'Inducement workers' was to be discontinued and people would be engaged in the ordinary way to do kitchen, cleaning and other work in the Centres.

(b) It was planned to issue butter, margarine, sugar and jam to the evacuees at intervals, weekly or monthly, according to the article, instead of at each meal-time as at present. Naturally, a portion of each would have to be retained for use in the kitchen. In the Centres where facilities for boiling water existed, it was proposed to extend this issue to coffee, tea and cocoa, and to extend the facilities for boiling water to other Centres.

(c) Every evacuee who wished to have his mid-day meal outside the Centre could do so and receive a corresponding allowance in his Recovery Scheme payment.

(d) It was also hoped to make revised arrangements for the children attending schools to use the School Meal Service.

(e) Efforts were being made to provide a number of new Centres of a much smaller size than at present. In some of these it was proposed to try the experiment of only providing living accommodation and leaving the evacuees to provide their own food: i.e. they would have their ration books and cook their own food. Such an arrangement, it was stressed, would be entirely experimental and would be stopped if it did not work out satisfactorily in practice.

(f) Although in the existing Centres the present practice of all main meals being prepared in the centre kitchen would have to be retained (since it would be impossible to provide proper cooking facilities for each family) the Ministry was seeking the advice of the War-time Meals Division of the Ministry of Food on feeding arrangements and it was hoped that some definite proposals would be forthcoming soon.

Patron now asked one representative from each Centre to meet him at the Calpe Institute, at which meeting he relayed the Ministry's proposals. He told the representative from the Royal Palace Hotel (the Centre where, according to Patron, most of the trouble had been) that if he wished to bring any ten to twelve people concerned in the agitation to see him, he would be pleased to meet them without putting any restriction on who came. Nothing resulted from this offer.

What did happen now was that Patron was subjected to a good deal of personal attack from Dr Wright and the Provisional Executive Committee. A Notice, issued by this body and disseminated amongst the evacuees, accused Patron of having achieved nothing tangible for the evacuees in the matter of food and lodging. It was claimed that the improvements now being effected, and future ones, were entirely due to the activities of the Provisional Executive Committee, who had sent the Ministry of Health a list of propositions on the 18th August. Patron denied this allegation, affirming that said improvements had been the subject of negotiations with the Ministry for many months and had actually been approved in principle before the agitation had started. The agitation, he claimed, had merely resulted in a delay in their being put into practice.

The Notice went on to accuse Patron of acting in the name and for the Ministry, and *not* the evacuees. 'Therefore', it continued, 'if the evacuees wish to continue obtaining advantages, they must carry on supporting the Provisional Executive Committee, and not pay any attention to the rumours and tales from those parties at the service of the Ministry who are hoping, perhaps, to receive honours and compensation for supporting the many irregularities that have been committed against the interests of the evacuees . . . which can never have the approval of anybody, except by a few official employees.' (This was libellous!)

The Ministry now decided to prosecute Bellotti and Holliday, whilst the Provisional Executive Committee continued its campaign with a series of meetings. At one such meeting, held at the Royal Palace in early October, Dr Wright addressed some 100 to 120 evacuees. He told them that they had the same rights as everybody else in England, including the officials of the Ministry. He also told them that they had had the misfortune of being in the hands of the most inefficient of all the Ministries and that the Ministry of Health was composed of all the cast-offs of all the other Ministries who were not fit to work elsewhere! He claimed that nobody had done anything for them and that he felt, as an Englishman, that it was a shame that they should go back with a bad opinion of England and that it was his duty to do everything he could for them.

He went on to denounce the attempt by the Ministry of Health to get new House Committees elected. He argued that neither the Ministry, Major Patron nor anyone else had the right to enforce elections upon them, that the existing

House Committees could not be replaced by anybody, and that any evacuees who stood forward at the election at the dictation of the Ministry would be acting as quislings. He said that the elected Committees should continue to consider themselves the representatives of the evacuees and should ignore any attempt to alter the Committees.

He then read a Petition to be presented in Parliament. This requested a public enquiry into the treatment of the evacuees, that the evacuees be returned to Gibraltar at the earliest possible moment, that the evacuees be allowed to manage their Hostels by Committees elected freely and without pressure by Ministry officials. Dr Wright said that this Petition would be circulated to the Centres for signature and he informed the Meeting that since Parliament was the highest Court in the Land, anybody who endeavoured to stop, hinder or advise any evacuee from signing such Petition would be committing an offence. They were watching things very closely and would not hesitate to take legal proceedings against anybody who advised or hindered any evacuee from signing this Petition.

In answer to questions he said that the Ministry had no right to take down any Notices placed in the Centres (referring to the above-mentioned Notice from the Provisional Executive Committee) and that this was a matter completely at the discretion of the House Committees. In answer to other questions he gave the impression that the real running of the Scheme was in the hands of the House Committees. He further claimed that the Ministry had no right to move anybody, and that nobody should move from their rooms when asked to do so. (It must be added that the above resumee is as supplied by Patron to the Colonial Secretary).

Further meetings were held in early October. According to Patron, a man at the National Hotel called Bottino, who was not an evacuee as he had been in Spain for some years, had asked for a Meeting, for which permission had been granted. This meeting had been attended by Gustav Bellotti and Bruzon, Chairman of the Provisional Committee, and by about 50 people from the National. After considerable abuse directed at Patron, the meeting had proceeded to elect two scrutineers who were to receive nominations for a House Committee and would act in co-operation with the Provisional Committee.

Patron considered that committees elected on the lines proposed above could hardly be considered representative, and if tolerated would result in the election of a Central Committee with which, due to the methods employed, it would be very difficult for him to work with. Patron also alleged that the methods employed by the Provisional Committee had gone beyond acceptable lengths. He claimed that in the presentation of their Petition to the Houses of Parliament they had made a room to room canvass and had taken down the names of anybody who refused to sign and threatened them with reprisals both there and on their return to Gibraltar. He further claimed that at the meeting at the National, Bruzon had appealed to the women to pray for the success of Bellotti in the forthcoming Court Case, as on that depended the success of the Provisional Committee.

Those prayers would seem to have been answered! The case opened on the 13th October, 1943, and Judge Hargreaves gave judgement at West London County Court in favour of Bellotti and Holliday against the Minister of Health. The Judge stated that there was nothing to justify the view that either of the defendants was organising rebellion against authority, and he saw no reason to doubt that their motive in taking meals up to their rooms was simply the desire for hot meals. Their conduct, said the Judge, was a not altogether unnatural result of the failure of the Ministry, after three years, to provide the type of meals that the residents might reasonably expect. He could not find sufficient justification for such short notice as was given, or for such drastic measures as were taken.

So that was that! What about Major Patron's position now? As has been seen, he had been having a rough time since the 'Bellotti affair', subjected to abuse and criticism from the agitators, and the strain soon began to tell! By early October, 1943, he was complaining that it had become almost impossible to have a position from the Government of Gibraltar, to sit on the Inter-Departmental Committee to advise the Ministry of Health, and at the same time, to represent the evacuees. In the prevailing atmosphere of agitation and legal cases it was impossible to reconcile all these functions. He insisted that the agitation was a purely artificial one and that 'the decent and level-headed people' were getting very tired of the whole thing. In the circumstances—and this was before the legal judgement had gone against the authorities—Patron was thinking of resigning all his posts as from the 1st January, 1944.

Writing to the Colonial Secretary in mid-November, 1943, Acheson of the Colonial Office expressed the opinion that Patron was not really serious about resigning his posts. However, if he was, 'it would be better not to attempt to dissuade him.' Continued Acheson: 'I have reached this view with regret. He is very sincere in his desire to help the evacuees and to act in a public-spirited way, and as you know we here like him very much and think he has done much valuable work for the evacuees. But he has . . . been feeling his position and the personal attacks most unjustifiably made on him acutely, and in the frame of mind he was in a few weeks ago . . . I am sure the right course is to let him follow his own inclination.'

On the 21st November, 1943, a General Meeting of Delegates was called by the Provisional Executive Committee, at which representatives from 28, out of a possible 32 Centres, were present. Also present was the AACR's Hon. Treasurer, Mr M Ghio, on a brief visit to London. A proposition expressing disapproval of the way in which Major Patron had conducted matters affecting the welfare of evacuees and requesting him to tender his resignation forthwith was unanimously carried.

Evacuees in London enjoying 'the sights'.

Evacuees in London having a good time on the river!

Evacuees in London—note the boxes containing gas masks.

GIBRALTAR EVACUEES FROM ALL OVER LONDON BROADCAST TO–"THE ROCK"

These pictures, taken in a B.B.C. studio, show talented Gibraltar evacuees in ndon giving their own broadca… concert to Gibraltar.

They came from various centres all over London, where they are now living, to give an enthusiastic and entertaining performance.

Above, six-years-old Laura Diaz, is photographed singing "Mi Jaca," in which she was accompanied at the piano by Mrs. D. Caruana.

On the right (top) is a scene from the Spanish operetta, "La Rosa del Azafran", being sung by (left to right) Miss Orensia Ghio, Miss Elena Cruz, Miss Angeles Usifredo, Miss Noelia Mosquera, Miss Araceli Lopez, Mr. Louis Gomila, Miss Luisa Lopez, Miss Carmen Ghio, Miss Maruja Lopez and Mrs. L. Gonzalez. They were accompanied at the piano by Mrs. Frances Calamaro.

Below—a glimpse at the enthusiastic audience of Gibraltar evacuees (and some of the artistes) enjoying the concert.

Extract from *The Gibraltar Chronicle* of the 29th July, 1942.

The British School for Gibraltar Children, Funchal, Madeira, 1940.

The British School for Gibraltar Children, Entrance Hall, Funchal, Madeira, 1940.

The British School for Gibraltar Children, Funchal, Madeira, 1940.

THE BRITISH SCHOOL
FOR
GIBRALTAR CHILDREN

SCHOOL RULES

School will begin daily at 9 a.m. sharp. All pupils must be in their places in their Class Room before the hour.

Each pupil must learn and remember his or her School--Number, and upon entering the School must first of all hang hat, cap or coat on the peg bearing that number.

A bell will ring one minute before the time marked for each lesson on your time-table, and immediately this signal is given pupils must go immediately to their places.

A break of a quarter of an hour will be given from 11 o'clock to 11.15. During the break boys must go to the play-ground at the back of the building: girls can play on the ter-races in the front and at the side of the building.

At the end of the break each class must fall in in line and walk quietly with the teacher to the respective Class-Room

No talking is allowed in the Class-Rooms. Attention and respect must be paid to the teachers.

It is strictly forbidden for pupils to touch any of the electric bells. Offenders will be punished.

Special care must be taken not to damage or deface any of the School furniture or the walls or floors of the building.

English is the only language allowed to be spoken in the School.

Those who speak Spanish may be punished.

It is strictly forbidden for pupils to touch the taps in the garden, and the water from those taps must never on any account be brought to the mouth nor drunk. The water laid on in the house is drinking water.

At the close of school pupils travelling by the special buses must without delay get their things together and go to their respective bus, according to the number on their ticket, which they must keep from the previous journey to school that morning.

Only those who show their tickets will be allowed to enter the bus. Those intending to come to school by bus the following day must get a book of tickets from their teacher be-fore they leave school today.

The British School for Gibraltar Children, Lazareto Group, Funchal, Madeira, 1940.

The British School for Gibraltar Children.

Main Group, Funchal, Madeira, 1940.

Watching a drill class in action.

The front door of the School with the Union Jack and the Portuguese flags prominently displayed.

A lesson in progress.

Visit of the Civil Governor of Madeira to the British School for Gibraltar children at Funchal.

Madame Teixeira Dias, wife of the Civil Governor of Madeira, walking through the school grounds

The first school certificate class receive their awards in front of the whole school.

; *Indrapoera* embarking returning evacuees alongside the Loo Rock in Funchal Harbour with her escort vessels May 1944. The warship in the foreground is a Portuguese destroyer.

Excavations in progress at Commercial Square (now John Mackintosh Square) for the construction of bombardment shelter. July, 1939.

Gibraltar underground. Sleeping quarters for men inside the Rock.

Military exercises on the Rock.

Street scene in Main Street, Gibraltar. (IWM).

When the Secretary of the Provisional Executive Committee, writing from the Royal Palace Hotel, sent a copy of this resolution to the Governor of Gibraltar, on the 27th November, 1943, His Excellency's terse comment to the Colonial Secretary was that such letters were best ignored!

At the end of the year 1943, the Governor, General Mason MacFarlane, paid a short visit to London, during which he called at some of the evacuee Centres. In his New Year Message to Gibraltar, the Governor said that in almost all cases he had been most agreeably surprised, 'in view of the publicity which has been given to certain difficulties and conditions', at the standards of board and accommodation. He added that in most of the Centres he had found a very happy family spirit, and that the relations between the evacuees and those in charge of the administration of the Centres were in most cases 'delightfully cordial and friendly.' In the one or two cases where he had found definite overcrowding the families concerned had been offered more spacious accommodation, but they had refused to move to another Centre as they were very happy where they were and did not want to leave the staff of the Centre they were in.

Regarding the food, the Governor said that much had been done to provide items normally not procurable in England, and the rations were good and plentiful. The children, especially, were extremely well looked after and were getting plenty of milk. In most Centres they had very cheerful nurseries and plenty of entertainment was being provided over the Christmas season, and in many cases the children were rehearsing shows of their own.

Particularly relevant to the main theme of this chapter was the Governor's statement that 'the Calpe Institute for boys in which, as in many activities, Major Patron has given much assistance—is a great success and a very nice place.' His Excellency said that he had spoken with a fair number of evacuees and that all seemed well satisfied with their work and conditions. 'I found them all remarkably cheerful, they had practically no grouses except minor ones, were on the best terms with those in charge of the Centres and had only one main and oft-repeated question: 'When can we get back to Gib?'

Despite these assurances, the hunt for Patron's scalp continued! On the 18th January, 1944, the AACR wrote to the Colonial Secretary saying that the Association was repeatedly receiving reports expressing dissatisfaction at the inefficacious manner in which the Evacuation Commissioner was exercising his powers. The letter claimed that what improvement there had been in the conditions under which the Gibraltarians in London lived, were due, not to Patron, but to the Evacuees Provisional Executive Committee, ably aided by Dr and Mrs Newcome Wright. 'Rubbish', commented the Colonial Secretary, Miles Clifford, in the margin!

The letter criticised Patron for his belief that it was wrong for the evacuees to give publicity to their complaints and because he favoured submission to the dictates of the Ministry of Health. It was also pointed out (and this is perhaps the most significant part of the letter) that whereas the Evacuees Provisional Executive Committee had been elected by popular vote in true democratic spirit, Major Patron's appointment had been official, and the evacuees did not want him.

In conclusion, the AACR Committee requested that the Evacuees Provisional Executive Committee be given official recognition as the competent body to look after the general welfare of the evacuees in conjunction with the Ministry of Health. Alternatively, it was suggested that a similar body to the Committee should be elected by the evacuees in a democratic manner. 'The adoption of either would render the post of Patron unnecessary.'

By this time, General MacFarlane had been replaced by General Eastwood as Governor of Gibraltar. In his comments to the new Governor on the above letter, the Colonial Secretary said that he did not admit any of the AACR's contentions, and neither had General MacFarlane. He also considered that Patron had been treated 'with abominable ingratitude.' 'He has given freely of his time and from his purse in the interests of the evacuees who prefer however to rely on allegations of a handful of irresponsible people.' He added that if Patron wished to retire—'as I would in the circumstances'—the Government could not prevent him, but 'I hope he won't.'

On the 25th January, 1944, the Colonial Secretary sent back a very cold reply to the AACR Committee. He said that His Excellency had noted the contents of their letter of the 18th 'with surprise and regret' since he felt it would be most impolitic for the Association to take sides in a dispute of which it had no first-hand knowledge, and which, if left to itself, would die a natural death to the benefit of all concerned.

On Patron, the Colonial Secretary had this to say: '. . . during his recent tour of the Evacuation Centres, General MacFarlane was left in no doubt as to the generous assistance and unremitting voluntary work of Major Patron on the evacuees' behalf, nor of the esteem in which he is held by the great majority of them. The Government is greatly indebted to this gentleman and would regard it as a matter of concern if the ungenerous response which his efforts have met in certain quarters should move him to resign from the duties which he has so cheerfully accepted and so sincerely discharged.'

The letter concluded by suggesting that the AACR Committee should take advantage of Patron's presence in Gibraltar to meet him and discuss the whole affair so as to 'clear the air.'

On the very day that this letter was being written, the Minister of Health won his appeal over the Bellotti eviction case! The Master of the Rolls, who heard the appeal together with two Lord Justices, ruled that the Minister had the right to evict. However, he strongly criticised the Ministry for the way it had handled the affair and in particular the attempt to evict by using force and intimidation.

The meeting between Patron and the AACR representatives, in the presence of the Colonial Secretary at the AACR's insistence, duly took place on the 8th February, 1944. At the meeting it was agreed that any non-representative or self-constituted Committees should be abolished, and that a fresh start should be made. A properly supervised ballot in each Centre would elect delegates to a Central Committee and the delegates, also under proper supervision, would elect an Executive Committee with which Patron and the Ministry could deal when occasion required. (It does sound very much like the scheme proposed by the Ministry in September, 1943, and rejected by Dr Wright and the Provisional Executive Committee!) By this time, another organisation had appeared amongst the evacuees, 'the Gibraltar Union', formed by Agustin Huart—no friend of the Provisional Executive Committee or the AACR!

The problem now was how to get the existing committees to dissolve themselves! As Acheson of the Colonial Office pointed out to the Colonial Secretary on the 3rd March, 1944, 'there is no means in this country whereby persons who want to form themselves into committees and undertake activities within the law can be prevented from doing so.' He doubted whether the Provisional Executive Committee would be willing to dissolve itself. In any case, concluded Acheson, the whole tempo of events had been changed by the recent air raids, and he reckoned that when the announcement of the decision to start repatriation was made the evacuees would lose interest in matters concerning the organisation of their life in England.

Patron went ahead with the attempt to get the proposed new representative system off the ground—but he did not get very far! A letter to Louis Bruzon, Chairman of the Provisional Executive Committee, on the 13th March, asking his Committee to resign met with short shrift! A similar letter to Huart met with the response that his Committee would reluctantly accede to the request, provided other Committees did likewise! In any event, as anticipated by Acheson, the developments of March and April, 1944, soon pushed all else into the background. The talk now was of repatriation!

After reading this chapter, the reader may well feel somewhat confused! Who was right—Patron and the Ministry or Bellotti, Wright and company? Unfortunately, there is no ready answer to this question. It may even be that the question is too simple a one given the complexities of the whole matter. All one can do is to offer some tentative conclusions.

That Major Patron worked hard in the interests of the evacuees is accepted by all except the most extreme of his opponents. That the Governor and Colonial Secretary of Gibraltar and the officials at the Colonial Office and the Ministry of Health should be fully behind him is a commendation which must be tempered by the fact that Patron firmly believed in co-operating with such official bodies, sometimes possibly to the extent of not presenting the evacuees' point of view forcefully enough. Writing about the problems of food quality and presentation in July, 1943, Patron himself would appear to be admitting as much: 'It is possible that in my desire to co-operate, I have not been emphatic enough in bringing forward these points.'

The AACR were less fullsome in their praise of the Evacuation Commissioner's work. Whilst unconditionally accepting that he had always displayed the utmost activity in matters concerning the evacuees, the Association's Committee 'reluctantly' came to the conclusion that his efforts, in what they related to the welfare of the majority of the evacuees, had been singularly unsuccessful. It was, nevertheless, admitted that certain minor sections of the evacuees had benefited to an appreciable extent from his generous assistance.

Further insight into the working of Patron's mind comes from the following extract from one of his letters to the Colonial Secretary: '. . . it must be borne in mind that the Scheme is designed for working class people who have been accustomed to living under conditions applicable in Gibraltar and will have to return to those conditions there, and although they may be resident in Kensington, it is hardly fair to judge the Scheme by Kensington standards. The small number of people with means who are accustomed to a higher standard of comfort should not really be in the Scheme, and if they choose to do so as an economy, they cannot expect to have the whole Scheme raised to their level, or conditions adapted to suit their requirements.' The evacuees 'forget completely that their children are receiving better education and are better looked after than ever they were; that the health of the people is better than in Gibraltar, and that their earnings are higher than they have ever been.'

Such statements would seem to be a recipe for the continuance of unsatisfactory standards and a negation of any attempt to seek improvements—at least by means of agitation and unofficial pressure.

On giving the evacuees a greater say in the running of their own affairs, Patron had this to say: 'The people's ideas of the true meaning of Democracy are distinctly hazy, and they are not accustomed to exercise the power to vote, so it appears to be necessary that any steps to give them more control of their affairs should be gradual and kept under proper control.'

Given all this, it is hardly surprising that Patron disapproved of the actions of Bellotti, Holliday and the Provisional Executive Committee. Rules were there to be obeyed, complaints should be made through official channels. It was precisely that attitude which created the unbridgeable gap between the Commissioner and the Provisional Executive Committee.

What were Dr Newcome Wright's motives in conducting his campaign, and what were conditions really like in the Centres? The first question cannot be conclusively answered without an excursion through that gentleman's mind! Was he genuinely concerned about the evacuees or was he out for publicity? Or was he just one of those people who cannot resist a poke at officialdom? According to the Ministry of Health (not the most reliable source in this instance!) his actions were 'somewhat difficult to understand', and they were 'hardly those of a solicitor who had only a professional interest in a case.'

Were conditions as bad as to justify the action taken? The difficulty here lies in the human propensity to forever claim to represent 'the majority.' Thus, according to Patron, 'there is a small minority of discontented people, not always with much right to be called Gibraltarians, who are vocal out of all proportion to their numbers.' The Provisional Executive Committee, for its part, claimed to be acting 'in representation of the evacuees in general', and the Colonial Secretary had remarked that Patron was held in great esteem 'by the great majority' of the evacuees! Talking to some evacuees today, some forty years later, the overall view would seem to be that the food, conditions and organisation at the Centres were good considering that it was war-time. But there are a few who do not go along with this!

CHAPTER TWELVE

The Evacuees in Madeira

The evacuees who went to the beautiful island of Madeira had a comparatively easy time, though they too, of course, had to suffer the pain of separation from home and close ones. As seen in an earlier chapter, it soon became apparent that the total of 2,000 which the Portuguese Government were prepared to accept could not entirely be made up of people capable of supporting themselves. In the end, the evacuees were divided into three categories:

A—self-supporting;

B—in a position to contribute towards their expenses in accordance with a scheme drawn up by the Government of Gibraltar;

C—without means (subject to legislation requiring any breadwinners in Gibraltar who were earning money to make some contribution to be determined by a Means Test Committee).

The evacuees arrived in Madeira in three contingents: on the 21st and 23rd July, and on the 13th August, 1940. The first two contingents were composed exclusively of Category A evacuees, and the total number of persons in each category who actually reached Madeira was as follows:

	Adults	Children	Total
Category A	710	205	915
Category B	548	165	711
Category C	283	70	353
		Grand total:	1,979

During the first days that followed the arrival of the first contingent in particular, the British Consul at Funchal, Mr Cyril F W Andrews, was expressing concern that the evacuees might not be able to maintain themselves in the Island, owing to the limited means at their disposal in comparison with the rates charged at the different hotels and boarding houses at which they first stayed. Other reasons given by the Consul were the loss on the exchange for English notes and the limitation on the sums allowed to be exported by the Gibraltar Treasurer. The Consul suggested that it would help if the Portuguese Government could be prevailed upon to suspend the Tourist tax in the case of the evacuees.

However, such difficulties were rapidly overcome through evacuees finding private accommodation on reasonable terms in and around Funchal, and as a result of hotel proprietors and managers finally recognising that the new arrivals were not tourists, but persons of limited means, and that it was far better for their establishments to remain open with at least a fair number of guests at low rates than to close again. Two hotels only, considering themselves 'luxury hotels', closed after a few days, the reason given being that they were unable to remain open at the price that could be afforded by most of the guests.

Category B evacuees were distributed among the various hotels and boarding houses in and near Funchal, all of which made special terms very much more favourable than those applying to tourists in the ordinary 'season'. In some cases, and in particular in one of the largest hotels where approximately 280 evacuees from Category B were accommodated, two or more persons were sharing one bedroom, but the British Consulate was keeping a careful watch on the comfort and general welfare of the evacuees. Most of the establishments concerned were doing their best to adapt their food to the somewhat different tastes and customs of the Gibraltarians, and facilities were provided to the women to do their own laundry on the premises.

As regards Category C evacuees, it was decided from the outset to treat them as one community, and, with the help of the Civil Governor of Madeira and other local authorities, two large buildings and two smaller ones (known collectively as the Lazareto) to the west of Funchal were hired from the County Council of Madeira. The buildings were in a very healthy situation overlooking the sea. One of the buildings, a modern structure originally destined for a hospital, was divided into rooms, including a large dining room, and was well provided with kitchen facilities, bathrooms and toilets. The other and larger building, when taken over by the British Consulate, was nothing more than two very large dormitories, one on the ground floor and one on the floor above. The two floors had then been partitioned into cubicles of various sizes, with a corridor down the middle. Some necessary repairs had been done to the roof and new windows and shutters had been installed (the old ones were broken and had been replaced by rough boards which would have proved quite inadequate and certainly too dark in the winter). A new kitchen had also been built to enable the inhabitants to have their meals on their own premises thereby avoiding overcrowding for meals. Sanitary conveniences as well as extra facilities for drinking-water were provided next door to the building by the local authorities. The expenses involved in these alterations were met by the British Government.

Of the two smaller houses, one was also used as living quarters and the other was converted into an infirmary. Once Category C had been housed in these buildings it was found that there was a certain amount of undesirable overcrowding. The Consulate then obtained, at a very reasonable rent, a large unfurnished house with garden (Quinta das Cruzes) in which about eighty evacuees were accommodated.

Every encouragement was given by the caterer to both men and women in Category C to assist in the kitchen and to submit ideas regarding any particular dishes they might be accustomed to. Facilities existed both in the open air and in the buildings for the evacuees to do their own laundry. The inhabitants of the Lazareto could also bathe on the beach below, and a bathing attendant was hired to prevent accidents. Category C evacuees were provided with pocket-money allowances, and a doctor was also hired for them. He was on daily duty at both the Lazareto and Quinta das Cruzes, and the infirmary and hospital at the Lazareto had a male nurse in constant attendance. Another doctor was hired for Category B evacuees.

The needs of the evacuees were clearly well catered for (educational facilities will be dealt with later). How did the Gibraltarians settle in and how did Madeira react to their presence? The evacuees, by all accounts, were given a warm welcome by the Portuguese authorities and people. It would appear that the trade of the island had been on the point of bankruptcy when the evacuees arrived, and the Portuguese authorities not surprisingly welcomed their arrival. Hotels which had been closed for some time were now able to open, many flats and villas were hired by the evacuees. All the shops had had to replenish their stocks and were looking prosperous. The evacuees were becoming popular because they were taking an interest in the life of the island.

In view of the comparatively large number of aged and infirm in Categories B and C, the standard of health maintained was remarkably good, and the change and diet had not affected the evacuees as much as might have been expected. No cases of epidemic were reported in the first few months of the evacuation except for one suspected case of typhoid fever at the Lazareto, where there was also a mild outbreak of skin irritation, akin to 'prickly heat'. Mild digestive troubles among persons in Categories B and C were fairly widespread at the outset. In general, the evacuees settled in well.

Soon after the arrival of the Gibraltar evacuees in Madeira it was realised that provision would have to be made for the continuation of the children's education on British lines during their indefinite stay there. Evacuee children of all ages in the three categories totalled 438, and it was estimated that not less than 300 children were of compulsory school age under the Gibraltar Education Ordinance, plus a number of slightly older boys and girls whose attendance at school appeared desirable.

It was therefore decided to establish 'The British School for Gibraltar Children', to open as early as possible in October, 1940. The news was welcomed by the majority of parents, whose children had had no schooling since May, when they had first been evacuated to Morocco, and who in many cases were becoming restless and in need of some form of discipline.

The establishment of a school for so large a number of children and in the space of a few weeks only was no simple matter. Adequate premises at a reasonable rent had to be selected, a suitable headmaster and teaching staff found on the spot, and numerous other problems solved.

The school opened on the 9th October, 1940, and was run under the auspices, and to a very large extent at the expense, of the Imperial

Government. A Gibraltar Advisory Committee was appointed to help the British Consulate in the project. A small number of 'volunteer helpers', selected from Category A evacuees, helped to relieve the small consular staff of much heavy routine work connected with the establishment of the school.

To meet at least a portion of the school's expenses, it was decided to charge school fees at the following rates:

Children of Categories A and B—20 to 40 escudos (about four to eight shillings) a month according to standard. The children of Category C were to be educated free.

An ideal building was acquired. It was spacious, but not overlarge. Situated in healthy air at an altitude of about 250 feet above sea level, just behind and within less than five minutes drive of the centre of Funchal. It had just the necessary ground for play-grounds, with views commanding, on the front, part of the town, the harbour, sea and coastline, and, at the back, the hills and mountains towards the interior of the island. The place was originally a private mansion. It had been rented early in 1939 as a private nursing home by a leading surgeon, who had reconditioned the whole building and added an extra wing at the back to accommodate two operating rooms (now used as classrooms), but had been compelled after some months to give it up as a result of war conditions. The rent paid by the Consulate was £16.10s a month as from the 1st October, 1940. About £123 were spent in installing extra sanitary conveniences and minor adjustments. Desks and benches were made to order by local carpenters. Other furniture items were teachers' desks, blackboards, staircarpet and semi-fixtures taken over from the previous tenant.

Originally, the intention had been to use this building for the education of the children of all three categories of evacuees. However, when the matter of daily transport between school and home was examined, it was realised that the cost in respect of the children of Category C, most of whom lived in the Lazareto buildings some distance from Funchal, would be considerable.

Furthermore, suitable accommodation for classrooms for the fifty to sixty children of school age in Category C was available at the Lazareto. It was therefore arranged for these children to have their daily lessons out there, although they were considered as part of the main School under the supervision of the Headmaster, in whose absence one of the three teachers living at the Lazareto was responsible for their order and discipline.

The post of Headmaster was given to Mr Nigel Power, born in Madeira and a member of a prominent British family on the island. He had been educated in England and abroad, and had for some years specialised in private teaching and was favourably known in Madeira.

The seventeen members of the teaching staff were all evacuees from Gibraltar, and in their selection the greatest care was taken to choose teachers who were as nearly English as possible, preference being given to this fact rather than to mere knowledge of subjects or teaching experience. The need to secure an English atmosphere in the School was strongly stressed.

The names of the Staff were as follows:
1. Mr Francis Carbutto. 2. Mr Ernest Pons, later Father Pons 3. Miss Mercedes Carboni. 4. Miss Teresine Imossi. 5. Miss Marilou Canessa. 6. Miss Victoria Baker. 7. Miss Ellen Romero. 8. Miss Amelia Imossi. 9. Miss Elsie Teuma. 10. Miss Teresine Coelho. 11. Miss Molly Attias. 12. Miss Laura Warne. 13. Miss Florence Ross. 14. Mrs Queenie Richardson.
In the Lazareto Branch: 15. Mr Esteban Macarri. 16. Mr Anthony Milan. 17. Miss Louise Parody.

In addition to the salaried teaching staff, the following arrangements were made for special subjects:

(a) Religious Instruction.
The majority of the children were Roman Catholic and, with the approval of the Bishop of Funchal, two British ladies, Mrs H J King and Mrs F de C Keogh, attended the school regularly to give religious instruction.

(b) Physical Drill.
Miss P Porrall volunteered and attended the School three times a week. Every child at the main building had two lessons in physical training every week. There was no physical training at the Lazareto Branch of the School.

(c) Singing.
This was under the charge of Miss Marjorie Discombe, and, according to the British Consul at Funchal, this contributed 'to the English atmosphere of the School, the children being taught English songs.'

The question of the daily conveyance to and from the School of the children of Category C did not arise, since nearly all of them had their lessons in one of the Lazareto buildings where they lived. The few who were maintained with their families at the Quinta das Cruzes only had a two-minute walk to the main school.

However, some arrangement had to be made for most of the children of Categories A and B. Owing to local transport regulations, the only way in which it became possible to organise a special bus service was by hiring a number of buses for the exclusive use of the School. Five buses, each carrying about thirty persons, were therefore hired. Tickets for travelling on these buses were sold to the children and teachers in books of twenty.

In addition, a special bus was run daily to the School and back by the Grand Hotel Belmonte in Monte (about four miles north of Funchal), where a number of evacuee families were maintained. Another distant place from which eight children had to travel was the hotel at Camacha (about seven and a half miles north-east of Funchal). The hotel proprietor provided free transport for these children as far as the Campo de Barca, Funchal, where they changed to a No. 4 bus; they returned by this same bus at 12.45 pm and connected with the Camacha bus at 1.00 pm.

This system of transport seemed to work well, though one evacuee recalled that after a year police officers had had to accompany the children because hooligans had stoned the buses!

Reference has already been made to the importance attached to the creation of an English atmosphere in the School. In fact, everything possible was done to achieve this. The speaking of Spanish was forbidden in the School, in the school grounds and school buses. Offenders were severely reprimanded, and if necessary punished.

Apart from the teaching of English school and folk songs, every effort was made to ensure that religious instruction was given in English, and, according to the Consul, a boys football club and a girls netball club also helped to create an English atmosphere.

School hours were from 9.00 am to 12.45 pm, the decision to limit the classes to the morning having been taken largely for reasons of economy in the conveyance of pupils and teachers. The School opened on Saturday mornings as well.

On the 26th November, 1941, the Civil Governor of Madeira and Madame Teixeira Dias, the Deputy Governor, Dr Branco da Camacho, the Consul and his wife visited the School. They were received by the Headmaster and members of the School Advisory Committee, and the children were drawn up in front of the building to welcome the visitors. The Union Jack and the Portuguese flags were hung over the front door, and the children sang the first verse of the Portuguese National Anthem, followed by three cheers for the Civil Governor, and the first verse of the British national Anthem, followed by three cheers for the King.

The guests were then taken round the school, where they saw the children at play and at their lessons, and they also attended one of the drill classes. The visit lasted one and a half hours, after which the Civil Governor and his wife expressed their admiration for everything they had seen and the pleasure that the visit had afforded them. The visit was prominently featured on the front page of the *Diario de Noticias,* one of the two leading newspapers of Madeira.

Indeed, the opening of a British School with British teachers proved to be very good propaganda. Many of the local inhabitants were impressed by the action of the British Government, who, they said, took care of the well-being of its citizens, providing them, not only with shelter and upkeep but with an education for the younger generation.

Another important feature of the Madeira evacuation in the early days was the formation of a guild run by Lady Liddell, the wife of the Governor of Gibraltar. The object of this guild originally had been to help the poorer classes of the evacuees with clothing. However, it soon extended its activities to look after the poor natives of the Island of whom there were many.

The guild also became a source of very good propaganda to counter the German element and sympathisers on the Island. Thus, at Christmas time, 1940, mugs with chocolates and marked 'A present from Hitler' were distributed among the poorer native classes. This action was counter-acted at once by Lady Liddell with presents of clothes and food to the children.

Every opportunity was taken by the ladies of the guild to infuse the Island with a British atmosphere. Christmas trees with presents for the children were arranged in all the hotels. Theatre shows were given by the evacuees and all the funds collected were given to the poor.

Evacuees were contributing one escudo a week each towards the native poor. Such activities transformed the life of the Island in a matter of five months.

On the 10th July, 1941, the *Gibraltar Chronicle* gave a summary of the activities of Lady Liddell's Guild for the three months ending May 31st. This showed that 194 oz of wool, 55 dress lengths, 63 other garments and money grants to the value of 70 escudos had been given to Gibraltar evacuees.

For men of HM Forces, including prisoners of war, 119 knitted comforts, 10 flannel vests, 24 handkerchiefs and 8 pairs of pyjamas had been provided. Garments (nearly all children's) sent to England for air-raid victims numbered 133, with a considerable quantity of used clothing. About 112 children's garments had also been provided for the children of poor Portuguese in Madeira. An appeal of April 22nd for air-raid victims had raised the sum of 2,822 escudos as well as the used clothing mentioned above.

Of course, not all was smooth sailing even in the relatively comfortable conditions of Madeira. One problem was the persistent refusal of the Portuguese Government to allow relatives in Gibraltar to visit their families in Madeira. As early as the 19th September, 1941, the Governor of Gibraltar was suggesting to London that approaches should be made to Lisbon to exempt the evacuees from the general order prohibiting foreigners from visiting Madeira. In support of his plea he pointed out that it had been estimated that the evacuees were spending about £20,000 a month to the economic advantage of the island.

The Secretary of State for the Colonies supported this request which was transmitted to the Foreign Office and in turn to Lisbon. No response was received from the Portuguese Government until the 6th February, 1942, when it was stated that the military authorities maintained that such visits would be inconvenient at the present time!

On the 10th August, 1942, Governor MacFarlane informed the Secretary of State for the Colonies that he had received a petition signed by 184 Gibraltarians seeking permission to visit their families in Madeira whom they had not seen for two years. Further approaches to the Portuguese Government were equally abortive.

A different approach was tried on the 17th December, 1942, when the evacuees wrote to the Civil Governor of Madeira requesting him to submit to the appropriate authorities in Lisbon their plea for permission to be granted to their menfolk in Gibraltar to visit them in Madeira. The men made a similar request to the Gibraltar authorities.

This appeared to have solved the problem when the *Diario de Noticias* of the 17th January, 1943, announced that the Ministry of the Interior had agreed to the granting of visas to husbands and relatives of Gibraltarian families evacuated in Madeira. This caused great excitement amongst the evacuees, but uncertainty too, due to the lack of official confirmation of the announcement in the press. A month or so later, on the 10th February 1943, it was officially stated that the Portuguese authorities had agreed to allow visits of thirty days by husbands and relatives—but only cases of sickness or bereavement would be considered. Gibraltarians pointed out to their Colonial Secretary that this was not what they had been asking for!

What transpired next is not clear from the documentary evidence available, but a report from Dryburgh dated September, 1943, states that small parties of men continued to come from Gibraltar to visit their families. It would thus appear that the problem had been resolved.

Another matter which created difficulties in the early stages of the evacuation concerned mails between Madeira and Gibraltar. At the end of January, 1941, the British Consul at Funchal informed the Gibraltar authorities that the Portuguese Government was deliberately holding up mails in both directions between Madeira and British territories. The Governor of Gibraltar surmised (in March, 1941) that this action was due to Britain's enforcement of blockade measures—the British Government was insisting that all local mail from Madeira could not be sent to any country other than Portugal or the United Kingdom, and the Portuguese were retaliating to this irksome condition by refusing to load mail bound for Gibraltar. The Governor pointed out to London that no mails had been received in Gibraltar from Madeira for nearly three months and that the lack of news from their relatives was affecting the morale and efficiency of the menfolk in Gibraltar.

The problem was resolved when the Foreign Office agreed to dispense with the abovementioned restrictions, and normal mail service between Gibraltar and Madeira recommenced in late May, 1941.

Yet another problem arose over who should look after the interests of the evacuees in Madeira. On the 15th August, 1940, the British Consul appointed an Advisory Committee of Gibraltarians 'to constitute a link between himself and the evacuees', to investigate any complaints or claims on their part and to 'represent their interests generally.' This arrangement worked well for a while, but on the 16th April, 1941, the Consul informed the Committee that he did not think that their existence was any longer necessary. He felt that the evacuees should now be treated in the same way as the rest of the British community in Madiera—i.e. directly under the control of the British Consulate. He had therefore 'come to the conclusion that the Advisory Committee ... has become superfluous.'

Messrs. King and Bentubo of this Committee were quick to transmit their complaints at this decision to Governor Liddell: ' ... we beg to suggest with all respect, that as both in Jamaica and in London our evacuees have a Committee or some responsible official to look after their interests although resident in British soil, that it is even more desirable that Gibraltar evacuees in this foreign Island should have their interests looked after by a representative and responsible committee selected from their own people, and that such committee should, of course, act in close co-operation with the Consular Office on the spot.' The Consul's action in deciding to abolish the Committee was described as 'most surprising and unprecedented.'

Mr P G Russo, Acting Chairman of the Board of District Commissioners, commented that it appeared that the position and conditions of the Madeira evacuees had deteriorated and that he felt that the Consul's action was 'high-handed'. He compared the situation in Madeira with that in the United Kingdom which seemed much more 'democratic.'

The Governor transmitted these feelings to the Colonial Office with the observation: 'I should have thought that HM Consul would have welcomed the suggestion and proposals put forward by the Advisory Committee representing the evacuees. I understand that in the United Kingdom and in Jamaica there exist Advisory Committees composed of evacuees, exclusively, and appointed by themselves and I should have thought that a similar practice should have been adopted in Madeira.' He further pointed out that a considerable feeling of discontent existed amongst the evacuees regarding the attitude of HM Consul and his staff.

The Secretary of State for the Colonies endorsed these feelings in a communication to the Foreign Office. The Consul's reasons for disbanding the Advisory Committee were described as unconvincing. 'The Gibraltarians in Madeira, though a part of the British community, are in a special position. They were all evacuated to Madeira at the same time from the same colony for reasons connected with the war. Their evacuation from Gibraltar was compulsory, and His Majesty's Government have recognised a special obligation towards them by providing at the public expense for those of them who are unable to provide for themselves. All these factors give them a community of interest which is not to be found in the ordinary course of events amongst the British residents in any foreign country and does not extend to the other British residents in Madeira.' Lord Moyne therefore felt that the wishes of the evacuees should be regarded with sympathy and asked the Foreign Secretary, Mr Eden, to urge the Consul to reconsider his decision and agree to the appointment of an Advisory Committee to be chosen by the evacuees.

There the matter rested, for despite these high-powered representations, the fortunes of the evacuees in Madeira continued to be controlled by the Consul and his staff.

The actual conditions, financial and otherwise, of the evacuees in Madeira are not easy to ascertain, given the conflicting reports which emanated from the island now and again. A letter sent to the Governor, Lord Gort, on the 8th February, 1942, by a Lieutenant-Colonel F C O'Rorke was very disparaging about the evacuees. He wrote to say that he was appalled at the money being spent by the Gibraltar evacuees, criticised the classification of the evacuees, and the evacuees' own discontent. Category B, he claimed, seemed to have 'money to burn'— a handbag for £2.10s, waterproofs for £5 and £7, £10 for a gold ring; they used taxis and buses, bought clothes and shoes often, and generally indulged in reckless spending. The letter was also critical of young men 'loafing about while our sons are saving the country.'

These statements would seem to have had the effect desired by the author when the Governor informed the Chairman of the Board of District Commissioners in April, 1942, that his attention had been drawn to what would appear to be overspending of foreign currency by certain evacuees in Madeira. Consequently, although it was appreciated that evacuees should not be required to exist without spending any money over and above the cost of bare maintenance, it had been decided to reduce the remittances in the case of Category B to £2 per head per month and in the case of Category C to £1 per head per month.

A few months later, on the 27th July 1942, the Colonial Secretary of Gibraltar informed the Consul at Funchal that he had received representations from heads of families in Gibraltar claiming that the price of foodstuffs in Madeira had increased, that hotel keepers had had to reduce the quantity of food supplied at mealtimes, and that consequently evacuees were finding it necessary to buy extra food elsewhere. He asked the Consul for his comments before deciding whether family remittances for Categories B and C should be increased.

The Consul replied that he could not agree with the claim that evacuees in Categories B and C had to augment the meals provided for them in their respective establishments by the purchase of food elsewhere, and he was strongly against increased remittances being allowed on that score. The Consul did admit that the cost of living had gone up considerably in the past year or so and that he had had to agree to an increase in the charges at one or two hotels, and that others were bound to follow. Nevertheless, he was satisfied that the food provided remained adequate both in quantity and quality. Some evacuees, he claimed, were over-eating resulting in high blood pressure or liver trouble. It was therefore desirable that food should be reduced in some cases!

Despite all this, evidence of financial difficulties being experienced by some of the evacuees as time went by may be gleaned from the ever-increasing number of applications made to move 'down' a category, and growing problems over the payment of school fees. At the beginning of August, 1942, the British Consul informed the Financial Secretary, Gibraltar, that the Foreign Office had instructed him that school fees need not be collected from the beginning of the next school year (September, 1942) but that this abolition of fees would be subject to the following qualifications:

a. abolition of fees would be effective only when arrears had been paid off;
b. an appeal for voluntary contributions would be made to parents able to pay;
c. stationery and bus transport would continue to be charged in respect of children of Categories A and B except in specific cases where such charges had been waived by the Means Test Committee or an appeal to the Consul.

By September, 1943, the rise in the cost of living necessitated an increase in the daily maintenance of Category C evacuees whilst transfers from Category A to B and from B to C continued. At the same time, the Consul responded to a communication from Gibraltar about complaints received from Madeira (largely to do with the quality of the food and bad treatment received at some of the hotels and pensions) by insisting that these were without proper foundation. He accounted for the complaints thus:

'Although the mass of evacuees seem grateful for everything we have done for them—and this gratitude is sometimes shown in quite a touching manner—there are among the fold a few black sheep whose principal occupation, probably because they have nothing else to do here, is to grumble and complain as a matter of principle.

I have from the beginning found these people full of suspicions and jealousies of each other . . . '

It may be added that if these 'black sheep' existed they had nothing else to do because the evacuees were not permitted to compete in the local labour market. This inevitably led to boredom and restlessness. The *Gibraltar Chronicle* reported in October, 1943, that although the evacuees lived virtually as hotel guests, their life of comparative luxury was illusory to the outsider. 'To the evacuees themselves it is convincing proof of the wearisomeness of enforced inactivity for a long period.'

By late 1943, thoughts of repatriation were beginning to predominate. In September, six men left for Gibraltar to engage in essential civilian work, and nine women and children departed for Spain and Tangier. At the same time the evacuees were organising a petition to the Governor of Gibraltar asking that repatriation should be effected as soon as possible.

The arrival of the Repatriation Census Forms from Gibraltar on the 11th February, 1944, not surprisingly caused great excitement amongst the Gibraltarian Community in Madeira. In that month six young men left for Gibraltar and 34 persons moved to Tangier. Further excitement was aroused in March, 1944, by the news, published in the press and by radio, that a party of evacuees from London were being repatriated to Gibraltar. Seven men left that month for Gibraltar for service in the Gibraltar Defence Force or work of national importance. Seven other persons left for Tangier and four for Spain. Two more evacuees left for Spain in April and five for Tangier—all from Category A.

The first official repatriation party, totalling 977 evacuees, left Madeira aboard the *Indrapoera* on the 28th May, 1944, arriving at Gibraltar three days later. This reduced the number of evacuees in the Island to 699, the Lazareto closed down and the remaining residents were moved to Quinta das Cruzes. The school population was now down to 115 with ten teachers.

The trickle of evacuees to Tangier and Spain continued throughout the summer of 1944, whilst proposals were being considered for despatching high priority evacuees 'left behind' from the first party on the 28th May and others by Portuguese ships to Lisbon and thence overland to Gibraltar.

The year 1944 ended with further small repatriation parties—36 in September, 76 in October and 21 in November. By the end of the year the number of Gibraltar evacuees in Madeira was down to 520. The Hotel Belmonte closed on the 31st December, the majority of the evacuees there being transferred to Pensions in town.

In April, 1945, the Spanish steamer *Cabo de Hornos,* diverted from her route on her return voyage from South America, picked up 134 evacuees and took them to Lisbon, whence they travelled overland to Gibraltar. These were evacuees authorised to return under Government Notices 213 and 214 (applicable to those who had accommodation awaiting them in Gibraltar). Further small parties left during the course of that month.

By this stage, as a result of repatriation, the number of children attending school had been considerably reduced. Notice was given to surrender the existing premises on the 31st May, 1945, with a view to transferring the School to smaller premises in a sufficiently central locality to render it possible to discontinue the hire of a school bus. Smaller premises were secured on the 1st June, 1945, in one of the annexes of the Savoy Hotel.

Notice was likewise given to all the School Staff with arrangements made to re-engage a certain number at the end of May for further service depending upon the number of children still in attendance. Because of the small number of pupils remaining it was also decided that the Headmaster would be replaced by a senior woman teacher at a considerable saving in salary.

Further repatriation led to the closing on the 31st May, 1945, of Quinta das Cruzes. Ninety-nine repatriates left on the 11th May on the Portuguese steamer *Carvalho Araujo* for Lisbon, thence overland to Gibraltar.

The event of outstanding interest in June, 1945, was the unexpected news communicated by the Ministry of War Transport that a ship would be despatched from Gibraltar to Madeira to repatriate some 200 evacuees. The Polish liner *Batory* consequently arrived in Madeira on the morning of the 24th June and left direct for Gibraltar that same evening with 193 repatriates.

It had been hoped that this repatriation would have embraced the whole community since only a small number were ineligible under Government Notices 213 and 214 and it had been hoped that emergency arrangements would be made for these cases. However, despite the Consul's plea on their behalf, the Gibraltar Government replied that the extreme difficulties of housing accommodation in the Colony rendered it impossible to permit the return of persons whose names had not been previously authorised.

With the school population down to ten pupils, and two teachers, the decision was taken to close down the School at the end of July, 1945. Repatriation proceeded at a slow rate, and a further three years were to elapse before the process had been completed. The last to leave, numbering 32, did not do so until May, 1948.

CHAPTER THIRTEEN

Gibraltar During the War

How did the Rock itself fare whilst so many of its children were thousands of miles away? What was life like during the war years? To those familiar with life in Gibraltar today, many things would have seemed strange. The absence of children would have stood out, as would the heavy concentration of uniformed men. Very few women had been allowed to remain in the Fortress—only those working in hospitals or involved in confidential work in HM Dockyard. However, some 2,000 Spanish women came into Gibraltar every day to work as domestic servants and shop assistants.

This was to cause problems! Gibraltarian women evacuated from Gibraltar did not take kindly to the thought of their menfolk being looked after by Spanish females. Complaints arising from rumour and gossip amongst the Gibraltarians in the United Kingdom were transmitted to Gibraltar in late 1941 and elicited the following reply from the Acting Colonial Secretary, Mr Dryburgh. Spanish women 'have always come into Gibraltar to work and still do so. Practically all domestic service has always been done by Spaniards, as Gibraltarian women rarely took up this kind of work. There are also shop assistants, These have naturally increased in number since the evacuation of the Gibraltarian girls. Laundry work for the thousands of men on the Rock also accounts for large numbers of the Spanish daily workers. The average daily total of Spanish women entering the Garrison is 2,360. Of these, 336 (domestic servants) have permits to stay in the Colony overnight. The number with permits to reside prior to the war was 1,300.' Such comments would seem to have missed the whole point of the complaints!

Another feature of war-time Gibraltar were the many restrictions in existence. Many areas, including Europa and the Upper Rock, were 'out of bounds', there was a curfew imposed, and the town's gates were closed every evening. An order of the 17th January, 1941, announced that the Gate at Four Corners would be closed from 10.00 pm to 6.00 am (those with special passes could go through from 11.00 pm to 5.30 am). Bayside Bridge, Casemates Square, Landport Tunnel and Waterport Basin would be closed from 11.00 pm to 5.30 am. The frontier gates with Spain were closed at 11.30 pm throughout the war. The Curfew Order of the 7th August, 1941, forbade anyone being out of doors from 10.00 pm to 5.30 am without a written permit.

In October, 1942, a further list of restricted areas was announced. Included were the following:

(a) the whole area north of a line commencing from the foreshore of Eastern Beach and passing to the south of positions then known as Caledonian Canal,

Devil's Dyke, North Fence, Cross Ditch to its junction with the Road to Spain and thence to the north of Stone Jetty, with the exception of the Road to Spain;
(b) the east side of the Rock south of the southern edge of Catalan Bay;
(c) Smith Dorrien Avenue;
(d) West Place of Arms from the wall joining North Bastion to the junction of Corral Canal;
(e) Corral Road, that is to say, the road between West Place of Arms and the junction of Glacis Road, Smith Dorrien Avenue and Inundation Road;
(f) Landport Tunnel and Landport Bridge;
(g) within the boundary-line drawn from the Unclimbable Fence from its beginning on the north face of the Rock to the bend north east of the property known as Arengo's Palace, thence on a line westwards to the south end of Calpe Married Quarters, thence to the west face of Calpe Road to Willis's Road and along the Western edge of the Catchment area and Reservoir to Moorish Castle and on to the north face of the Rock; and
(h) the whole area of Windmill Hill Flats, Europa Flats and Europa Advance and included within the following limits, the coastline between Monkey's Cave and the south end of Little Bay thence along the cliff edge of Viney Quarry to the Unclimbable Fence and continuing along the southern limits of the Upper Rock to Monkey's Cave.

Many black-out exercises were held, but there was no black-out imposed since it was reckoned that the Rock in complete darkness was a more easily identifiable target than with its lights on which made it difficult to distinguish from neighbouring Spanish towns.

Gibraltar underwent some drastic changes during the war years, the most notable being the transformation at North Front, where beautiful gardens, a racecourse, football and cricket pitches disappeared to make way for the building of an airfield—one of the great constructional achievements of the war. Gibraltar 'under ground' also developed dramatically as many miles of tunnels and chambers were dug out of the limestone. Royal Engineer tunnellers constructed an underground city, with its own telephone exchanges, frozen meat stores and water distilleries, an up-to-date bakery and hospitals. The Governors responsible for all this work and for keeping the Fortress at the ready were Lieutenant-General Sir Clive Liddell until April, 1941, General Lord Gort from April, 1941 to May, 1942, and Lieutenant-General Mason MacFarlane from May, 1942 to January, 1944.

Attacks on the Rock were few and far between, were restricted to the occasional Italian raid (either by air or from under water), and caused little damage. Nonetheless, Gibraltar was in the thick of war activity, and its value was proved time and time again: as a source of protection for Britain's sea-borne trade and transport, as the base for Force H, the Royal Navy's offensive fleet in the area, as a stepping stone for thousands of refugees, as a psychological symbol, an example of Britain's continuing fight against the

Axis Powers. Gibraltar provided valuable support for the war in the Middle East, and proved indispensable in the North African campaign. In the words of General Eisenhower: 'Britain's Gibraltar made possible the invasion of north-west Africa. Without it the vital air cover would not have been quickly established on the North African airfields.'

Gibraltar suffered very little physical damage during the war. Attacks by Italian aircraft were usually followed by exaggerated claims which were quickly denied by the authorities in Gibraltar. There were eleven air raids in 1941, but none of them approached the intensity of the attacks of September, 1940, already described in an earlier chapter. Most of them were of short duration, and on none of these occasions did any bombs drop on the Rock.

On the 2nd and 3rd January, 1941, an aircraft with French markings approached the Rock but was driven off by the anti-aircraft guns of the Royal Navy and the Fortress. Four further raids (one in March, one in April, and two in June) hardly troubled the Rock's defences. On the 12th July at about three o'clock in the morning two unidentified planes were heard droning overhead. The searchlights of the fortress went into action and two distant explosions were heard. It was subsequently revealed that a bomb had fallen near the Calle Duque de Tetuan, La Linea, killing six and wounding eleven people. Another bomb had fallen in La Linea but had not exploded. The Governor of Gibraltar offered to send medical supplies or any other help that might be required. The funeral of the unfortunate victims was attended by thousands of people, the opening of the annual fair, which should have taken place on that day, being postponed until the Sunday.

In the early hours of the morning of Monday, 14th July, the searchlights and the shore anti-aircraft batteries were again in action when two planes believed to be of Italian type approached the Rock from a northerly direction. The searchlight beams picked them up and caused them to swerve towards Campamento. Two bombs were dropped which exploded on the beach off the old racecourse. One report stated that an Italian plane had crashed near Los Barrios.

Two more abortive attempts were followed by a further underwater attack by the *Scire* on the 20th September, 1941. According to a communique from Rome, a naval craft had penetrated Gibraltar harbour and sunk a 10,000-ton and a 6,000-ton tanker, and a 6,000-ton munition-laden steamer, as well as damaging a 12,000-ton liner which ran on the rocks. Such claims were quickly denied in London—a hulk had been sunk but the rest of the enemy's claim was described as 'exaggerated'. The true facts were revealed many years later: a 2,000-ton storage hulk had been sunk, the 10,000-ton Motor Vessel, *Durham* had been damaged, and an 8,000-ton Naval tanker had been immobilised.

Despite all this, the Axis Powers claimed that German and Italian planes had carried out heavy raids on Gibraltar causing severe damage. Such claims were denied in the *Gibraltar Chronicle* of the 29th August, 1941: '. . . . signs of enemy attack are vitually non-existent. One has to search hard to find three or four houses hit by bombs last year and damage is negligible. . . . . No German bombs have ever fallen in Gibraltar and the nearest the Italians got this year was at the Spanish town of La Linea where men, women and children were killed.'

1942 saw a further decrease in attacks from the Italians, only eight air raid alarms being sounded. On the 1st April, a small number of enemy aircraft approached the fortress from the north and were engaged by the AA defences. Some bombs were dropped but there was neither damage nor casualties. The Italians claimed otherwise! A local News Letter, regularly sent for dissemination amongst the evacuees in the United Kingdom and titled *Echoes from Gibraltar,* commented: 'The local population has derived quite a lot of amusement from the fantastic versions of the attack given by the Italian stations. According to them, the achievements of the Italian pilots were beyond expectation for, after fighting their way through a huge fighter screen, they attacked all their objectives without any difficulty and caused huge fires. We can only say that the pilots who gave these details must have been suffering from delusions as not only did they fail to reach a single objective but their retreat was anything but dignified.'

The next raid, by three planes, came on the 29th June, 1942. A few bombs were dropped at North Front but there were no civilian casualties or damage. An underwater attack by the Italians on the 14th July, using a base on the Spanish coast two miles from Gibraltar, succeeded in crippling four steamships. A similiar attack on the 15th September damaged the steamship *Ravens Point.*

The Italians reverted to aerial attack on the 24th September, 1942, but the few bombs that were dropped fell harmlessly into the sea. The results, according to *Echoes from Gibraltar,* were 'entirely negative for though, as usual, they claimed to have inflicted widespread damage we have as yet been unable to find any trace of it. The Rock is still very much on the map!'

Four further raids in October, 1942, failed to land a single bomb on Gibraltar, though the raid of the 20th caused casualties and damage on Spanish territory. Two air raid warnings on the 8th and 14th November were of short duration with no bombs dropped on the Rock.

The main attacks of the year 1943 came from the underwater exploits of the Italians; the air raid warnings could be counted on the fingers of one hand. On the 8th May the steamship *Camerata* was sunk and two other vessels damaged, and on the 4th August the last Italian underwater operation against Gibraltar took place, three ships being damaged: the steamship *Stanridge* was in fact the last merchantman successfully attacked at Gibraltar during

World War Two. The following month, September 1943, Italy surrendered, an occasion celebrated in Gibraltar by a great ack-ack searchlight display.

Air and sea attacks apart, what was life really like in Gibraltar during the war years? 'Grim', 'monotonous', 'drab', are words used by people living there at the time. 'Gibraltar is today one of the quietest places in the world. Life is so normal and unexciting that it has become monotonous and the course of the war in all its fronts is the only topic which can, and does arouse interest.' (*Echoes from Gibraltar,* February, 1942).

Reuter's special correspondent on the Rock, John Nixon, writing in The *Gibraltar Chronicle* on the 12th August, 1941, gives us some further indication:

'Gibraltar today is the eighth wonder of the world. Nestling at the base of the gaunt rock concealing one of the strongest works of man, the tiny town bravely carries on. Its shops still offer a glittering array of goods, from silk stockings to ivory curios, the hotels still serve five-course meals, the street lamps still come on each night: there is no black-out.

Every morning thousands of Spaniads flock across the border into the fortress—swarthy workers for the dockyard, servants, seamstresses, and girls who work in the well-stocked shops. At nightfall they hurry home to their own country by bus or on foot, all carrying shopping bags filled with food.

Every evening soldiers, sailors and airmen pack narrow Main Street seeking a little relaxation after their hard day's work. These are the men who are not sparing themselves to make and keep this outpost impregnable.

Voices and heavy-booted footsteps drown the blare of jazz bands in the cafes. Some prefer the cinema—there are four here. There are, too, football and hockey grounds, tennis and squash courts, and swimming. Occasionally keen amateurs produce a play or give a concert.

Though food is plentiful, prices have risen greatly, and now the cost of living is approximately the same as in Great Britain. Cigarettes are cheaper, but beer costs up to 1/6 a half pint. Big American cars—most of them distinctly aged—provide a taxi service, but for most people the only alternative is to walk. Car horns are banned entirely; the only form of warning allowed is heavy thumping by the driver on the car side.

The streets begin to clear between nine and 9.30 pm when the cafes close. By curfew time—11.00 pm—Gibraltar resembles a deserted town. But although the streets are empty, the work of the fortress goes on. Never has so much thought and labour been expended here. The monotony of life in a confined space and the impossibility of granting leave is a strain; but the men who man this fortress are working wholeheartedly and pulling their full weight in the Empire's war effort.'

Writing again in September, 1941, the same author describes the scene in Main Street:

'In the afternoons and evenings in the narrow ugly Main Street, hundreds of soldiers and airmen off duty for a few hours, as well as sailors and merchant seamen on shore leave, throng the well-stocked shops augmenting their rations with chocolates, sweets, biscuits or fruit, or selecting silks and curios to send home to their families and sweethearts. Others sit and sip their beer at one of the many cafes to the tune of the latest jazz or a Spanish 'paso-doble', while yet others crowd one of Gibraltar's four cinemas, stopping outside to buy fruit, almonds or nuts from a hawker's barrow.

But in spite of this apparent gaiety, no one forgets the war for more than a few moments .... Aircraft roar overhead daily, frequently skimming the house-tops as they prepare to land; the sound of blasting, which goes on day and night, may cause the Andalusian midinette in the local 'Woolworths' to glance enquiringly at the uniformed customer of the moment to be assured she need not dash for the nearest air-raid shelter; or the crash of a heavy battery at target practice will drown music and conversation alike. Again lorry-loads of cheering dusty tunnellers, engineers or infantrymen coming off their shift, will force pedestrians on to the too-narrow pavements.'

In contrast, an article in *El Faro* of Ceuta in its issue of the 14th August, 1941, quoted a report from Algeciras that there was an increasing food shortage in Gibraltar due to shipping losses. The *Gibraltar Chronicle* commented that such a statement might have been printed as a consolation for hungry Spaniards! As if to underline this *Presente* of Tangier reported on the 15th August, 1941, that as a result of a campaign to round up beggars in Spain, about 3,300 had been arrested in Granada!

Echoes from Gibraltar also made reference to articles appearing in the British press which seemed to give a warped impression of life on the Rock.

'The people on the Rock are having a jolly good time'. This expression seems to represent the general opinion about life in Gibraltar but it is far removed from actual fact.

In the first place, it is obvious that the absence of our loved ones in the United Kingdom, Madeira and Jamaica has cast a blight over our domestic life, for a town without children is a town without joy, and Gibraltar lacking family life, lacks too that atmosphere of quiet happiness which characterised its pre-war days.

In the second place, the town is now a fortress in every respect and at the close of day, when the work people from Spain have gone back over the frontier, the streets and places of entertainment are so crowded with men in uniform that it conveys the impression of some huge barracks. 'Ennui is the greatest bugbear.'

However, 'everyone leads a healthy existence. Hard work is followed by peaceful rest and thanks to the nutritious diet the health of the population is kept on a very satisfactory level.' The same journal described New Year's Day, 1942, as 'the saddest New Year's Day Gibraltar has ever known.' There were obviously no celebrations due to the curfew.

One aspect not touched upon by any of the above reports was the violence and general lawlessness that often errupted in the town. With so many Servicemen around, of various nationalities, a hard day's work would often be followed by a hard drinking session! Fights were common. On the 2nd February, 1943, the City Magistrate warned that thefts by members of HM Forces were on the increase in Gibraltar, and later in that month the Attorney-General regretted that cases of housebreaking and larceny in Gibraltar were becoming excessive and increasing and that the police had their work greatly augmented as the result of so many evacuated homes being at the mercy of 'these marauders'.

Attempts were made to combat boredom. Dances, varieties and concerts were held, the Gibraltar Symphony Orchestra under the direction of Mr W F Edwards proved a great success, the Gibraltar Musical Society, the Gibraltar Dramatic Society, and the Gibraltar Garrison Literary and Debating Society all met regularly.

Radio Distribution did its utmost to extend and amplify its programmes which, according to *Echoes from Gibraltar,* 'are daily becoming more attractive.' The same journal (this was in 1942) added that 'arrangements have been made to bring to the microphone the most well known local artists and on several occasions "Bashery and his boys", "The Trini Trio", singers, musicians and speakers have made appearances. Radio Distribution also relayed the BBC feature 'Gibraltar Calling', by means of which the families of those stationed in the Garrison were able to contact their relatives.

The *Rescue* resumed her weekend trips to Tangier in 1942, and those with their families in that town were thus able to visit them regularly. 'A few days outside the Fortress is a tonic to those who are stationed in it for months at a time.' *(Echoes from Gibraltar).*

Nor was sport forgotten, despite the loss of the playing fields at North Front. Football underwent a recovery in 1942, with old rivals 'Britannia', 'Prince of Wales' and 'Europa' turning out regularly as well as Service sides. In the summer of that year cricket was resumed on a makeshift pitch at the Alameda after an absence of two years.

There was the occasional accident. On the 31st January, 1941, an explosion occurred at North Front during the excavation of a new tunnel. A quantity of explosives used for blasting operations accidentally detonated, killing six soldiers and one civilian, a Spaniard. On the 4th May, 1941, a Blenheim aircraft crashed against a tree, killing one Spanish woman and injuring another. On the 31st October, 1942, an aeroplane from Malta carrying evacuees crashed on landing at North Front aerodrome. There were several casualties including a number killed. But the most 'famous' accident occurred in July, 1943. The Polish leader, General Sikorski, had landed in Gibraltar when returning from a visit to Cairo. The following evening the Liberator in which he was to have flown to England failed to gain height after leaving the runway and crashed into the sea off Eastern Beach. Everyone on board was killed except the pilot.

Military exercises, of course, were commonplace in Gibraltar during these years. The war was never far away as the following notice in the *Gibraltar Chronicle* of the 26th April, 1941, illustrates:

MILITARY EXERCISES

'For the next few days the Garrison will, at intervals, be practising certain military exercises connected with their duties in the defence of the Fortress. These will also include imaginary damage to roads and buildings, the control of traffic, and the treatment of casualties.

There will be black-outs on certain nights, and searchlights may be exposed, and gun-fire may be heard at times.

The public will not be called upon to take part in these exercises, but their co-operation in observing certain restrictions may be required at times.

The public are reminded that the first black-out exercise is from dusk on Monday to dawn on Tuesday.'

Training was part and parcel of the serviceman's existence. Troops would be seen in and about every day taking part in exercises of various kinds. Bren gun carriers clattering through the streets would awaken the comparatively few remaining civilians to remind them that there was a war on! The roar of aero-engines would proclaim that the air arm of the fortress was also keeping itself fit. Machine-gun posts, AA batteries and coastal guns were manned day and night, and in the harbour, units of the Navy were always ready at a moment's notice to take part in some operation or other.

On the second Wednesday of each month, all civilians were required to wear gas masks from 11.00 am to 11.30 am.

In early November, 1941, another exercise was announced: 'a small combined naval, military and air exercise will be taking place .... the area affected will be North-West of a line exclusive Catalan Bay—inclusive Rosia Bay. Rattles and certain small explosions may be heard and flashes seen.' Practice Black-out and Fire-Fighting exercises were also held from time to time.

Echoes from Gibraltar commented in July, 1942: 'We no longer wake up startled at the sound of the anti aircraft defences going into action. We wake up, but with a mental note of gratitude to the men who are devoting all their time to perfecting themselves in the use of their weapons, for we know that they have now reached such a high degree of proficiency that any attempted attack will be met with a very warm reception. We listen unconcernedly to the deep reverberating detonations caused by those valiant tunnellers within the Rock and the sight and sound of many planes is no longer a source of wonder.'

Whilst Gibraltar kept itself in trim for any eventuality, amazing improvements were being carried out to the Fortress defences. The task of enlarging and completing the system of tunnels that honeycomb the Rock continued unceasingly day and night throughout the war. John Nixon reported on this work in the *Gibraltar Chronicle* on several occasions. On the 29th July, 1941, he observed:

'When I was conducted through some of the miles of tunnels I saw how masses of rock had been blasted out to make room for barracks and everything necessary for thousands of men to live—and fight—for a prolonged period. I saw large three-storey barracks in huge man-made caverns in the heart of the Rock, and hospitals fully equipped with operating theatres and X-ray apparatus.

This incredible underground city also contains power stations for generating electric light, well-fitted washrooms, complete with built-in handbasins and chromium-plated taps, and cookhouses, at least one of which is alone capable of feeding 1,000 men at a time.

Vast quantities of oil and water are stored in subterranean tanks, and there is ample storage for food and even tobacco and boiled sweets!'

On the 9th September, 1941, Nixon wrote:- '.... tunnellers are boring their way inside the heart of the Rock in conditions made Dantesque by the ear-splitting rattle of penumatic-drills, the dim light, the dust and their half-naked sweating bodies. In and out of the Rock's face hundreds of men are employed on the less skilled, but equally hard, task of removing the immense quantities of spoil from the blasting of the tunnels.

On the 11th November, 1941, came a further report:-

'Nearly ten miles of new tunnels have been driven through this vest-pocket mountain in just over a year ....

Some 3,000,000 cubic feet of rock have been excavated in this period—and all the rock broken by blasting is being used. Some goes into concrete-making, some into road-construction and some into providing protection for buildings against bombs. An average of half-a-mile of tunnel is being added monthly.

Exploring the system, I descended the world's longest all-concrete staircase—531 steps which drop one down 450 feet. Every few yards I passed an embrasure cut through to the face of the rock, and in each of the resulting emplacements were two or more guns. I also saw searchlights designed to throw their beams through slits in the rock on to attacking forces below. It is said that they can even penetrate smokescreens.

Trucks and ambulances can drive right into the Rock, in which there is a turn-round for vehicles bigger than the circle of road round Eros in Piccadilly Circus.

Huge underground rooms whence operations will be directed in emergency are equipped with office furniture, and every table is labelled ready for immediate use. Some of the new chambers I saw would accommodate two tennis courts with room to spare ....

The underground fort is to be all-electric. Already electric lighting is installed, and in time all cooking and heating will be done by electricity generated by underground power-stations.

The enemy will not be able to interrupt the Fortress's communications with Britain as it is now possible to transmit and receive with wireless aerials which are completely protected. During a siege the defenders would still be able to get word home to their relatives—every man will be allowed to send one cable a month, circumstances permitting.' (The *Gibraltar Chronicle*)

What had been some four miles of tunnels outside the Rock at the outbreak of war had become about 24 miles by the end of it. Over a million cubic yards of stone had been removed! Today, parts of this amazing engineering feat can be enjoyed by tourists—it is a sight well worth seeing.

The attitude of Spain was a constant source of anxiety and provoked further evacuation of civilians during the course of 1941. By early March the Governor was urging the immediate evacuation of a further 1,000 civilians who would be useless under siege conditions. There was also the problem of some 800 British subjects, including women and children, still residing in La Linea and district. On the 22nd May, 1941, the *Arundel Castle* left Gibraltar bound for the United Kingdom; on board were 349 evacuees. A further 500 departed on the 30th May aboard the *Nea Hellas,* and another 152 were evacuated on the 4th July.

As if to justify such moves, on the eve of the fifth anniversary of the Spanish Civil War (18th July, 1941) General Franco made a speech in the course of which he clearly indicated that Spain's sympathies lay with the Axis and expressed the conviction that the Allies would lose the war. A further small evacuation followed on the 27th July.

By October, 1941, the Spanish press was looking forward with Falangist enthusiasm, to the invasion of England. The periodical *España* of Tangier stated on the 16th October:

'In all parts of England there are signs that this terrible hour has arrived, the real hour for England, which more than once the people who were her Allies have experienced.' Around the same time, a Hitler Youth delegation arrived in Seville, where the National Secretary of the Movement presented ten .22 Mauser rifles and 12,000 rounds to the Falange Youth.

By the end of 1941 important developments were taking place in the war. The attack by the Japanese on Pearl Harbour in December was quickly followed by a declaration of war by Germany and Italy on the USA. In the East, the Germans were finding the Russians a tough nut to crack! On the 30th December, a further 200 civilians were evacuated from Gibraltar.

There were also a number of attempts at sabotage in Gibraltar. On the 4th March, 1942, a Gibraltarian, José Key, was arrested for having in his possession information on the movements of ships and aircraft in Gibraltar. He was sentenced to death on the 18th May and executed in London.

In early July, 1943, Gibraltar's fire service was called upon to subdue a fire when a petrol dump near Devil's Tower caught alight—the second fuel blaze in a week. Flames shot up nearly one hundred feet, illuminating the north face with a red glare. The blaze was brought under control in about two hours. Damage to surrounding installations was negligible. It was not disclosed whether foul play was suspected.

In the same month, M15 received news of a projected bomb attack on ammunition ready for the Sicily landings. Luis Lopez Cordon-Cuenca, a Spaniard employed on maintenance in the dockyard, was an agent working for the German Secret Service. He was arrested, tried on the 19th August, and found guilty on the 25th. An appeal lodged with the Privy Council was rejected on the 13th December.

Another Spaniard, Jose Martín Muñoz, also a dockyard employee, was arrested following an explosion in the fuel enclosure on Coaling Island on the 30th June, 1943. He was tried on the 11th October and also sentenced to death. Both Cordon-Cuenca and Muñoz were executed in Gibraltar on the 11th January, 1944.

One notable development in Gibraltar during the war was the formation of an Association for the Advancement of Civil Rights at the end of 1942. As will be seen in later chapters, this Association was to become heavily involved in the problems which were to accompany repatriation and was also destined to be at the forefront of the move for greater self-government in Gibraltar. One of the first projects it concerned itself with was that for enabling Gibraltarian men to visit their families in the United Kingdom—the so-called 'Splea Scheme'.

The first batch to be given such leave numbered 88 and left Gibraltar in July, 1943, to spend six weeks with their families. A second party, numbering 120, left in October, 1943, and another during the Christmas holiday period. In February, 1944, it was agreed in principle to extend the Scheme to Madeira.

Such, then, were the main themes of life in Gibraltar during the war. It is now time to return to our evacuees.

CHAPTER FOURTEEN

Repatriation—A Question of Priorities

The year 1944 saw important developments in the War and significant changes in the situation of our evacuees. The surrender of Italy in September, 1943, removed any danger of a German invasion of Spain, Gibraltar was then relatively safe from attack, and by the end of the year the Chiefs of Staff had decided that there was no longer any objection on operational grounds to the return of the civil population to Gibraltar. However, if the evacuees thought that a return home was imminent, they were soon to be disappointed; indeed, for several thousand of them a move further away from home was yet in store! It is interesting to note that in the matter of the repatriation of civilians to Gibraltar a trend developed which was quite the reverse of that of 1940. In 1940, we saw the Governor of Gibraltar pressing London for the evacuation of an ever-increasing number of civilians from the Fortress, whilst the British Government tried to resist these demands. Four years later, the roles were reversed: the authorities in London, according to the Colonial Secretary of Gibraltar at the time, seemed 'more concerned with getting rid of the evacuees than with the conditions to which the latter must return', whilst the Government of Gibraltar insisted that there must be 'no wild rush' in the return!

As early as October, 1943, the Colonial Office in London were turning their minds to the arrangements that would have to be made in due course for the return of the evacuees to Gibraltar, even though their return at this stage was not regarded as imminent. The Colonial Secretary in Gibraltar was urged to apply himself to the preliminary preparations which would have to be considered. It was suggested that the main problems encountered would be at the receiving end, in particular in the matter of accommodation and education. The Colonial Secretary curtly replied that the Government of Gibraltar was well aware of the problem 'but until the Governor receives a reply to a questionnaire he has recently addressed to the Chiefs of Staff on future military commitments here, it is a little difficult to put any very realistic planning into effect.' It was pointed out to London that the return of the evacuees would have to be controlled and that it would have to be related to the availability of accommodation in Gibraltar. On the matter of PRIORITIES, the Government of Gibraltar seemed inclined at this stage to give preference to the return of the evacuees in Jamaica, followed by those in Madeira: 'both have had, relatively, a worse time than the United Kingdom evacuees—no opportunities for employment, organised leave scheme possible and, particularly in the case of the Jamaicans, grave disabilities in regard to their mail.' Such an assessment would appear to have ignored the fact that whilst those in Jamaica and Madeira had enjoyed a peaceful time, those in the United Kingdom had often lived with the threat of instant extermination! In early November, 1943, the matter of repatriation was discussed by the Colonial Secretary, the Financial Secretary and the Board of District Commissioners. It was then agreed to set up a Resettlement Board and to carry out a Census to help decide on the question of priorities. The Repatriation Sub-Committee of this Resettlement Board first met on the 7th December, 1943.

At the end of 1943, the Governor, Lieutenant-General Mason MacFarlane, visited London, primarily to discuss the question of repatriation. At a meeting at the Colonial Office on the 16th December the Governor proposed that the first batch of evacuees should arrive in April, 1944, and that the initial target should be 4,000 persons. He felt that priority should be given to the families of the men in Gibraltar and to the Jamaica evacuees. The Spanish evacuees should go to the bottom of the priority list. The Governor added that 18,000 was the maximum that could be accepted at the moment until more accommodation was available. In the light of subsequent developments, the comment of the Secretary of State for the Colonies at this meeting is very pertinent. He made it clear that in his view *it would be quite impossible to contemplate a situation in which any evacuees who wished to return to Gibraltar were prevented from doing so for lack of accommodation. If, as seemed probable, permanent accommodation could not be made ready in the time available, temporary accommodation would have to be provided.*

The problem of the Spanish evacuees was a difficult one. The Home Office stressed that Britain did not want them to stay in England even if they wished to do so. It was pointed out that it had been agreed (in April, 1941) that Gibraltar should take back any Spaniards evacuated to the United Kingdom if it was not considered practicable or desirable to return them to Spain or to keep them in Britain. According to London, the majority of these Spaniards were not genuine political refugees, but had merely taken refuge in Gibraltar at the outbreak of the Civil War because conditions there were better than in Spain. On this assumption, it did not seem unreasonable to the Home Office to hope that they would wish to return to Spain after the war if conditions in Gibraltar were not as favourable as previously. It was also hoped that even some of the genuine political refugees might feel that it was safe to return to Spain after a lapse of five or six years, 'particularly if the power of the Fascists in the rest of the world is broken.' That was to prove a forlorn hope! The Gibraltar Government had been dreading the moment when this subject would be raised by Britain, and they now consoled themselves with the thought that at least these Spaniards were at the bottom of the priority list. The Colonial Secretary even suggested that the rider 'when accommodation is available' should be added to 'after the war'. 'Our accommodation problems are so serious that the return of unwanted aliens is not reasonable on any other basis.'

There was the additional problem of the 400 or so Spaniards at present residing in Gibraltar, taking up accommodation needed for Gibraltarians.

In his New Year Message to the Fortress, the Governor had this to say on the subject of repatriation:

'It is my firm intention to commence repatriation as soon as the progress of the war and the shipping situation permits. In this I had the wholehearted support of all the ministries involved, with whom I discussed the situation.

We got down to fixing provisonally a good deal of detail. Priorities will be left to our local repatriation comittee here. First priorities will be the near relatives and dependants of all of you who have borne the heat and burden of the day here for the past three and a half years. Jamaica will get highest possible priority in the earlier categories.

We fixed provisional numbers and dates. We discussed rebuilding and new building problems here. In fact we went a long way towards setting the ball rolling. But in wartime there are always unforeseen factors. And I am not going to make any definite promises until final decisions have been taken at home and the word go has been given. I don't want to give you cause for disappointment and I don't intend to do so.

But I can give you this assurance. That all the ministries concerned in London are now determined to commence repatriation just as soon as the many factors involved make it possible for the War Cabinet to give a definite decision. We are a very great deal nearer the realisation of our hopes than we were a year ago. For my part, I and the local Government are going right ahead and flat-out to ensure that all possible preliminary work and arrangements are completed so that when we get the word we can go right ahead. As I told you, I am promising absolutely nothing. But I hope and pray personally that it won't be long. . . .'

A few days after this statement it was announced that, after nineteen months as Gibraltar's Governor, Lieutenant-General Sir Noel Mason MacFarlane had been appointed Deputy President of the Allied Commission in Italy.

Priorities and the rate of return were the main topics of discussion throughout January, 1944. Regarding the latter, two distinct schools of thought were clearly emerging; that which argued for the quickest possible return of the evacuees regardless of problems likely to be encountered at the receiving end, and the view that the return should be dependent upon the availability of accommodation. The City Council of Gibraltar subscribed to the former: 'the problem of overcrowding has troubled Gibraltar for over a century and the solution of this problem of restraining people from returning to their native land would not appear to be warranted.' The Board of District Commissioners, on the other hand, argued that 'the accommodation available previous to evacuation was well below that required for the then civil population. Besides the civil population of Gibraltar many persons were evacuated from the vicinity. These latter will not return necessarily to the vicinity, but will expect to be accommodated here. It is assumed that the Spanish refugees will not return to Gibraltar.' The Board therefore strongly recommended that evacuees should not be allowed to return until the Government was assured that accommodation was available for them.

By the end of January, 1944, the Repatriation Census organised by the Resettlement Board had been completed. On the 5th February, the Colonial Secretary informed the Colonial Office that the maximum that Gibraltar could absorb at the moment was 500 a fortnight, beginning on the 1st April, with a ceiling of 4,000 in the first four months. Apart from the major problem of accommodation, there was also the matter of fuel. Before the war the large majority of Gibraltarians had used charcoal for cooking and heating which had then been obtainable readily and cheaply in Spain. Now it was all needed for the domestic transport industry and if one could get it at all it cost £25 a ton delivered at San Roque. The local gas was extremely bad and very expensive, and the only alternative the Gibraltar Government could think of was the use of Primus Stoves and/or oil cookers, if these were obtainable. (It subsequently turned out that they were not!). Despite all this, the Colonial Office proposed that the rate of repatriation should be speeded up after the first two or three months, a suggestion totally rejected by the Colonial Secretary in Gibraltar.

On the 10th February, 1944, the Resettlement Board produced an estimate of the number of civilians who would be requiring accommodation in Gibraltar once the repatriation was complete. It makes interesting reading:-

1.	Gibraltarians at present in Gibraltar		3517
2.	British subjects other than Gibraltarians	1386	
	less Dockyard	1062	324
3.	Total Gibraltarians and other British subjects excluding Dockyard at present in Gibraltar		3841
4.	Jamaican evacuees (excluding Spaniards) (This figure does not include births and deaths since 1940)		1414
5.	Madeira evacuees (all classes, no aliens)		1861
6.	Evacuees in Spain		102
7.	Evacuees in Tangier		719
8.	Evacuees in the United Kingdom	12,000	
	Less Spaniards	242	11758
9.	TOTAL TO BE ACCOMMODATED EXCLUDING ALIENS, REFUGEES AND DOCKYARD 'IMPORTADOS'		19767

10. The following aliens and refugees would have to be taken into account:

(a)	Spanish refugees now in Gibraltar	483
(b)	Spaniards in Jamaica	80
(c)	Spaniards in the United Kingdom	242
(d)	Total Spanish refugees	805
(e)	Other aliens now resident in Gibraltar	144
(f)	Swedes in Jamaica	2
	GRAND TOTAL:	951

FINAL GRAND TOTAL: 20,718

(These figures were partly estimated, but clearly accommodation would be required for approximately 20,000)

A few days later it was announced that the new Governor of Gibraltar was to be Lieutenant-General Sir Ralph Eastwood. Upon his shoulders were to fall the many problems which accompanied the repatriation of civilians to the Rock!

By late February, 1944, London was again experiencing air raids. One such raid damaged an evacuation centre which made it necessary to re-house some 1,100 evacuees in emergency accommodation. Although no evacuee was killed during the raid, one, Joseph de Soiza, died subsequently of suspected heart failure. Injuries amongst the evacuees included cuts, lacerations, bruises and shock. Continued attacks on this scale, claimed the Colonial Office, would cause acute problems of accommodation in London and might give rise to an extremely embarassing situation. In these circumstances, bearing in mind the unavoidable risks of continued residence in London, the Colonial Office reckoned that it as necessary to examine as a matter of urgency the question of sending the maximum possible number of evacuees back to Gibraltar. Since there were good prospects of troopships leaving the United Kingdom about the middle of March, the middle of May and the end of June, capable of carrying considerable numbers, the proposal was now made to Gibraltar that full use should be made of these ships—could Gibraltar accept 1,000 evacuees by each of these three opportunities? The pressure was now really on the Governor and his Colonial Secretary! The former insisted that this rate of influx was unacceptable.

Another effect of the heavy pressure on accommodation in London caused by the February air raids was the proposal by London that the next Splea Party, due to leave Gibraltar in early March, should be cancelled. The Splea ('Special Leave') Scheme was that by which Gibraltarian men were given special leave to visit their families in the United Kingdom. The Governor was most concerned about the political effect of such a move at the present time 'when there was so much personal anxiety.' Despite his representations, the Colonial Office remained adamant, and the Splea Scheme was halted.

The Colonial Office also informed the Governor that in order to facilitate repatriation arrangements and to relieve congestion in London it was proposed to send the first repatriation party at an early date to a special accommodation centre in Scotland and the second to accommodation some miles outside Coventry.

Pressure continued to be exerted upon the Government of Gibraltar to accept more and more evacuees. On the 3rd March, 1944, the Ministry of War Transport stated 'that while shipping opportunities are now in sight which should enable us to send to Gibraltar during the second quarter of this year as many evacuees as you can absorb, the prospects after June are quite indefinite and do not look like being anything like as favourable again.' The Colonial Office chipped in a few days later: 'As you will understand, now that military considerations no longer demand the absence of the civil population from Gibraltar, heavy pressure will be exerted from a variety of sources in this country to secure the repatriation of the evacuees, and it is important in the interests of the evacuees themselves that their return should not be delayed longer than is absolutely necessary.'

On the 10th March, 1944, an official announcement was issued simultaneously to the Press in London and Gibraltar, and posted in the Evacuation Centres in London:-

'It is nearly four years since a large proportion of the civil population was evacuated from Gibraltar. This evacuation was rendered necessary solely in the interests of the prosecution of the war, and it has always been the intention that the evacuees should be repatriated as soon as the war situation permitted. Arrangements are now being made for a limited number of the evacuees to return to Gibraltar. At present these arrangements apply only to the evacuees in the United Kingdom. They will be extended in due course to those in Madeira and Jamaica also.

It must be clearly stated that no promises can be given regarding the repatriation arrangements. Progress will depend upon the availability of ships for the journey and to the extent to which accommodation can be released and made ready in Gibraltar. It will probably be a considerable time before all the evacuees can return. But a beginning is in sight.

The selection of individuals and families for repatriation is in the hands of a Committee in Gibraltar. Those selected for the first party will be notified immediately.'

The *Gibraltar Chronicle* of the 11th March, 1944, commented as follows:-

'Decisions behind the official announcement
FAMILY REUNION BEFORE REBUILDING GIBRALTAR
PLAN SPEEDED UP.

SUBJECT TO THE OVERRIDING CONSIDERATION OF SHIPPING, UPON WHICH THE WHOLE SCHEME DEPENDS, DETAILED PLANS HAVE NOW BEEN COMPLETED FOR THE REUNION IN GIBRALTAR OF ALL FAMILIES SEPARATED FOR MORE THAN THREE YEARS BY COMPULSORY WAR-MEASURE EVACUATION.

In the hands of Ministerial departments in Whitehall today is a complete list of priorities, on the basis of which this great family reunion move will be carried out.

This list has been compiled by the Resettlement Board in Gibraltar after an exhaustive analysis of the recent civilian repatriation census.

All arrangements which it is possible to make from now on for the return of wives, children and dependants from all evacuation centres—London, Jamaica and Madeira—will involve a strict application of the priorities which the list lays down.

Behind the official announcement yesterday that initial steps have been taken for the first party of evacuated Gibraltar civilians to return lies a decision which affects the whole policy of planning Gibraltar's future.

BOARD'S BIG TASK

THE RETURN OF FAMILIES HAS PRECEDENCE OVER ALL SCHEMES OF RECONSTRUCTION, EVEN TO THE EXTENT OF RISKING INCONVENIENCE OWING TO LACK OF ADEQUATE ACCOMMODATION.

The priorities affect principally the wives, children and other dependants of married men who have remained in the colony on essential work throughout the war, and the near relatives—mothers, fathers, sisters, brothers—of unmarried men similarly placed.

'MAKE THE BEST OF IT'

One of the biggest tasks confronting the Resettlement Board following the recent local census, I understand, was to define the relative priority of evacuated dependents in order to reach a fair decision all round.

As part of the repatriation plan it was finally decided to include with families and direct dependents whenever possible any other near relative who formerly lived with a family in Gibraltar and who would otherwise be left unaccompanied at the evacuation centre after the family's return.

THE RIGHT COURSE

Reasons for the 'reunite the families first' policy was outlined to me yesterday by Mr P G Russo and Mr I Eames Hughes, chairman and secretary respectively of the executive sub-committee of the Resettlement Board. This is what they said:

''Bearing in mind the natural desire of families for reunion as speedily as possible, the Board has now undertaken—if shipping can be made available—to receive the people back at a quicker rate than was at first thought convenient or possible.

This the Board holds to be a right, though not an ideal, course. It means, unfortunately, that some people will return to conditions that are far from ideal—to a Gibraltar very different from the one they remember, a Gibraltar with rationing difficulties, a major housing problem, and above all practically no education facilities. They must be ready to accept these conditions. The only alternative would have been to put back the repatriation years—literally years''.'

Events were not to bear out the main theme of this article. 'The return of families' was not to take precedence over 'schemes of reconstruction'. The alternative of putting back the repatriation of some of the evacuees was, indeed, the one eventually taken!

The Government of Gibraltar was determined to let the evacuees know in no uncertain terms the conditions to which they would be returning. This was the clear purpose of the statement issued for repatriates on the 12th March, 1944. It read:

'The Government of Gibraltar while welcoming the prospect of your return has felt it necessary to warn you that conditions will not be ideal. The Rock is more overcrowded than ever, is shabbier and more uncomfortable. All houses whether they have been under requisition or not have inevitably deteriorated during the last four years. Some houses do not exist any more and those who lived in them, if they return among the early categories, will have to make do with temporary and possibly uncongenial accommodation.

2. The Government recognises the need to remedy this situation and has laid its plans accordingly, but owing to the lack of skilled labour and a serious shortage of building materials it cannot begin to put these plans into effect before the repatriation without postponing the latter for years. Neither you nor your relatives in Gibraltar would wish to contemplate continued separation on this account nor does the Government itself wish to defer your return for one day longer than can be avoided.

3. You must know too, that food and clothing are rationed, just as in England, and that the cost of living has risen. Furniture and other household goods are almost unobtainable. In the early stages of repatriation there will be no educational facilities for your children, and it will be some time before they can be provided on any satisfactory scale. There are, too, certain necessary restrictions on movements within the fortress.

4. These things are told to you not to discourage you from returning but in order that you should do so with your eyes open as to present conditions, ready to make the best of things and prepared to exercise patience and forbearance until such time as the Government's extensive plans for improvement can be carried out.

The Colonial Secretary commented to the Governor that such a notice 'should leave no-one in doubt and absolve the Government from unfair criticism by the disgruntled.'

CHAPTER FIFTEEN

The Return of the First Half

With the first contingent of evacuees due to leave the United Kingdom came shattering news from the Colonial Office. As preparations proceeded for the invasion of Normandy, the whole of the South of England became an armed camp with severe restrictions placed upon entry into or exit from the United Kingdom. The object, of course, was to prevent any leakage of information to the Germans regarding the impending operations against them. Clearly, the repatriation of evacuees from the United Kingdom to Gibraltar was quite incompatible with such precautions. On the 24th March, 1944, the Governor was informed that if arrangements for the first contingent had not been so far advanced, it would have been necessary to defer the whole scheme. As it was, approval had been given, 'though not without considerable hesitation', for the contingent to proceed, on the understanding that certain special security measures were taken.

Thus the first contingent of Gibraltar repatriates, 1,367 of them (1,170 in the *Duchess of Richmond* and 197 in the *Antenor*) got away—but only just! On Thursday, 6th April, 1944, they arrived at Gibraltar little knowing how close they had come to an extended stay in the United Kingdom! For them, and for their relatives and friends awaiting them, it must have been a very emotional moment. Happy faces abounded, and the *Gibraltar Chronicle* called the day 'good Thursday', the biggest 'Easter Egg' anyone could wish to have. 'If the town was not bedecked with flags', continued the report, 'it was certainly wreathed in happy and contented smiles.' The furniture and personal belongings of the repatriates followed a week or so later on board the *Empire Forest*.

For some of the repatriates, babies born in England, it was, of course, their first time on the Rock. To them, Gibraltar must have seemed as strange as England had been to the evacuees in 1940. The scenes at the dockside were naturally enthusiastic as hundreds of dockyard employees joined officials in giving the Gibraltarians a rousing welcome.

The first repatriate to set foot ashore, reported the *Chronicle*, was 23-year-old Miss Elena Chini, of Willis's Passage, who was formerly at the evacuation centre at Courtlands, Richmond. Following behind her was her mother. Miss Chini told a *Chronicle* reporter: 'We are very happy to be home. We thank God and England for our safe return.' Third off the ship was Mrs Margarita Barcia, aged 64: 'How glad I am to be back on my Rock again', she exclaimed. Children, whose ages ranged from two years to eight, were soon scrambling ashore, and before long the parties had been taken to dispersal points and quickly whisked away to their homes by excited relatives and friends.

Those without accommodation went to one of the four transit centres—the Hotel Cecil, Gavino's Asylum, Loreto Convent North and St. Mary's Senior School. A *Chronicle* reporter went along to the Cecil a few days later to see the dining arrangements. He reported that 1,650 meals were being served daily, and that local business firms were co-operating with the authorities to achieve an exceptionally high standard of catering. On the day of arrival the firm of Messrs Saccone and Speed had presented free of charge 60 dozen tins of beer and 100 bottles of cordials, and Messrs Baglietto and Co had also donated refreshments. A Mr Abelardo Escobar had presented 600 lbs of fish and 100 lbs of prawns. Lunch on the Friday, continued the report, had comprised four courses—including the best butter—and had equalled that obtainable in the best of Gibraltar's hotels.

How did the repatriates find Gibraltar after nearly four years' absence? The older generation were obviously thankful to be home—to them, Gibraltar was still the best place in the world! The younger generation, whilst glad to be back, had seen the wonders of the outside world which Gibraltar could not rival. The glamour and excitement of London would not slip so easily away from their minds. One significant benefit derived by the younger evacuees from their stay in England was a great fluency in the English language. Of course, all would appreciate the climate of Gibraltar after the winter frost and fog of London!

The Association for the Advancement of Civil Rights wrote to the *Chronicle* thanking the officers and crews of the ships which had brought the evacuees on behalf of the repatriated families, and a telegram was also sent to Lieutenant-General MacFarlane thanking him for 'having initiated this great work of bringing to us our dear ones after nearly four years hard separation.' The telegram added: 'Gibraltar will ever be grateful to Your Excellency.'

At the end of April the Governor proposed to London that to offset the 'very natural disappointment and distress' caused by the postponement of repatriation plans from the United Kingdom, a 'token' repatriation from Madeira should be organised.

In the United Kingdom, the Colonial Office arranged in early May for 500 evacuees, due to return to Gibraltar with the next repatriation party, to be moved to Scotland, this to release accommodation in London urgently required for other purposes. Given the continuing ban on travel to and from the United Kingdom, the evacuees concerned were warned that they might have to remain in Scotland for some time. The evacuees, 511 of them, went to the Neilston Hostel in Renfrewshire, and their situation was to give rise to yet another polemic between the Gibraltar Government and the AACR.

While the Colonial Office and the Governor continued to argue over the number of evacuees who should or could be returned to Gibraltar, the AACR made representations urging the removal of the evacuees from London to safer areas, and the early repatriation of the Jamaican party. Regarding the former, the Governor held out no hopes, commenting that 'we must face the consequences of air-raid casualties.'

On Wednesday, 31st May, 1944, a contingent of 977 repatriates arrived in Gibraltar from Madeira aboard the Dutch steamer *Indrapoera* (see page 131), thus bringing the number of those home to 2,344 out of the 15,000 or so who had been evacuated. 699 evacuees still remained in Madeira.

The War now took on yet another dramatic turn. On the 6th June, 1944, the invasion of Normandy finally got under way—this was D-Day (D for Deliverance). Prospects that the lifting of restrictions on travel from Britain would soon follow were tempered by the beginning of flying bomb attacks on Britain, and London in particular. These V1 pilotless jet-propelled planes carrying one ton of explosives at more than 300 mph on a predetermined course, were launched against Britain from the 13th June onwards. The British people nicknamed them 'doodlebugs'.

There were casualties amongst the evacuees as a result of these attacks. Francisco Pereira of Linden Hall Centre, who had been admitted to hospital, died on the morning of the 17th June; Mrs Laura Fernandez, not living in an evacuee centre, was killed on the 19th June; Mrs Joaquina Ryan and her son Andrew were killed on the 30th June; Rosa Vella and Dolores Garcia suffered the same fate on the 18th July. In addition there were the usual cases of cuts and bruises and shock.

The increased danger of casualties as a result of the V1 attacks prompted the Colonial Office to urge the Governor to agree to a speeding up of repatriation. The Colonial Secretary also wrote to the Governor on the 1st July: 'We have had reports of two deaths and several injuries at the Ilford Centre and I think it is incumbent upon you to get the whole of the priority class back in one contingent if possible.' The Governor had little option but to agree to accept about 3,000 priority cases at once instead of in two spaced-out parties.

One evacuee reminisced forty years later about these V1 attacks. 'Some time after D-Day, the flying bombs started coming over London and its suburbs. I can still remember the ominous buzz, the sudden silence, the whistling sound as the bomb fell and the explosion as it landed. Whenever the air raid warning sounded during school hours the children had been taught to stand up, form into two lines and march downstairs quietly to the air raid shelter. No hurry, no panic.

'The air raid shelter, situated next to the playground, was a brick and concrete structure which offered protection from blast but certainly not from a direct hit. The children would sit in the shelter during the air raid and carry on with their lessons while the bombs fell around them. During the time of the flying bombs the children spent hours in the shelter as the missiles flew over continuously.

'One afternoon there was a sudden sound of a terrific explosion. The shelter was filled with dust, the children cried out in fright and the teachers tried to calm them down. When some sort of order had been restored, one of the teachers went outside to investigate. On her return she told us that a flying bomb had fallen on the hospital about a couple of hundred yards away from the school. It had scored a direct hit. Later, we knew that several people had been killed. The victims included a Gibraltarian lady, Mrs Ryan, who had been visiting her son Andy, a patient in the hospital at the time. Both were among the very few Gibraltarian casualties from bombing raids in England.

'There were no further lessons that day. The children were told to go home. The cottages where we lived in had been damaged by the blast. Windows were shattered and the plaster in some of the rooms had fallen from walls and ceilings. The whole of the homes were in a turmoil with people rushing about trying to discover what had happened. Later, when the extent of the bomb damage had been ascertained, many of the Gibraltarians offered to help with the victims. Needless to say, since two of the victims had been Gibraltarians, well known to everybody, and the circumstances of their deaths had been so tragic, the whole community was engulfed in a wave of grief, sadness and anger.'

The Association for the Advancement of Civil Rights in Gibraltar bitterly complained that they had warned the Governor on the 26th May that the opening of the second front would very probably result in savage reprisals against London. 'We rightly foresaw the danger, and, unfortunately, Gibraltarian casualties have in fact already resulted, and . . . if the worst comes to the worst, English women and children are sure to be made to leave London, as in 1940. Not even this course is open to our women and children, and under the circumstances, the responsibility for these totally unnecessary casualties, and for those which will inevitably occur, can only fall on the British Government . . . the limit of patience and endurance has now been reached.' Notice was then served of a forthcoming public demonstration.

The Association also complained that since the ban on travel from the United Kingdom, necessitating the postponement of further repatriation, there had been several cases of arrivals in Gibraltar of Dockyard personnel not engaged in urgent business of national importance. It was also alleged that 'evidence from a very reliable source described as appalling the conditions under which 511 Gibraltarians, women and children, in Neilston Hostel are existing.' The Colonial Office repudiated this last allegation.

The public demonstration was staged on the 4th July, 1944. The demonstration (consisting of 2,000 people according to official sources, and over 5,000 according to the AACR) included women and children, and went off peacefully. The demonstrators assembled in Market Place, marched quietly through Main Street, where shops were closed and all business had temporarily halted, passed Government House and into the Alameda where they dispersed in orderly fashion. Banners carried at the head of the procession had such inscriptions as: 'Bring our Dear ones before it is too late'; 'Jamaica is Hell'; 'Ban must not apply to our Evacuees'; 'Free Women and Children from the Bombs'. The President and Committee of the AACR headed the march.

On the 6th July, 1944, the Colonial Office was again pressing for an increase in the numbers to be returned to Gibraltar:

'I am much disturbed at possibility of casualties amongst evacuees from enemy action. The possibility of providing alternative accommodation outside London is being considered but accommodation and railway transport difficulties are serious and I should be most grateful if you would consider whether it would be possible even at cost of further inconvenience to you to accept a higher figure.'

The Governor was clearly in a difficult position now! As the secretary of the Repatriation sub-committee of the Resettlement Board, Eames Hughes, observed:

'It has always been a sore point locally that "you put our women and children in a place from which you evacuated your own." This was in 1940: and from Press reports recently, it looks as if we may be open to the accusation of repeating the process now.' This last was a reference to the evacuation from London to safer areas of English women and children currently taking place.

The AACR pressed the point in a letter to the Colonial Secretary on the 11th July:

'In view of the conditions at present prevailing in London which have resulted in the re-evacuation of English women and children, my Committee directs me to enquire what arrangements are being made regarding the Gibraltarian women and children whose early repatriation is not likely.'

The *Gibraltar Chronicle* poured salt into the wound on the following day, reporting that 'Doodle-bug' expresses carrying children from the flying bomb areas had again been running at frequent intervals from the London stations accompanied by teachers, nurses and members of the WVS. By mid-July 150,000 mothers and children had left London and southern England for safer areas. Were the Gibraltarian evacuees to be left behind?

On the 18th July, 1944, broke the news that many of the evacuees in London were being transferred to Northern Ireland, pending their repatriation. There, they would be accommodated in camps. The first batch of some 3,000 were already setting off as the news broke in Gibraltar. A BBC commentator who saw them off at a London station reported:

'I have just been passing along the train saying good-bye. Everyone seems to be eating and they all have baskets of food. Some are eating fruit and I saw one youngster having a hard boiled egg. They are very excited about the journey.

Government officials and members of the WVS are here to see them off. The people are standing in the corridors to wave good-bye as the train leaves. The train is off now and they shout "good-bye and good luck". We wave back and cheer ....'

A week or so later, on the 24th July, a second contingent of 3,100 evacuees arrived at Belfast to bring the total number there to 6,600. The evacuees were housed in sixteen (later increased to seventeen) Camps; eight of these were in County Antrim, four in Londonderry, three in County Down, and one in Belfast. The full list was as follows:

Camp No. 1: Clough, County Down.
Camp No. 2: Cargagh, Cough, County Down.
Camp No. 3: Crossgar, County Down.
Camp No. 4: Saintfield, Belfast.
Camp No. 5: Tawnybrack, Kells, County Antrim.
Camp No. 6: Moorfield, Ballymena, County Antrim.
Camp No. 7: Castlegore, Ballymena, County Antrim.
Camp No. 8: Dunnaird, Broughshane, County Antrim.
Camp No. 9: Drummock, Broughshane, County Antrim.
Camp No. 10: Aghacully, Augafatten, County Antrim.
Camp No. 11: Breckagh Bridge, Aughafatten, County Antrim.
Camp No. 12: Corby Bridge, Rathkenny, County Antrim.
Camp No. 13: Ballyarnett, Londonderry.
Camp No. 14: Molennan, Londonderry.
Camp No. 15: Warbleshinney, Cullion P.O., Londonderry.
Camp No. 16: Tagherian, New Buildings, Londonderry.

Less than 200 evacuees now remained in London, two Centres still being kept open by the Ministry of Health. These evacuees were nearly all relatives of people in hospital.

On Wednesday, 2nd August, 1944, 3,161 evacuees arrived back in Gibraltar from the United Kingdom aboard the *Stirling Castle.* The party had embarked on the 18th July, but a mechanical breakdown in the ship had delayed departure for about a week. Two of the passengers had been born on the way: Stirling Lima on July 24th and Hortensia Arsina on July 27th. The captain had presented a miniature silver cup to the former, and a silver spoon to the latter on behalf of the ship. The disembarkation went very smoothly, taking only four hours. This party was the third contingent of evacuees to be repatriated, the second from the United Kingdom since April 6th, and brought the total number of evacuees back home to 5,505. Still to be repatriated were 7,000 in the United Kingdom (mostly in Northern Ireland), some 700 in Madeira, the 1,400 in Jamaica, and about 750 in Spain and Tangier.

The voyage report of the Senior Medical Officer aboard HMT *Stirling Castle* makes interesting reading:

'On my embarkation seven days after that of the evacuees I received numerous applications on the grounds of ill-health for the transfer of evacuees from Troop Deck to Cabin Accommodation. Many of these requests were well founded as I discovered that aged and infirm evacuees, and expectant mothers, had been berthed regardless of their condition. The Ship's Staff, in my opinion, were justified in their judgement that a complete reberthing as requested by the Ministry of Health Medical Advisor was impracticable at this stage. Therefore I reviewed all requests and adjusted conditions as far as possible, but I was only able to allot a proportion of the Hospital Accommodation to people who were classified by us as aged and infirm.' The Medical Officer submitted that people should have been medically classified and berthed in accordance with their condition and ability to conduct themselves aboard a ship, and that they should also have been medically examined with regards to freedom from infection before embarkation.

He concluded: 'I would also like to ask how it came about that cases of Pulmonary Tuberculosis (some active), at least one helpless Imbecile and many persons quite unable by age or infirmity to take care of themselves got included.'

At about the same time, the Gibraltar Government turned its attention to the matter of those Gibraltarian evacuees in Tangier and Spain, the vessels *Alert* and *Rescue* being chartered to bring those in Tangier. The first parties returned to Gibraltar in early August, 1944.

The Government of Gibraltar continued to resist the pressure being placed upon it to raise the number of evacuees they were prepared to receive. On the 8th August, 1944, the Governor pointed out to London that once the expected third party arrived from the United Kingdom he would have taken back some 7,000 evacuees in five months, whereas his predecessor had only been prepared to receive 4,000 in twelve months. In addition he had undertaken to receive the entire Jamaica contingent. Until service establishments were further and substantially reduced and new accommodation could be provided no more evacuees could be accepted. 'I consider it absolutely essential to call a halt for many of those now returned are living in a deplorable condition of overcrowding or in transit centres which cannot be tenanted indefinitely ....' The Secretary of the Repatriation sub-committee of the Resettlement Board echoed these sentiments.

The question might be, and was, asked: if they all lived in Gibraltar before the war, why could they not now return to their homes? Well, let us consider some interesting figures. Immediately before the evacuation the civilian population of Gibraltar had been about 20,000, of which nearly 16,000 had been evacuated. By the time the third party of repatriates from the United Kingdom and the Jamaica contingent returned (both were expected before the end of 1944) there would only be between 13,000 and 14,000 civilians on the Rock, yet the authorities were claiming that by that stage there would be room for no more. According to official figures, the difference between 20,000 and 13/14,000 was accounted for by:

1. 2 or 3,000 who had formerly lived in Spain and would not now be able to return there;
2. those who had lived in War Department lettings, not now available;
3. those who had lived in buildings since demolished;
4. those who had lived in buildings since bombed;
5. those who had lived in grossly overcrowded conditions, now aggravated by the increase of family units due to marriages and by the maturing of many children to puberty during evacuation, both to an extent not compensated by deaths. (On the other hand, it could be surmised that the war period must have resulted in a considerable decrease in births!)

The conclusions drawn by the Secretary of the Repatriation sub-committee of the Resettlement Board from these figures were:-

1. It would be *impossible* before the end of the year to take in more than a few hundred additional evacuees (over and above present priorities).
2. Any substantial repatriation from Northern Ireland was *out of the question* until temporary houses had been built and/or the Garrison was drastically reduced.

The Colonial Office, whilst appreciating such difficulties, insisted on the 9th September, 1944, that 'every means of speeding up the return of all the Gibraltarians who were evacuated... must clearly be examined and all possible action taken to find room for the returning population, 6,500 of whom are living in accommodation in Northern Ireland which is only suitable for their temporary home. This was obtained on the footing that it was to be accommodation during a period of transit to Gibraltar. It provides no opportunities of employment for those who are able to work and it is impossible to contemplate that these evacuees should remain there indefinitely.'

The cessation of flying bomb attacks by mid-September, 1944, restored priority of return to the Jamaican contingent and consequently reduced the chances of an early return for those in Northern Ireland. The Colonial Office explained that the latter could not be returned to London because of the severe housing shortage there, nor could they remain in Northern Ireland! The Governor was informed that the conclusion had been reached that it would be extremely difficult to hold the position in Northern Ireland throughout the winter. What were the alternatives? The Colonial Office insisted that the solution must be to return the evacuees to Gibraltar, and that such a return could not be delayed until the Government of Gibraltar had solved its housing problems. The suggestion followed of an approach to Spain for the use of a site where a temporary camp could be erected for the evacuees whilst more permanent accommodation was built in Gibraltar. The Defence Security Officer in Gibraltar described the idea as 'outrageously idiotic!' The Governor discussed the matter unofficially with the Spanish Consul General who gave it as his opinion that the proposal would be very ill received in Madrid or locally and that it was quite impractical.

The Governor, in rejecting the idea on the 7th October, 1944, highlighted inherent problems. '.... we cannot force the people to submit to Spanish authority, and, clearly, no Spanish Government will be prepared to grant us extra-territorial rights over the Settlement, a Settlement which must, inevitably, remain in being for a number of years. Nor would there be any means of keeping the people in the Settlement if they did not like it (and they would not), and, once in Gibraltar, to which they must have full freedom of access—there is otherwise no point in bringing them here—I am advised that they could not, as British subjects, be expelled therefrom, and they would soon be camping in the streets.' A host of other problems were enumerated, such as the difficulty of executing normal legal processes, administering to health requirements, the inadequacy of sanitary and electricity services in La Linea, the political instability of Spain and so on.

Counter-proposals were then made to London. Why not move the evacuees to Camps in England, preferably within reach of large towns where employment would be available? Or why not Tangier ......?

Meantime, repatriation continued. A party numbering 488, the third contingent from England, arrived at Gibraltar on the 2nd September, 1944. It had initially been planned that this contingent would comprise over one thousand persons. However, the ship originally designated to carry the repatriates was unable to sail with the convoy due to engine trouble, and its replacement did not have the capacity for so large a number. This inevitably caused great disappointment in Gibraltar. Two further parties from the United Kingdom arrived at Gibraltar on the 5th and 25th October respectively, carrying in total some 500 repatriates. Some of these came from Northern Ireland, where they had been for just a few months. Others in that country were destined for a much longer stay!

More often than not, the heavy personal luggage of the repatriates was transported in a separate ship weeks after their arrival, and this gave rise to additional problems. In November, 1944, it was reported to the Secretary of the Resettlement Board that the heavy baggage belonging to the Gibraltar evacuees had recently arrived 'in a dreadful state of pilferage.' Many packages, crates, bags, etc. had been wantonly forced open with obvious intention. The percentage was exceedingly high and a matter of grave concern. The amount of loose clothing which had fallen out of crates, etc, through being forced open, had already filled eleven large bags! It seemed that the pilferage and stealing had taken place whilst the ship was at Casablanca.

The people affected were naturally in a state of concern as in most cases they were in urgent need of the clothing and other items thus lost. They felt that it was grossly unfair that their belongings should have been tampered with in such a way, and claims for compensation followed. The Colonial Secretary's comment was that this was disgraceful and that the same thing had happened to his wife's baggage on the *Stirling Castle*.

Delays regarding the repatriation of the evacuees in Jamaica provoked a Memorial from the AACR on the 13th September, 1944, directed to the Secretary of State for the Colonies, and backed by a peaceful demonstration in front of the Governor's residence. The Governor agreed to forward this Memorial to London with his strong recommendation, and eight days later it was announced that the arrangements for the repatriation of the evacuees in Jamaica had been finalised. The entire contingent, some 1,500, arrived in Gibraltar on the 26th October, 1944, almost exactly four years after leaving their homes.

These returns completed the homecoming of all people from Gibraltar listed under the priority scheme so far used as the basis of repatriation. It also meant that the repatriation scheme had passed the half-way stage, with 7,000 evacuees already home. The return of the remaining 7,000, mostly accommodated in Northern Ireland, was to pose more difficult problems! As the year 1944 dragged to a close with no apparent progress in the repatriation of the remaining evacuees, so public opinion, largely channelled by the AACR, increased its pressure on the authorities.

CHAPTER SIXTEEN

The Northern Ireland Saga

With half the evacuees back, attention now centred on the repatriation of the rest, most of them in Northern Ireland camps. The major question which emerged was whether they should be returned immediately regardless of conditions in Gibraltar, or whether they should remain in exile until permanent buildings had been erected, a process likely to take at least two years. The Association for the Advancement of Civil Rights in Gibraltar and the Government joined battle on this issue. Meantime, repatriation proceeded at a trickle.

Much of the Authorities' attention, both in the United Kingdom and in Gibraltar, was taken up by the evacuees in Northern Ireland. The initial reaction of these evacuees on arrival at the Camps had been one of relief and gratitude. After the hazards of the flying bomb attacks, the peace of the Irish countryside must have seemed idyllic. An extra-ordinary long spell of fine weather, a plentiful supply of milk and poultry, the wonderful hospitality from the local inhabitants in the form of village dances, concerts, invitations to their homes, and the general kindliness and sympathy of the people as compared with the coldness and aloofness of their former London neighbours, all contributed to a general feeling of well-being.

However, as time went by all that was to change! The weather (inevitably!) broke, and dissatisfaction grew because of the inability of obtaining employment, the residential qualification which prevented the unemployed evacuees from receiving Unemployment Insurance, a delay in the delivery of the evacuees' luggage, and, above all, the realisation that repatriation was not just around the corner.

As one Ministry of Health official put it to the Governor of Gibraltar:- 'The Government of Northern Ireland are likely to have a very difficult time unless there is some steady repatriation. It was the one question on everyone's lips in all the camps.'

He was right, as a spate of telegrams from Northern Ireland Camps to Gibraltar during the month of August, 1944, show:

'Gibraltar Evacuees have survived the 1940/41 Blitz and Flying Bombs and have gone through hardships of four years communal living. As if this was not enough we have now been brought to Camps where general and particularly sanitary conditions are appalling.' A plea for early repatriation followed.

'Conditions here unbearable. My health further deteriorating. Pray once more have me and family repatriated earliest possible.'

'Gibraltarians Northern Ireland unanimously and anxiously request Your Excellency expedite arrangements general repatriation soonest possible. To alleviate housing problem evacuees living at present Nissen Huts are all willing live temporarily in Gibraltar similar huts.'

'.... the weather in this camp in winter is almost unbearable.'

'Submit inadequate conditions. Residence this Camp will have terrible effects on women and children and request very urgent repatriation in bulk to prevent further sufferings in coming winter.'

And there were many others in the same vein!

There was the other side of the coin! The Secretary of the Resettlement Board, Eames Hughes, informed the Colonial Secretary that he had discussed conditions at the camps with Dr Dotto who had been there, and from his account they were not nearly as bad as the telegrams suggested.

The Ministry of Health, too, asked one of their officials, A P Fitzgerald, to investigate the allegations. He reported that a visit to Camp No 15 had not revealed any complaints or any incidents of note and that everything appeared to be going well. 'Eight or ten families .... have been very unsettled since arrival and complain no matter what is done for them.' The suggestion that the general conditions in Camp were appalling was dismissed as 'a gross misstatement.'

In general, continued the report, although there were problems connected with the lack of employment and unemployment benefit, the majority of the Gibraltarians were settling down. Every camp was operated by a carefully trained staff and there had been numerous expressions of gratitude received from individual Gibraltarians and from entire camps. Two 'unsolicited testimonials' were included in support of this statement:

An article, translated from the Spanish, from Camp 5 at Kells read as follows: 'Now that we have settled down in this great and lovely country—Northern Ireland, whose hospitality is world famed, it is my utmost desire to dedicate the present article to make due our acknowledgement and express our grateful thanks to High Officials of the Ministry of Home Affairs. To the Press, and especially to the staff in charge of our Camp for the warm welcome and multiple sympathies shown unto us at the time of our arrival to this blessed spot. Not only at this first stage are we benefited of their great kindness, but it still goes on without end to our greatest satisfaction. The high spirits now prevailing in our temporary homes is best proof of the eagerness of Mr McCromack, Officer in Charge: Miss Reid, Deputy, and the whole staff under their supervision at the said camp. In fact, life is worth living in the company of such grand people.

Life under the present circumstances is carried on smoothly and in complete harmony, and excellent understanding. Food is plentiful and of a great variety and suitable to our tastes. As days go by everything tends to improve, so much so that the management may rest assured that the whole Camp will for ever appreciate their unenvious and arduous task.

Everywhere we go we are certain to find smiling faces and sympathy from everyone: country folks, townspeople, who all have a friendly hand and readily come to our aid. Who do all in their power to satisfy our necessities and wishes.

I therefore, and on behalf of the residents of Camp 5 wish to make public our testimony and guarantee that their kindness will for ever live in our hearts.'

The second 'unsolicited testimonial' stated that 'the Gibraltarians at present residing at Emergency Camp No 6, Ballymena, wish to express to the Authorities and peoples of Northern Ireland, through your medium, their appreciation and gratitude for the friendly reception given to them ever since they set foot on Irish soil.

We realise the great amount of work which the transportation and accommodation of thousands entail, more so as the matter had to be attended to at such short notice, and this makes us admire all the more the way in which everything has been organised here.

If any doubts or suspicions ever existed in our minds as to the kind of reception which would be given us, or about the conditions under which we were to live in this country, these disappeared as soon as we arrived here and began to feel the warmth of your welcome.'

The Colonial Secretary of Gibraltar commented that this Report and conversations with 'one or two responsible persons' who had been in the camps satisfied him that the claims made in the telegrams were 'not founded upon anything but an uncontrollable and quite understandable itch to get back to the Rock.'

Be that as it may, the complaints continued! On the 1st November, 1944, the Secretary of State for the Colonies was informing the Governor that the evacuees were refusing to co-operate in further broadcasts to Gibraltar on the grounds that they conveyed a false impression to the people in Gibraltar that they were happy and contented when in fact they were not.

A circular posted in the Camps stated:

'The Executive Committee is prepared to launch an energetic propaganda campaign, using various means, in view of the negligence on the part of the Authorities in attending urgently to the various matters submitted to it by this committee. One of these methods will be a display of ''sandwich-boards'' through the streets of Belfast. For this purpose Camp Committees are asked to solicit the aid of volunteers from each Camp to carry these boards.

It goes without saying that the Executive Committee is responsible for the propaganda which is to be launched, and we know that the campaign will be supported by all the evacuees.'

This Notice, which had been translated from the Spanish, was signed by L Bruzon, Chairman, and dated the 26th October, 1944.

In late November, 1944, the Governor informed the Colonial Office that he was being bombarded with telegrams from Northern Ireland complaining of conditions there and demanding their immediate return. He insisted that this was impossible and asked that the evacuees be informed authoritatively that the remaining stages of repatriation were linked to such problems as reduction of the garrison and new building and that the process had, perforce, to be slow. He again urged that the evacuees should be returned to England.

Exchanges between the Gibraltar Government and the AACR became quite heated at this stage when the latter's Secretary, E Salvado, informed the Colonial Secretary that 'a very great anxiety and concern is felt in Gibraltar for the sufferings that are being endured by our people in Northern Ireland', and then referred to the 'present muddle in the housing situation and its causes.'

The Colonial Secretary, Miles Clifford, curtly replied:

'Your reference to the present muddle in the housing situation is neither understood, nor appreciated; it was your wish and the wish of those who remained in Gibraltar throughout the war, that since the return of the evacuees had to be controlled (as it clearly must be controlled) we should first re-unite those who have been separated. That the Government has done, and has in barely seven months brought back approximately 9,000 people including—at your frequent insistence—the whole of the Jamaica contingent: when repatriation was first considered it was laid down by the then Governor that we could not expect to bring back more than a total of 4,000 at a monthly approximation of 500. I am to suggest that it is incumbent upon your committee to place these facts before its members, to the end that they may be persuaded to take a more reasoned view of a situation which has been brought about wholly by the war and which is deplored by none more than this Government and His Majesty's Government at home . . . with the best will in the world we cannot do the impossible—you cannot put a quart into a pint pot!'

When the Executive Committee of the evacuees stated that the vast majority of them blamed the Ministry of Health in London for having dumped them into such miserable living quarters, the Colonial Secretary's sardonic comment was that they had been happy enough to escape the flying bombs at the time and that they had to realise that His Majesty's Government could not shift them back and forth as occasion and their convenience demanded!

At the same time, Governor Eastwood pointed out that no promise had been made to the evacuees that they would be repatriated very soon. Yet, he added, 'evidence was accumulating that the evacuees themselves were fully persuaded that their stay in Northern Ireland was to be a brief one while they were in transit for Gibraltar.'

Such a belief was now resulting in accusations of bad faith being levelled at the Government of Gibraltar. 'I shall be grateful', he wrote to London, 'if action is taken to inform the evacuees that, while His Majesty's Government and the Government of Gibraltar were anxious that they should be removed from the danger of flying bombs, the latter held out no prospect of their being returned to Gibraltar in the near future. Any indication that their transference to Northern Ireland heralded an early return which, if given at all, was given without my knowledge or connivance, represents, I fear, one of the major factors in their present discontent.'

Notwithstanding such statements, the AACR held a public meeting on the 6th December, 1944, in which it was alleged that the remaining evacuees in Northern Ireland were living in appalling conditions. A six-point resolution was presented to the Gibraltar Government calling for the immediate repatriation of all evacuees and suggesting measures for overcoming the accommodation difficulties currently impeding such a move.

On that same day, a deputation from Northern Ireland, consisting of Messrs L F Bruzon, A Bellotti, and A A Felipes, met the Duke of Devonshire at the Colonial Office in London. At that meeting, the deputation referred to the situation at Camp 5, where, it was alleged, the evacuees were being 'starved into submission by a Head Warden.' According to them, no meals had been allowed to the evacuees at the Camp for two days, except for children up to the age of seven years. In addition, the evacuees had been deprived of firewood and paraffin for lamps. The dispute had arisen because the evacuees wanted the domestic staff to be chosen from amongst themselves in rotation, whereas the Warden preferred to appoint a permanent staff, selected by himself. The evacuees felt that it was unfair that they should be deprived of the opportunity, in turn, of earning a little extra money. Police had been called in and were patrolling the camp.

These complaints were investigated by a Ministry of Health official, whose report differed somewhat from the version just given! Following the arrival of the Gibraltarians in Northern Ireland it had been agreed to employ a number of them—male and female—in each camp kitchen as labourers and cooks on a weekly rotational basis. The object of this arrangement had been to distribute the work available amongst evacuees willing to take it up and to provide an opportunity for the largest possible number of persons to augment the pocket money allowance which at the time was only one shilling and sixpence a week.

After a reasonable trial, however, it had been realised that it was quite impossible to run the kitchens properly or to ensure the preparation of satisfactory meals under such a system, because of the inevitable employment of incompetent, lazy and dishonest persons and the dislocation caused by a change of Gibraltarian cooks each week.

The opportunity to alter the system had come in September, 1944, when the allowances to the Gibraltarians were increased. Wardens were accordingly instructed to select Gibraltarian staffs on merit only and to employ them on a permanent basis. In the majority of the camps the new arrangement had yielded satisfactory results, but in Camp 6 (Moorfields) the Camp Committee had strongly opposed it. Due to this and to their offer to ensure that only efficient workers would be nominated for kitchen duties the Warden had agreed to continue on the old basis. However, the improvement hoped for by the Warden, both in personnel and in efficiency, had failed to materialise and, in consequence, unfavourable reports on the Moorfields kitchen arrangements had been received from two of the Ministry of Health's outdoor officers who had visited the camp respectively on the 2nd and the 16th November, 1944.

On the 24th November, the Warden of Camp 6 had been informed by the Ministry that the continued employment of Gibraltarian kitchen workers on a rotational basis could no longer be sanctioned. The Warden had been instructed to arrange for the selection and appointment of a permanent Gibraltarian staff and to submit his proposals to the Ministry after discussion with the Camp Committee.

The Committee, when consulted, had again refused to support the Warden's arrangements and would agree only to the permanent appointment of one Gibraltarian cook whom the Warden had already found unsuitable. Moreover, the Committee had also intimated that if the Warden insisted on the installation of a permanent Gibraltarian staff, they would disclaim all responsibility for any trouble which might follow.

Mr McDevette, the Camp Warden, had therefore informed the Committee of Camp 6 on the 1st December that due to the complete failure of the rotational system of labour, a permanent staff of Gibraltarians selected by the Warden would be appointed as from Sunday, 3rd December, 1944. When the Committee had replied that 'the idea of a permanent staff would not be entertained by their people', the Warden had informed them that if the staff chosen by him were not available for duty as required on the Sunday morning, no food could be cooked or provided for any persons other than children up to seven years of age, invalids and members of the permanent staff.

The only workers who had reported for duty on the 3rd December had been those appointed by the Committee themselves and excluded all persons selected by the Warden. It had then been made clear to the Chairman of the Committee that in the circumstances the Warden had no alternative but to prepare meals only for invalids, certain children and members of the permanent staff. Two police officers had been on duty at the Camp during both Sunday and Monday.

Not only had the Gibraltarians refused to co-operate, but they had contacted their compatriots at Camp 5 (Tawnybrack) who had supported them to the extent of sending by taxi from Camp 5 to Camp 6 all dinners provided for the residents of the former.

On the 4th December, the Ministry had received a letter from the Gibraltarian Executive Committee requesting the immediate removal of the management at Camp 6. All children had absented themselves from school from the Moorfields Camp School on Monday and Tuesday, 3rd and 4th December, though the school had been open and the teaching staff on duty.

The Ministry had then instructed the Group Warden to tell the Gibraltarians at Camp 6 that unless they agreed to the appointment of a permanent Gibraltarian kitchen staff at that camp, the Ministry would install a permanent Irish staff and that if this were done Gibraltarians would not in future be employed in Camp 6 kitchen on any basis.

The Camp 6 Committee had again refused their co-operation and on Tuesday, 5th December, a staff of non-Gibraltarians had been selected and engaged to commence work on the following day. The normal service of meals had been accordingly resumed at Camp 6 on Wednesday, 6th December, the day of the deputation's visit to London. No further incidents had occurred at the time of the Ministry of Health official's visit, though his feeling was that it was possible that more might be heard about the incident as the Gibraltarians had been talking 'rather wildly about being forced into submission by starvation', a claim described by the official as 'a travesty of the facts'. The policy of the Ministry, he concluded, was that the rotational system of employment in the kitchens must cease and that there was no question of allowing the Gibraltarians to dictate to it in connection with the employment of staff, or indeed, any other matter.

What were conditions really like in Northern Ireland? One viewpoint is provided by a comprehensive set of notes produced by a Miss Whitehorn, Regional Assistant of the British Council, and dated the 1st January, 1945: 'It is not easy to give a true picture of the life of the Gibraltarians in Northern Ireland. Naturally, all opinions are tinged with the sentiments or prejudices of the observer. The Gibraltarians, on their side, suffer from the usual characteristics of all those torn up and removed from their natural surroundings. Possibly this may be accentuated by their Mediterranean temperament and lack of education. I think it is true to say that with most of them, their longing to return to their Rock has almost become an obsession and nothing told them of the unsatisfactory conditions there . . . has any influence now. Lack of work forces the Gibraltarian man to brood on this all day—from his half Nissen hut he hears so many voices of varying authority, from his camp warden to the Governor of Gibraltar, and so many well-wishers, busy-bodies, and others, are telling him one thing and another, that he becomes bewildered and disgruntled. Under these conditions, he is more than ever a victim to his predisposition to believe every rumour, and his inability to reason out matters of this kind. He has nothing to concentrate on but his own grievance, and often he is unable to see and appreciate what is being done for his immediate welfare. There is some danger that he will become his own enemy. His Ulster neighbours welcomed him with their native friendliness and hospitality. Not understanding his background, aware that he receives certain benefits that they do not, they listen to his endless, and, to them, sometimes unreasonable complaints and begin to judge him as 'ungrateful' and 'truculent'. In one other way the Gibraltarian does not make things easier for himself. This is in his tendency to jealousy. It had often been possible for the authorities to offer some entertainment or service to one or a group of camps only, but, fearful of the resentment it might cause to the less fortunate ones, this had to be abandoned.

The main preoccupations of the Gibraltarians are:

1. Return to the Rock

Many of the Gibraltarians say that if they could only be told authoritatively *when* this will be, they would do their best to settle down. They do not believe the housing position to be so acute, and have produced a long list of houses said to be empty, which has been submitted to the authorities. It seems fairly obvious that this is mostly wishful thinking, but a reply on this from Gibraltar would help.

2. Lack of work

Any money made in London is slowly disappearing; their future is uncertain, and having paid their insurance money in England, they do not understand the law in Northern Ireland which grants benefit only to those of five years' residence. It is not easy to explain to them that Ministries cannot make presents, and that with the Assistance Board's grant, they are, in fact, better off than with unemployment benefit. They only see that 8/6 a week for a married couple is very little in terms of foot-wear, fares, cigarettes, etc. It is noticeable that in Camp 17, where everyone is employed, there are no troubles or complications.

3. Camp Life

Although no doubt the majority of Gibraltarians were used to somewhat primitive conditions on the Rock, they have since known the conveniences of modern luxury flats in London. Many have become more self-respecting and to endure outside sanitation, rain, snow, and, in some cases, rats, is hard, especially for the old. Also, most of the camps are in isolated places, where 'bus services are not very frequent.

4. Lack of suitable clothing

There have been many complaints from the Gibraltarians that they and their children are short of clothes, particularly shoes, which wear out rapidly under camp conditions. Many Gibraltarians have no more coupons, or have sold them, anticipating their return. The Womens Voluntary Service can provide a certain amount of coupons, free of charge, and arrangements are being made to secure a number of clogs and mackintoshes.

Against these difficulties the following points should be mentioned:-

1. Camps

Included in these are the Primary Schools, sick-bays, CCR huts and entertainment.

2. Food
Very few real complaints. Milk is unrationed and apparently almost unlimited.
3. Health
The sick-bays are practically empty, except for a few old people. The nurses living on the spot struck me as a very nice competent lot on the whole.
4. Welfare—general
I had the impression that there was little of which the Administration had not thought in the way of encouraging any sort of occupation or interest the Gibraltarians might show. For instance, a float of coupons had been arranged to get material for the women, and a most successful bazaar of their work held at Ballymena, which produced a number of orders. Wood was found for toy-making, which has become quite a feature in some camps. It is hoped that a Gibraltarian Concert Party and/or Jazz Band will be run on business lines round the many Service camps and clubs, from talent drawn from all Camps.
5. General attitude towards the Gibraltarians
The natural friendliness of the Northern Irish people has been noted. Mention should be made also of the Stormont officials. I was present at the monthly meeting between these officials and the Gibraltarian Executive Committee .... and was always impressed by the human understanding and courtesy with which the Gibraltarians were treated, and the humour which at times helped to turn an awkward corner. No doubt the sorrows of a minority are not so unusual to the authorities in Northern Ireland, and one often suspected that in their attitude might lurk some vestige of the real Irish enjoyment of a scrap with the law and a tender feeling for those who indulged in it. At any rate, the dreariness of the solemn and superior person was avoided.

To *CONCLUDE*—one feels that life in the camps is definitely demoralising for the men without work, and for the aged. One cannot think the same about the children, who go to good schools, are well fed on the whole and enjoy the open air of that wet, but not unhealthy, climate. If the Gibraltarians are to stay months or years, one greatly hopes that at least the young people may come to feel themselves one of a larger community, and acquire more generous habits of mind such as have been denied them up to date through poor quality education. It may be hoped that they will eventually form a body of more enlightened opinion, should they ultimately wish to return to the Rock.

What is wanted for the adults is an immediate statement as to when they will return. Then if they must remain in Northern Ireland, a determined effort will have to be made to encourage every sort of occupation or trade in the camps, if possible on a profit-making basis.'

On the 15th January, 1945, a small party of about 170 Gibraltar evacuees returned home. They came from Northern Ireland and were the balance of the priority classes whose repatriation had recently brought the first part of the homecoming programme to a close. Most members of this party belonged to families which had been split during the evacuation—wives who had gone to Jamaica whilst their husbands had been sent to the United Kingdom. Included in the passenger list was an old lady of 65 who had had a leg amputated shortly before returning and who had stood the sea trip very well.

On the 29th January, 1945, the Colonial Office appointed Sir Findlater Stewart to examine the problems of repatriating the Gibraltarians still in the United Kingdom and Madeira. Meantime, the possibilities of moving them to Tangier, or even French Morocco, were being considered!

In February, Sir Findlater Stewart visited four of the Northern Ireland Camps at Cargagh, Tawnybrack, Saintfield and Ballyarnett. In an early communication to the Governor, he wrote:

'Allowing for the winter climate of Ulster, and Nissen huts, everything possible has been done and is being done for the evacuees. But they will never be happy till they get back to Gibraltar or within reach of it. And by sending them to Ireland, where there is no work for them (there are 20,000 Irish unemployed) and no unemployment benefit, we have got ourselves on the wrong foot. I don't believe we can maintain the position very long.' Stewart also visited Gibraltar from the 23rd March to the 7th April, 1945, and he was subsequently to submit a full report and his recommendations.

Evacuees continued to trickle back home; a further party from Madeira on the 14th April, 1945, was soon followed by another contingent from Northern Ireland, 285 of whom arrived at Gibraltar on the 23rd April aboard the *Carthage* in convoy en route to India. This was the seventh party of repatriates from the United Kingdom. It was also announced that providing shipping could be arranged similar parties might be expected to arrive at least each month and perhaps more frequently. This new repatriation influx consisted mainly of persons who could return to accommodation provided by friends or relatives or to their own pre-evacuation homes.

On the 8th May, 1945, the German armed forces in Europe surrendered—VE Day. The war was practically over but the repatriation process still had a long way to go. An eighth party from the United Kingdom, consisting of 282 persons, arrived in Gibraltar on the 11th May, 1945.

Stewart's interim report finally reached the Gibraltar authorities in June, 1945. On his visit to Northern Ireland he had this to say:-

'The camps were composed of Nissen huts, 36 feet long. There were well fitted communal kitchens, adequate dining rooms, washing and sanitary facilities and the huts used for living accommodation were partitioned across the middle, each half, approximately 17 ft × 16 ft, being occupied by one family. The average Gibraltarian family consists of about four persons, but owing to the great unwillingness of families to separate there were occasional cases of gross overcrowding, as many as seven or eight people sharing one half hut, while others in the same camp were occupied by only two people. I was impressed by the energy and good will of the staffs at the camps I visited and by the great efforts they were making to make the best of the admittedly rough conditions under which the evacuees are living. The camps are fully staffed with nurses; doctors pay frequent visits and everything possible is done to promote the welfare of the evacuees, particularly the children. It is significant that in the camps I visited—with a total population of about 1,200 adults and 150 children under five—there were no children in the sick bays and only two adults, both bedridden old people.

Nevertheless, the evacuees are unhappy. They have a number of grievances about their conditions, but these are of relatively little account in comparison with the effects of climate (they have endured one of the worst winters known in Northern Ireland) and their feeling that they are marooned in an alien land with no certainty of return. This feeling of isolation is particularly acute among the old people, and I was assured at all the camps, and by the General Committee whom I saw in Belfast, of the unanimous desire for the establishment of a firm programme for return on which people could begin to plan their future.'

Stewart's main conclusions were that:

1. all evacuees should be removed from Northern Ireland as soon as possible. ('There may well be serious trouble in the camps if the evacuees have to pass another winter in the present living conditions.')
2. They should be returned to Gibraltar or to a Mediterranean climate; failing that they should be transferred to urban areas in Great Britain.
3. The removal of the worst features of the housing conditions in Gibraltar was an essential preliminary to the return of the mass of the evacuees.
4. The only practicable alternative site for a camp was Tangier (the possibility of one in Spain was discarded).

The month of June saw further repatriation from Northern Ireland and Madeira. On the 20th June, 1945, a contingent of 778 repatriates arrived in Gibraltar from Northern Ireland aboard the Polish ship *Batory* after a three and half day journey. Youngest passenger on board was Richard Charles Mansell, three months old, and born in Northern Ireland. A further batch from Madeira arrived a few days later. By the end of the month, 10,950 evacuees were back in Gibraltar out of the 16,700 who had been evacuated.

The trickle continued in July: about 40 repatriates arrived from Northern Ireland on the 23rd aboard the Norwegian steamer *Bergenfjord,* and a further 423 arrived three days later on board the British liner *Ascania,* also from Northern Ireland.

In charge of the latter party was Mr G B Newe of the Ministry of Health and Chief Inspector of Camps in Northern Ireland. He reported to the Colonial Secretary that conditions in the camps were now much more satisfactory than they had been a few months ago. Health had been excellent and the only complaints that had been received had been of a trivial character. News had been transmitted to the evacuees that conditions in Gibraltar at the present time were far from ideal, and there was consequently not the same urgency of desire to return to the Rock.

Mr Newe did not view with alarm the prospect of the evacuees remaining in Northern Ireland for another winter. Conditions last winter had been made difficult by the extremely cold weather which was not likely to occur again (how he could have known this is something of a mystery!). Moreover, he continued, fuel supplies were much improved. He did not think that any announcement to the effect that a substantial proportion of those remaining could not return to Gibraltar until permanent building was provided would cause undue consternation and he added that the Ministry of Health officials had to some extent prepared the ground for such a statement. Newe also thought that the idea of a transference to Tangier would be popular with the Gibraltarians. In a later communication to the Colonial Secretary (dated the 2nd August, 1945), Newe added that 'Gibraltarians for their own ends, have been at pains to misrepresent the conditions in the Camps.'

Between the 8th and the 12th July, 1945, a Dr Kauntze visited Gibraltar, as a result of which a new element was introduced into the repatriation issue. Until then, lack of accommodation had been given as the major obstacle to the repatriation of the residue. Dr Kauntz now reported:

'Apart from actual difficulties of housing the return of evacuees is throwing a great strain upon the Hospital services. As I have already mentioned, the people who have been evacuated to other countries have started to use medical services to a much greater extent than before the war. There is real danger that if more people are brought into the peninsula the Hospital services will break down not only for want of accommodation but also for want of staff. At the present time there are 70 maternity cases being delivered each month in the maternity Hospital requiring a practically day and night service of midwives. In my view there are very cogent arguments on health grounds for refusing to allow any more evacuees to return to Gibraltar until the medical authorities are satisfied that:

(a) overcrowding has all been relieved;

(b) congestion in the Centres has been reduced to a point where windowless cubicles are no longer used;

(c) admission of additional evacuees will not overstrain hospital accommodation and the civil medical services.

Thus, health considerations were now added to the accommodation shortage as a reason for holding up repatriation!

At the beginning of September, 1945, the British liner *Eastern Prince* arrived at Gibraltar from Belfast bringing 236 Gibraltarian repatriates from Northern Ireland. The report of the Senior Medical Officer aboard highlighted certain problems connected with the repatriation:

'.... amongst the Gibraltarians carried on the above trip there were many who, by reason of old age and infirmity, were not, in our opinion, suitable persons to be carried on Troop Decks. Considerable inconvenience was caused by their presence on these Decks, and there was a considerable risk .... that in a rough sea fractures would be liable to be caused. It is pointed out that a fracture in a person of advanced years is a very serious matter indeed, not only in itself, but also because it might lead to hypostatic pneumonia and death. Also very many found it difficult to negotiate the troop deck ladders. In our opinion, these elderly people should not have been passed fit to endure the very rough and ready conditions of troop deck life, for reasons of health and humanity.

Furthermore it is emphasised that three of those embarked were in such a condition of health that they had to be admitted at once to the Troop Hospital. Of these one was blind, another was one legged, the third was very old and suffering from senility. These were accepted under protest, only because refusing to embark them would have incurred very great inconvenience to their families. .... The Troop Hospital is not intended for the transport of invalids being meant only for cases occurring during the voyage and requiring hospitalisation as an emergency. To fill its beds with permanent patients is seriously to impair its efficiency for its true purpose, which is to deal with acute illness as it arises.

It is urgently requested that such practices should not occur in future, as a condition might easily arise in which a large part, or even the whole of the Troop Hospital might be filled from one end of the Voyage to the other with feeble and infirm people, leaving no room for the admission of any other personnel. It is our opinion that such people should be carried either in suitable cabin accommodation, or upon Hospital ships, and that a very grave risk and great inconvenience and interference with the running of the ship is caused by allowing them to travel under the above mentioned conditions.'

The Ship's doctor substantiated the above remarks and added that no sanitary arrangements were provided in the Troop Deck accommodation of a vessel of this type. 'There are no sanitary arrangements provided in Troop Decks and this necessitates the climbing of steep ladders to the upper deck which is an arduous and dangerous task for elderly people.'

Among the repatriates in this party was Mr Louis Bruzon, Chairman of the Executive Committee in charge of the Gibraltarian evacuees in Northern Ireland. His arrival in Gibraltar was to add fire-power to the campaign for the early return of all evacuees. Talking to a *Chronicle* reporter on arrival, Mr Bruzon said: 'My thoughts are and will always be with the people who unfortunately I have left behind and are still living in exile in Northern Ireland. I have, for the present, nothing else to add.'

The rift between the Government of Gibraltar and the AACR meantime widened, repatriation being but one of the issues in the dispute. On Sunday, 16th September, 1945, the Association held a public meeting at which it was decided to send a letter of protest to the Colonial Secretary on the composition of a committee appointed by the Governor to review salaries and conditions of service in the Colonial Government. The letter read:

'At a public meeting held at the Theatre Royal on the 16th inst, it was unanimously decided that the following communication be sent to you.

My Association on the 28th October, 1944, wrote to you protesting on the appointment of Major Patron as a member of the Executive Council, in view of his activities as Commissioner of Evacuees in the United Kingdom.

Since that date events have confirmed our view of his unpopularity (A reference to the results of the City Council Elections held earlier in the year at which the AACR had swept the board, all their seven candidates being elected, whilst others such as Patron had polled few votes).

His appointment as Chairman of the Committee created by His Excellency the Governor .... to investigate conditions of service in the Colonial Government, comes to confirm the blatant disregard for public opinion held by the Government in recent times.

If further proof is required of this assertion it is given by the appointment of Mr P G Russo as a member of the said Committee. Perhaps it has not yet come to the notice of the Government that Mr Russo had as many as 450 votes in his favour at the recent City Council elections out of 3775 votes.

We must therefore lodge our most energetic protest on the appointment of these two gentlemen, as it is an insult to the people of Gibraltar.'

In a reference to repatriation, the President of the AACR, Mr Risso, criticised the activities of the Governor since his appointment and regretted that he had not paid a visit to the Gibraltarians in Northern Ireland camps so that he could see for himself the disgusting conditions under which these evacuees were living. 'We only know', said Mr Risso, 'that Sir Findlater Stewart went to visit them but nothing official about his report has been given to us.'

At the meeting held on the 16th September it was announced that the Association had decided to send a deputation to see the Secretary of State for the Colonies, and that said deputation would be visiting the Northern Ireland evacuees first. Mr Bruzon described the living conditions in the Northern Ireland camps as 'disgusting', and said that it was intolerable that they should remain there another winter. 'This should not be tolerated and should be regarded by the whole community as an insult.'

Following upon Dr Kauntze's report, the Governor informed London on the 13th September, 1945, that it was the unanimous opinion of the Executive Council and the medical authorities (with which he entirely agreed) that further parties of persons already authorised to return by the Resettlement Board (about 800) should not be sent until essential minimum nursing staff and equipment needed for the erection of temporary houses were available. At the same time, he urged that these conditions should be met as soon as possible since the interruption of repatriation arrangements already announced could lead to serious local repercussions.

The Secretary of State for the Colonies replied on the 29th September, 1945, that a shortage of nurses in the United Kingdom made it impossible to foresee when Gibraltar's requirements could be met. At the same time the Ministry of Health urged that the next repatriation party of about 450 persons, due to leave in early October, should be allowed to proceed. To stop this party at this stage, they argued, would have most embarrasing consequences. They did undertake to ensure that no sick persons or woman likely to give birth within the next few months would be included in this party. The Governor agreed to receive the party on these conditions, and the Senior Medical Officer concurred provided that 'the policy of allowing no further parties should be rigidly enforced until the Hospital Staff position has become ameliorated.'

It would appear that the Ministry of Health misinterpreted the conditions specified by the Gibraltar authorities for among those banned from returning were all complaints affecting gastrics, diabetics, epileptics, tuberculosis, old people, even those persons in possession of a medical certificate not requiring further treatment. The complaint came from the Sub-Committee representing the Gibraltarian evacuees in Northern Ireland that persons not very ill and requiring no hospital treatment were not being allowed to leave with the next party.

Mr Bruzon was quick to transmit such complaints to the Colonial Secretary. In a letter of the 12th October, 1945, he wrote:

'It seems that the Authorities are determined to penalize the evacuees in Northern Ireland in all conceivable ways and this new obstruction to their return to Gibraltar will only serve to add very considerably to the ever-growing feeling of indignation of the Gibraltarians.

Is it suggested by the medical authorities that aged and infirm who have been condemned to exist in Northern Ireland camps for fifteen months and whose repatriation was, recently, duly approved by the Resettlement Board should now pass away in exile?'

There followed another public meeting on the 14th October, 1945. Between 800 and 1,000 people attended to listen to Mr Bruzon. He informed them of the latest developments, that the repatriation of sick and aged people had been suspended because the medical authorities in Gibraltar could not accept responsibility for them. 'This', he said, 'was trying to the limit of endurance the patience of the people and they must protest most energetically against this new injustice.'

Referring to a recent statement that 2,000 evacuees would not be able to return to Gibraltar for two years, Mr Bruzon said that 'this was a challenge and an insult to the people of Gibraltar which they could not, and would not, tolerate.' He went on to argue that the position in regard to medical facilities was no worse then than it had been before the war and that with the advances which had been made in air transport during the war there was no reason why medicines could not be flown out from England if they were urgently required in Gibraltar. This excuse, therefore, was not good enough, especially since the majority of the sick and aged only required attention at home.

The AACR submitted three resolutions to the Gibraltar Government:

(a) Gibraltarians should not be prevented in any way from returning to Gibraltar if their return had been authorised by the Resettlement Board (whether or not this latter body should exist was also another matter).

(b) People whose return had not yet been authorised and who had an equal right to return to Gibraltar should be brought back before the winter or at least transferred to a more favourable climate.

(c) The authorities should be asked to furnish a reply before next Sunday, 21st October.

The Governor informed London that if the information being received from Northern Ireland was correct, then the Ministry of Health had gone beyond the agreed conditions. 'There is no objection locally to repatriation of old persons or any others not likely to need hospitalisation and if repatriation of any persons not in this category had been withheld it would be desirable if time permits to include them in the party.'

The AACR was informed of this policy. The general public were also informed via Government Notice No. 171:

'It is notified for general information that in view of reports by the Medical authorities regarding the serious and increasing danger to public health caused by the conditions of overcrowding in Gibraltar and the lack of medical facilities due to the inability to obtain the additional nursing staff that must be secured before further hospital accommodation can be provided, it has been necessary to postpone the repatriation of any further parties of Gibraltarians until the nursing staff position has improved. Every effort has been made and is being made by the Government and by the Secretary of State for the Colonies to obtain additional nursing staff.

2. This temporary postponement will not apply to the next party of about 450 persons who are expected to arrive in Gibraltar shortly from

Northern Ireland, but persons likely to need hospitalisation will not be included in the party.'

The Colonial Secretary came to the defence of the Government at a press conference on the 19th October, 1945. 'I have always urged that every exiled Gibraltarian should come home as soon as possible. The Government was warned months ago by the Board of Health that overcrowding, lack of hospital accommodation and shortage of nurses might soon constitute a danger to public health. I was anxious that repatriation should continue until the red flag went up. The local doctors have now hoisted the danger signal and their opinion is supported by the Colonial Office. The Government cannot ignore it.

Some people seem to have the impression that the Government is putting spokes in the wheels of repatriation. Please tell them that such is not the case. It is the Government's sincere and earnest desire to get everyone back with the minimum delay.'

Asked how he could justify public health as a reason against the return of more people when Gibraltar had the same hospital accommodation, the same number of nurses and there were about 2,000 fewer people than in pre-evacuation days, Mr Stanley answered that there were many threads, each perhaps small in itself, but which woven together had resulted in the medical ultimatum. Amongst such threads were the existing overcrowding, the abnormal number of maternity cases being treated in hospital, more tuberculosis patients and private institutions which had previously cared for the aged and infirm no longer having premises.

On the question of soon making up for the lack of nurses the Colonial Secretary was not despondent. Although the shortage in the United Kingdom was acute, he said that the question had again been represented to the Colonial Office as one of the 'utmost urgency'.

Referring to the criticisms which had been made regarding the choice of site for the permanent building programme (certain parts of the Alameda Gardens), Mr Stanley commented that when space was so drastically limited as it was in Gibraltar, the elimination of sites had to be at the expense of accommodation. (Such a comment ignored the suggestion which had been made that the Ministry of Defence might have released land for the purpose!)

The City Council of Gibraltar entered the fray in late October, 1945. In a hard-hitting speech, Councillor J T Ellicott accused the Services of being uncooperative over the matter of releasing accommodation for civilian use. The people of Gibraltar, he said, were receiving poor recompense from the Services for what they had been compelled to give up by the exigencies of the situation in 1940, and for the steady faithful service rendered by Gibraltarians throughout the war. Following upon this, Mr A Risso, the AACR's nominee to the Resettlement Board, resigned that position, and Mr Ellicott, the Council's nominee, followed soon after.

Repatriates coming down the gangway of the ship which brought them back to Gibraltar from Britain.

A repatriate carrying a child is assisted by British Tommies to carry her luggage from the ship. (IWM).

Tommies helping to carry the luggage of the repatriates across a rather wet quayside. (IWM).

The scene on the quayside as women and children repatriates come ashore from the ship. (IWM).

Repatriates being assisted by British Tommies to carry their luggage from the ship. (IWM).

His Excellency the Governor, Lieut. General Sir Ralph Eastwood, talking to one of the first families to come ashore. (IWM).

Happy and emotional reunions. (IWM).

Some of the repatriates moving off to their homes in an army lorry. (IWM).

Repatriates leaving an army lorry on arrival at their homes. (IWM).

Repatriates leaving the ship and being assisted by the military.

Typical quayside scenes on arrival of more repatriates.

Repatriates arriving from Jamaica. (IWM).

A Gibraltar family landing from the ship which brought them back from Jamaica. (IWM).

A dockyard policeman on duty at the bottom of the gangplank, suddenly sees a returned relative for the first time for four years. (IWM).

Wild scenes of welcome such as this were common at the dispersal points all over the town, as relatives found each other and families were reunited after four years' separation. (IWM).

Back Home! Repatriates were carried from the dockyard to the dispersal point nearest their home, in army trucks. Crowds of relatives swarmed round each truck on its arrival. (IWM).

His Excellency Lieutenant-General Sir T Ralph Eastwood, KCB, DSO, MC, Governor and Commander-in-Chief, Gibraltar, talking to a newly returned evacuee from Jamaica.

Lieutenant-General Sir Thomas Ralph Eastwood, KCB, DSO, MC, Governor and Commander-in-Chief of the Fortress of Gibraltar. (IWM).

Lieutenant-General Sir Kenneth Noel Anderson, KCB, MC, who took over as Governor and Commander-in-Chief, Gibraltar, in March, 1947.

LONDON HOME FOR EVACUEES

Fulham Road Hostel. On the extreme left is a Men's Club, the building next to it is a church, and the residential quarters are on the extreme right. (Gibralter Chronicle, 14th October, 1947).

Governor's Meadow, 4th August, 1947. Above: looking north, Below: looking south.

The construction of new blocks of flats at Alameda Estate (Spring, 1948).

The first two blocks at Alameda Estate in course of construction. (Summer, 1948).

'M' block from Rosia Road looking north. (September, 1949).

On the 24th October, 1945, Mr George Hall, Secretary of State for the Colonies, stated in the House of Commons that it would be impossible to repatriate the 3,000 or so evacuees who would still be in Northern Ireland after the end of the year before completion of a plan of permanent building in the colony, under which, if all went well, accommodation would become progressively available from about October, 1946.

On the 7th November, 1945, the day the AACR deputation left Gibraltar for London (Messrs A Risso, S P Triay, E J Alvarez and J T Ellicott), a Memorial for that Association, signed by 7,000 Gibraltarians, was presented to the Governor by Mr J A Hassan. The Memorial was very critical of the Governor and the Colonial Secretary.

The AACR deputation visited all the camps in Northern Ireland prior to moving on to London. Meantime, on the 22nd November, the liner *Celicia* put in at Gibraltar from Glasgow and Belfast with 503 repatriates from Northern Ireland—it was their first sight of home for five and a half years. The following day, the Senior Medical Officer, Dr R A Procter, was quoted as saying that despite the expected slight improvement no further repatriation of evacuees from Northern Ireland could be recommended!

The Daily Express of the 24th November, 1945, carried a report headlined:

'BURN CAMP'
threat by 1,000 exiles.

'One thousand Gibraltarians now in Northern Ireland awaiting repatriation threaten to burn down their camp because of bad conditions, said one of their spokesmen who called on the Secretary of State, Mr George Hall, yesterday.

The spokesman, Mr S P Triay, said the camps have no winter clothing and no furniture save beds. Medical services are inadequate and educational facilities 'practically nil'.

Under the present scheme, he said, the last Gibraltarian will not be home for two years.'

The AACR deputation was received 'most attentively' by the Secretary of State for the Colonies and was promised an early reply to their Memorial.

A few days later, the Governor cabled London to say that residents in Gibraltar had been receiving telegrams from relatives in Northern Ireland to the effect that a further list of repatriates to be sent by the next available ship had been published and that departure from the United Kingdom was expected round about the 18th December. He expressed concern about such reports and speculated to the Colonial Secretary as to whether they had anything to do with the visit of the AACR deputation in London. The Colonial Secretary, for his part, found the whole matter 'disquieting', and he also considered the possibility that the Colonial Office and/or the Ministry of Health had blundered 'in which case the consequences may be embarrassing.'

The AACR deputation returned on Saturday, 1st December, 1945. Referring to repatriation, Mr Triay said there was already existing machinery that would put the responsibility for the solution of the problem squarely on the shoulders of Gibraltarians. 'Give the City Council of Gibraltar all the powers now exercised by the Colonial Secretary in respect of housing, health and repatriation and let them do the rest', he said.

In an effort to solve the problem of shortage of nurses, the Medical Officer of Health had been sent to Eire, and he had some success—four nurses were recruited. The Colonial Office was quick off the mark, cabling the Governor on the 15th December, 1945, that 'in view of Procter's success in Eire and prospect of getting air compressor shipped before the end of this month would you agree to party leaving by next opportunity late January early February?' The Government of Gibraltar agreed to the resumption of repatriation in January, 1946.

The position regarding repatriation in January, 1946, was that of 16,700 persons evacuated 12,307 had been brought back. This left a total of 4,393 not repatriated, but since considerable numbers had taken up residence either temporarily or permanently in Great Britain and a few in Spain and Tangier, for practical purposes the number still to be repatriated was 3,059 (2,989 in Northern Ireland and 70 in Madeira). Of these, 614 persons in Northern Ireland and 47 elsewhere in Great Britain had been authorised to return to live with friends or relatives. It was expected that Nissen huts would be ready by the end of June to take 606 persons, and that the Shorthorn Farm Estate would be ready to receive 198 persons by the end of 1946. Temporary houses would accommodate a further 450 persons. Allowing for the fact that it would be necessary to allocate 500 places in temporary houses and Nissen huts for further relief of overcrowding, principally from the transit centres where there were 1,050 persons, the maximum that could be repatriated prior to the completion of the permanent homes was 754, leaving 1,691 evacuees in Northern Ireland and Madeira. This residue was to cause the greatest problems of all!

At the end of January, 1946, the Secretary of State for the Colonies paid an unofficial visit to Gibraltar. His arrival coincided with the receipt by the AACR of a reply to the questions raised by the Association's deputation the previous November. In his reply, Mr Hall rejected the suggestion that there had been an appreciable change in the Gibraltar Government's policy since the appointment of Governor Eastwood and Colonial Secretary Stanley. He was 'fully satisfied that repatriation and other major problems are being tackled by the Government with energy, resolution and understanding.'

On repatriation Mr Hall replied that though he was fully aware of the hardship caused by the delay, he was not prepared to override the opinion of medical advisers on the spot. It was impossible, he continued, to avoid the conclusion that there could be no satisfactory solution to the problem until permanent housing could be provided. Hard as the period of waiting must be, Mr Hall was convinced that the policy adopted would in the long run be in the best interests of the community as a whole.

Concerning the request that the City Council should be empowered to deal with repatriation, Mr Hall expressed the opinion that the problem was properly the responsibility of the Colonial Government. Regarding Northern Ireland, Camp conditions were being further examined and the deputation's observations were being borne in mind. Concrete suggestions for improvement were welcomed.

On the 29th January, 1946, the Association held a public meeting at John Mackintosh Square which was attended by nearly 5,000 people. Two resolutions were unanimously adopted: one considering the Secretary of State's replies as unsatisfactory and unacceptable, the other petitioning the Secretary of State to reconsider the acute problem of repatriation and those points that had not been conceded. The Central Committee of the Association then led the meeting in procession via Irish Town to the Convent to hand in the resolutions for submission to Mr Hall. All shops were closed while the procession passed and crowds lining the streets applauded.

The next repatriation party from the United Kingdom, numbering about 250, reached Gibraltar on the 3rd March, 1946, aboard the ss *Devonshire.* The Chief Security Officer of Gibraltar commented that 'the chief topic of conversation amongst these returning Gibraltarians was of the hardships they had endured in Northern Ireland and bitter complaints about the food, accommodation and climate there.' A further party arrived on board the ss *City of Paris* on the 17th April; this party of around 250 and further small parties from Madeira brought the total repatriated to 12,847, thus reducing the number of Gibraltarians awaiting repatriation from Northern Ireland and Madeira to approximately 2,500.

Attention continued to focus upon conditions in the Northern Ireland Camps. In April, 1946, two Colonial Office officials, Mr Crawley and Miss Mary Fisher, paid 'unheralded' visits to five of the Camps in County Down. Their general conclusion was that, with the exception of the employment problem, the evacuees were uncommonly well off and that most of them knew it! The lack of communal activity in the Camps was criticised; there had been no attempt to develop gardens or allotments. According to representatives of the Northern Ireland Ministry of Health and Local Government the Gibraltarians were reluctant to co-operate with each other, and none of them would contribute anything to the life of the Camp unless paid. Health was excellent and, contrary to the assertions of the AACR deputation, the evacuees were well dressed and shod.

One complaint which had *NOT* been made was of overcrowding, yet, by English standards, the Colonial Office officials found living conditions extremely crowded. 'I went into as many huts as possible in different Camps', wrote Miss Fisher, 'and it was quite common to find four or five Gibraltarians living and sleeping in one small room, to say nothing of the family fowls which shared the hut and roosted in general on a perch behind the door in the porch . . . Indeed, at one Camp we received indignant complaints from a respectable middle-aged man in a black suit that he and his family of nine had all lived in the same room in Gibraltar before the war and they were now being prevented from returning to it on grounds of inadequate space.' The visitors were also told that whenever extra space was given to a family, it was in general used for storage and that the children (of all ages) and parents still preferred to sleep in one room. The report added that all the huts visited were very clean and well-kept.

On grievances, the only real complaint encountered had been the desire for repatriation. Food was only a real grievance in one of the five Camps visited, and that because the evacuees were not consulted as to the menus for the week. 'It is perfectly clear that the Gibraltarians are having far more to eat than they would at home.'

The Colonial Office officials concluded that 'as far as physical welfare is concerned, the Gibraltarians are "in clover"; they have far more done for them than they would have at home; they have a great deal to eat and they are extremely healthy. Where the Camp Warden is good (which by no means means where he is most lenient) they are quite obviously not at all unhappy. There is a real danger of encouraging a natural tendency to idleness through the absence of available work and it would be worth doing anything possible to diminish the effect of this.'

Thus the argument regarding the conditions under which the evacuees were living in Northern Ireland continued. The gulf between the AACR's version and those of Government officials could not have been wider!

In July, 1946, the AACR issued a notice to the evacuees in Northern Ireland which included a questionnaire aimed at ascertaining how many of them were willing to return to Gibraltar regardless of conditions there. The Gibraltar Government soon followed with a request of their own to the Colonial Office for a list of Gibraltarians (*not* aliens) in Northern Ireland camps who desired to return at the earliest possible opportunity and were prepared to accept accommodation in Nissen huts: 'we shall then be in a much better position to reply to representations by the AACR element if we know the answer to the Nissen hut question.' Referring to the present AACR attitude towards resettlement, the Colonial Secretary wrote that 'they seem all out to give the impression that they are running the Resettlement Board, and although this is not quite the case, we would far rather have them take an active and co-operative part and shoulder responsibility as members of the Board than stand aside and merely criticise as they did before . . .'

The Colonial Office replied that the number of evacuees who had professed themselves anxious to return to Gibraltar irrespective of the accommodation available was 1,709—the Government of Gibraltar regretted that Nissen huts had not been specified as requested. Regarding this figure, Miss Fisher, the Colonial Office official who had been so critical of the Gibraltarians in her report of a few months earlier, made some surprising observations. 'My own impression is that (this figure of 1,709) will not all materialise when it comes to the point. It is a point of honour to most of the evacuees to declare that they are longing to get back; but, as you will have noticed, there was a high proportion of last minute withdrawals from the last repatriation party, and my feeling is that most of them have pretty well settled down in Northern Ireland camps and are well aware that from many points of view they are better off there than they would be in Gibraltar in present conditions.'

True or not, this 'impression' would not appear to be borne out by subsequent developments. At the end of August, 1946, the Chairman of the Executive Committee for evacuees in Northern Ireland (Mr Richard Jones had taken over since Mr Louis Bruzon's departure) complained that news had filtered through that Nissen huts promised to evacuees in Northern Ireland had been handed to people in Gibraltar transit centres thereby prolonging repatriation indefinitely. The Resettlement Board in Gibraltar denied these allegations, asserting that the allocation of Nissen huts to persons in transit centres in no way prejudiced the prospects of return for evacuees and was part of the general plan to facilitate return.

The whole issue flared up again in October, 1946, when the Secretary of State for the Colonies (Mr Creech Jones had taken over from Mr Hall) stated in reply to questions in the House of Commons that the possibility had to be envisaged that repatriation would not be entirely completed before two years hence. In answer to another question, the Secretary of State stated that 302 evacuees had been repatriated from Northern Ireland since May and that there now remained between 2,000 and 2,100 there.

The forecast of a further two years' wait provoked reactions from Northern Ireland, the AACR and the press in Gibraltar. Mr Jones of the evacuees' Executive Committee in Northern Ireland reported that the situation had become extremely difficult due to the Secretary of State's statement. He also complained about the decision of the Ministry in Northern Ireland to close some of the Camps, and in particular the decision to close down one of the most efficient and best organised Camps, where the welfare organisation was highly satisfactory, and where people could earn money by making small quantities of string work. The Camp referred to was No. 14 at Molennan in Londonderry. Jones concluded that 'if the Ministry continue to unheed advice on the impracticability of the closing of the said camp, transferring the residents—if necessary by force—to other Camps which have always complained of unsatisfactory conditions, it will only increase the general dissatisfaction which is spreading like a flame and can only result in what I am most anxious to avoid . . . that is the spilling of blood.'

The Gibraltar newspaper, *El Calpense,* chipped in saying that the information given by the Secretary of State in the House of Commons had been received with great indignation in Gibraltar. In an article, not always noted for its accuracy, the authorities were subjected to some harsh criticism.

The AACR held a General Meeting on the 12th November, at which the following resolutions were unanimously carried:

(a) That this Meeting cannot under any circumstances accept as good the recent statement by the Secretary of State for the Colonies that at least two years must elapse before all the Gibraltarian Evacuees can be repatriated.

(b) That this Meeting is firmly of the opinion that if the Colonial Government decides to make use of all available accommodation and to obtain the help of the Military Authorities in handing over a limited number of buildings the necessary accommodation can be found for the return of all the evacuees.

(c) That much as this meeting would regret it, it is their firm conviction that if the evacuees are not repatriated immediately (as suggested in b above) the only course open to Gibraltarians both here and in Northern Ireland is to act in such a manner as to bring home to the Government once and for all the dreadful plight to which our evacuees have been put purely for war reasons, but for which there is no justification in lasting one more day.'

The Gibraltar Government replied the following day assuring the Association that the accommodation position was under constant review, but that the immediate return of the evacuees was impossible. Regarding the threat contained in the third resolution, the Government commented that 'it would be regrettable if your Association were to adopt any course liable to hinder the efforts which are being made by the Government to enable repatriation to be completed with the least possible delay.'

The reply from Mr Bruzon, now General Secretary of the AACR, was: 'it is precisely because my Association is not satisfied that the Government is doing its utmost to enable repatriation to be completed with the least possible delay that they will be compelled to take action as indicated in the terms of the resolutions and which will be regretted by my Committee no less than by his Excellency.'

The local periodical, *El Calpense* had its own comments to make on these exchanges:

'The position in which the authorities now find themselves is not at all comfortable. Repeatedly they declare that they wish the repatriation of all the evacuees to take place with the least possible delay, but in spite of this no great progress seems to be made. We are the first to understand that this is not a small problem, but we are also convinced that with good will more could be achieved. While on the one hand it is said that there is not sufficient accommodation for the evacuees, we are continually seeing foreigners arriving at Gibraltar. Some are the families of Service personnel, and others are complete strangers . . .

Nobody . . . can have more right than the Gibraltarians themselves to live in their own town. And that right is even greater when these Gibraltarians have been the victims of so much suffering, through no fault of their own, but on account of the mistakes committed by others.'

After dismissing Government claims about accommodation problems, the article concluded: 'With good will everything can be achieved. When there is no good will difficulties are encountered everywhere. That is why so many difficulties are encountered when justice is to be meted out to Gibraltarians who according to the statement of the Secretary of State for the Colonies are condemned to an enforced exile in the worst of conditions for at least another two years.'

Some repatriation continued to take place. A party of 175 arrived on the 29th June aboard the *Ascania* and another of approximately the same number on the 24th September aboard the ss *Cheshire.* This brought the total repatriated to 13,188, leaving a total of 2,024 evacuees in the Northern Ireland Camps and 40 in Madeira.

The AACR was now maintaining that the problem of the remaining evacuees could be solved in several ways: by requisitioning vacant premises and taking over suitable accommodation not currently utilised for residential purposes, and by the requisitioning of accommodation occupied by persons who had more space than was needed to satisfy their essential requirements.

The Government replied that to requisition vacant premises would entail obtaining additional powers from the Secretary of State for the Colonies, would in any case not have any substantial effect upon repatriation, and in some cases could prove expensive. On the other hand, it was conceded that it was not easy for the Government to justify a situation in which any premises continued to remain vacant. Regarding the suggestion that government should requisition accommodation occupied by persons who had space surplus to their requirements, (Government admitted that there were 275 such cases), it was pointed out that to do this would oblige the Government to provide suitable alternative accommodation for the current occupiers, which was impossible, or to adopt a system of compulsory billetting, which the Government refused to do.

Apart from the measures suggested by the AACR, other schemes were under consideration. One was the requisitioning of accommodation in hotels—an informal approach by the Executive Officer of the Resettlement Board had indicated that there would be strong opposition from hotel managers to such a move. Other ideas being mooted included proposals for increasing the accommodation at the Little Sisters of the Poor and the erection of further permanent accommodation on land adjacent to the Gas Works.

The forecast that repatriation would take at least another two years to complete also gave rise to demands from the evacuees for a transfer to England. This was to lead to some interesting developments the following year.

CHAPTER SEVENTEEN

And so to Fulham Road

The total repatriation of all evacuated civilians was still some distance away; the final party was not to return until February, 1951! Nonetheless, the year 1947 saw a slow but steady flow of return, and the arrival of a new Governor was to have an important and favourable influence upon the process. As the accommodation in the Northern Ireland Camps deteriorated, so the pressure increased for a pre-repatriation transfer to England, and this was to culminate at the end of 1947 in the so-called 'Fulham Road Battle'.

The position regarding repatriation at the beginning of 1947 was that 2,019 evacuees were still in camps in Northern Ireland, 1,547 others were living in private accommodation in various parts of the United Kingdom but chiefly in London, and 39 remained in Madeira. Allowing for the fact that 525 had been authorised to return under various categories, there remained a balance of 3,080 still to be repatriated at a time when accommodation in Gibraltar could only absorb a further 545 persons! It was likely, however, that some of the evacuees would opt to settle down permanently in the United Kingdom.

The next contingent of repatriates arrived in Gibraltar on Saturday, 18th January, 1947, on board the RMS *Samaria.* Most of the party of 246 were aged and infirm (the party included 68 persons over the age of 70, ten of whom were octogenarians, and the Secretary of State had expressed fears that they would arrive considerably the worse for wear after a winter journey!). Also on board was a stowaway—twenty-year-old Albert Moss from the Northern Ireland Camps; he was allowed to land.

The *Gibraltar Chronicle* looked for the personal angles in this homecoming. 'Shouted greetings were exchanged from the ship to the quay. Gunner Gonzalez, of the Gibraltar Defence Force, was there to meet his mother, sisters, brother and a male friend after seven years separation.

One order over-ruled others. It was "ambulances first". One by one, they drew alongside (Wharf 49), awaiting those whose first weeks back in Gibraltar would be spent in hospital.

Little Margot Saliva, aged nine, said that she had been very sick on the way. She was shy, but obviously happy. Joseph Dine, of La Linea, had been away for seven years and was glad to leave the mud of Northern Ireland. Tony Vera . . . was returning home after thirty years at sea with the Merchant Navy. He means to finish his "life on the ocean wave" and settle in Gibraltar. The voyage, smooth to him, proved rough for the women and children all of whom were sick.

Mrs Margarita Dalmedo was returning to her sister Elena. Her four daughters, Flor de Lis (13), Mercedes (11), Mary Dery (6) and Margarita

(4), were gathered around, presenting the happiest family scene on board. Mrs Dalmedo said that the voyage had been excellent throughout, although she had been a little sick in the English Channel. Food and accommodation, she said, were very good and better attendance could not have been desired.

Mr Will Galvin, steward who looked after the Gibraltar party on board, described them as ideal passengers, doing exactly as they were asked and causing no trouble whatever. They had to organise their own entertainment to a certain extent, and although the sea had been rough for at least three days, they enjoyed themselves with sing-songs and kindred amusements in the lounge.'

Miss Edna Gray of Belfast, in charge of the party, told The *Chronicle*: 'We left Belfast at 3.30 pm last Tuesday and the first three days were rather rough. The trip itself was very pleasant so far as I was concerned, but many of the repatriates were very sick. The old people were affected most but complained least. They took everything very well.

They are all very happy to be back and we also are very happy to be able to bring them home, for which they are all longing. There are still about 1,000 left in Northern Ireland.'

At the end of January, 1947, it was announced that the new Governor of Gibraltar would be Lieutenant-General Sir Kenneth Anderson, a Scotsman. Lieutenant-General Sir Ralph Eastwood left the Colony on the 17th February, 1947. The outgoing Governor had not been the most popular of chiefs with the mass of the Gibraltarians as will have been gathered from some of his exchanges with the AACR at the height of the repatriation process.

An article in the *Sunday Pictorial,* entitled 'And this is what they call democracy' and written by Rex North, was very critical of the British administration of Gibraltar and particularly severe on Governor Eastwood.

'Lieutenant-General Mason MacFarlane . . . was a good soldier and a popular chief. His successor, Lieutenant-General Sir Thomas Ralph Eastwood, who has just gone home, was probably a good soldier, but certainly a bad Governor. Mason MacFarlane got rousing cheers from the local population when he left; the only people who saw General Eastwood off were the Services, who had to.

I am sure . . . . that he tried conscientiously to govern well and fairly. Unfortunately, he has left behind a few memories that Gibraltar will not forget in a hurry.

Even if you are living seven to a room or in a Nissen hut, you do not mind particularly the Governor having a palace. After all, that is one of the recognised 'perks'. But you do mind when, with 3,000 of your friends exiled in Britain and unable to come home, he converts a large cottage into a miniature palace at a cost of thousands because his normal residence is a bit hot in the summer.' (This refers to the work of refurbishment carried out at Governor's Cottage.)

'It is not important, but you are apt to notice that when soldiers' wives were allowed out there, Governor 'Mason-Mac' said that priorities would be given to men who had not seen theirs for the whole of the war, and that his own wife would be the last to come.

Twenty-four hours before the scheme closed down (possibly referring to the 'Splea' scheme and/or repatriation plans) because of the invasion of Normandy, Lady Eastwood arrived. Then—and this may be a coincidence—General Eastwood's son, a captain in the Rifle Brigade, was appointed to his father as Aide-de-Camp.

Later—and this may be another coincidence—his son's fiancee arrived out with the Wrens.' (This statement was later denied—the lady was not stationed in Gibraltar, was in the ATS and not in the Wrens, and only went to Gibraltar after the war was over on a short visit.)

'Nor did Gibraltar like it when General Eastwood showed a Fascist Spanish General from over the border around fortifications that Gibraltarians were forbidden to go near.'

Harsh words indeed! How justified were they? Certainly, Governor Eastwood never won the affection of the Gibraltarians in the way that 'Mason-Mac' had done and General Anderson was to do. Certainly, many Gibraltarians never forgave him for bringing Lady Eastwood on the day before the repatriation of Gibraltarians and the 'Splea' scheme had to be postponed due to the ban imposed on travel into and from the United Kingdom. Certainly, Gibraltarians were sometimes left with the impression that their Governor cared little about their problems.

There is, however, another side to the matter, and account must be taken of the difficulties confronting the Government of Gibraltar during General Eastwood's tenure of office. His military responsibilities might not have been as great as those of his immediate predecessors, but he had the extremely difficult task of re-converting Gibraltar from war to peace conditions and to cope with the many problems associated with the repatriation of the civilian population.

Mr J L Imossi, President of the Chamber of Commerce and a member of the Resettlement Board, defended Governor Eastwood's record: '. . . he had to face the worst administrative period ever known to Gibraltar . . . I have had the privilege of taking an active interest throughout these Governorships in matters affecting the administration of Gibraltar and I am therefore in a position to state that Sir Ralph Eastwood worked hard and conscientiously, but the results of his efforts could hardly be made public and the benefits of them will only be achieved in the course of time. On his departure he was given hearty cheers by those present, amongst whom the civilian element was well represented. In any case', added Mr Imossi, 'the whole issue at Gibraltar is dependent more on the Colonial Office than on the personal activities of its Governors, whose performance is always tied up with and subjugated to questions of politics in the United Kingdom and the requirements, actual or imaginery, of the Services.'

On Thursday, 20th March, 1947, the British liner *Ascania* arrived at Gibraltar, via Belfast, with 115 Gibraltarian repatriates on board, 100 from Northern Ireland camps and 15 from England. Also on board was the Governor-Designate, Lieutenant-General Sir Kenneth Noel Anderson, KCB, MC. According to Miss Mary Fisher, Colonial Office official accompanying the party, the repatriates, whose ages ranged from 91 years to 10 months, had taken the passage rather well although most of them had been sea-sick in the Bay of Biscay two days after leaving England.

Mrs Mary Onda, aged 91, commented: 'this was my second time on board a ship and I don't think I will be in another again. My first time was when I left Gibraltar on evacuation over six years ago.' The youngest passengers were Julie Gonzalez (18 months), Mari Carmen Grech (13 months), and Emily Estella (10 months). According to relatives, they had behaved like real sailors on the voyage.

Mr Charles Raggio, speaking on behalf of a number of the repatriated families, told a *Chronicle* reporter: 'We are all very happy to be back in our home town again. It was a very nice gesture of the Governor-Designate to be interested in the welfare of the repatriated families during the crossing. Yesterday morning General Anderson paid a visit to the old people in their cabins and the patients in the hospital and talked for some time with them all.' The new Governor-to-be had got off on the right foot!

General Anderson was to prove a very popular chief with the Gibraltarians. From the very outset he identified himself with their problems, showed interest in and concern for their welfare, and he was not averse to chiding the Colonial Office on occasions when he felt that they had done wrong by the Gibraltarians. His presence and influence as Governor was to be of invaluable assistance to the cause of repatriation and to the improvement of post-war conditions in Gibraltar.

One of General Anderson's early functions as Governor was a visit, on the 3rd April, 1947, to some of the 'slum' buildings on the Rock. Accompanied by Lady Anderson, he visited buildings in Willis's Road, George's Lane, Carrerra's Passage and Hargraves Barracks. His Excellency and Lady Anderson conversed for a long time with many of the tenants. Their visit to Danino's Building, Willis' Road, lasted over an hour.

On the 1st May, 1947, the Colonial Office issued an official communique directed at the Gibraltarian evacuees in Northern Ireland. It stated that consideration had been given to the possibility of moving the evacuees back to England, but that it was impossible at the moment to move so large a number of people, particularly in view of the housing problem in that country. In any case, continued the communique, it would not be possible to provide the evacuees with hotel accommodation such as that provided by the Ministry of Health during the war years. However, the possibility was being explored of providing before the winter, camp accommodation within reach of a centre which would offer the Gibraltarians work opportunities.

In the meantime, those evacuees capable of work were urged to travel to England (without their families) to find employment and accommodation. Since it could well turn out that finding accommodation in England for all the evacuees would be impracticable, as many as possible were now asked to make their own arrangements. '. . . if a number have not succeeded in making their own arrangements before a camp can be opened, there would appear to be no alternative to remaining in Northern Ireland.' (This sounds like gentle blackmail!)

The following inducements were offered:-

(a) Men who opted to travel to England in search of employment would be provided with one free travel voucher from the Camps to London, and free travel vouchers would also be issued to families joining the men once they had secured employment and suitable accommodation. Such vouchers would not be issued for journeys back to Northern Ireland or to a second destination.

(b) Limited accommodation would be made available in a London hostel for the working men on a purely temporary basis until they could find private lodgings.

(c) A special officer had been appointed to deal with the welfare problems of Gibraltarians in England, and he would help in any way possible to find them suitable employment.

(d) Financial assistance, according to individual circumstances, would be given to the men whilst they were looking for work, provided they reported regularly to an employment exchange.

What was the reaction in Gibraltar to this announcement? *El Calpense* gave a guarded welcome to it, claiming to have suggested such a solution months ago. Its general theme was that such a solution should have been implemented a long time ago, but that it was a case of 'better late than never'.

Luz, the mouthpiece of the AACR, was furious! In an article entitled 'OUR EVACUEES' of the 9th May, 1947, the newspaper commented:-

'What sort of an opinion has the Colonial Office formed of the legitimate rights of 1,500 Gibraltarians who after six years of unjustified punishment in the Camps of Northern Ireland are clamouring to be treated as British subjects?

What sort of an opinion has the Colonial Office in London formed of the meaning of the word 'urgency'?

What sort of an opinion has the Colonial Office in London formed of the limit of patience of a human being?

It is absolutely shameful—to say the least—that since the year 1944, when the Gibraltarian evacuees were hastily transferred for the convenience of the Imperial Government to Northern Ireland, and that after repeated promises that the matter was being given urgent consideration, this should be the third Secretary of State for the Colonies who, it seems, is not prepared to deal with the unfortunate problem of the repatriation of our evacuees with the sense of importance and urgency required.

That whilst every manner of arrangement is being urgently made for the early repatriation of German Prisoners of War and every facility is being given to Poles and other aliens to establish themselves in England, a handful of British subjects should be treated in the unjustified manner displayed by the recent official communique published in our daily press is in fact laughable. In accordance with this communique the journey of the evacuees to London is facilitated but if they are unable and cannot find employment they are not given facilities to return to Ireland to rejoin their families. This is but an example of the lack of imagination of those who are responsible for these arrangements.

Is it conceivable that after three long years the Colonial Office in London has not been able to find a completely satisfactory and acceptable solution for the cessation, once and for all, of the Gibraltarian evacuation, by providing a decent means of living to those unfortunate 1,500 British subjects who are suffering in Northern Ireland?

And what does the Government of Gibraltar think of all this? This is a matter affecting Gibraltarians who have an absolute right to live in Gibraltar in preference to the many imported people who are continually admitted in the Colony in addition to the foreigners who live here.

How long is the farce of the difficulties affecting repatriation to continue?'

The Governor, in a communication to London, commented that there was nothing unexpected about the reaction of the AACR 'since for the last two years the principal plank of their platform has been the need for the urgent repatriation of evacuated Gibraltarians, and if they were to take the view that the scheme described in the announcement will in a large measure solve this problem they would be depriving themselves of their political ammunition.' In His Excellency's opinion, *El Calpense's* view was a closer reflection of the general public feeling.

The Public Relations Officer in Gibraltar opined that, notwithstanding the AACR view that the 1,500 Gibraltarians in Northern Ireland had a right to reside in Gibraltar, 'the general impression may be summed up in the view that the scheme is necessary in view of the fact that, short of requisitioning premises, saturation point in accommodation in Gibraltar has already been reached. . . . . It can be said', he added, 'that the scheme is viewed favourably as a scheme, and that the getting of people out of Northern Ireland camps to England has an important psychological bearing, in that many feel that the name 'Northern Ireland' is associated with adverse climatic conditions and lack of opportunities as to work. A large number of people, including many who have been in Northern Ireland, are of the opinion that the obtaining of work in England is necessary to save the self-respect of any young men still in camps.'

In actual fact, the Scheme did not prove a huge success, only 185 evacuees availing themselves of its opportunities. That more did not do so was undoubtedly due to unwillingness to leave families behind. Moreover, there was little prospect of visiting the families remaining in Ulster as passages on the Irish Channel service were impossible unless booked weeks or months ahead.

Reporting on the Scheme several months later, Mr J L Keith, Head of the Welfare Department of the Colonial Office, said that over 140 evacuees had come over from Ulster so far (this was in September, 1947). Of the men, about a dozen had been employed on railway work, some on building work, some in the catering trade and one as an electrician. Of the women, half had been placed in residential jobs in hospitals and the remainder in residential hotel employment, after receiving very special guarantees from the employers.

The same Mr Keith was responsible for a report on conditions in Northern Ireland which was to have momentuous repercussions. Hitherto, Colonial Office reports on the matter had consistently claimed that the AACR's allegations on the subject were 'exaggerated'. The Keith Report was to put a different complexion on the matter.

Messrs Keith and Thomas, of the Welfare Department of the Colonial Office, visited Northern Ireland on the 4th July, 1947, to inspect the Gibraltar Evacuee Camps. Their stay included a comprehensive tour of the remaining eight camps (four in County Antrim and four in County Down). Only one of the camps was in reasonable proximity to Belfast, the others being scattered in outlandish areas.

Keith reported that the camps had been constructed in 1942 specifically as emergency accommodation to provide immediate shelter for the population of Belfast in the event of heavy air attacks. It had never been intended that they should be used for long term residence, but simply as transit centres. In the event, it had never been necessary to use the camps for their original purpose, and they had stood idle until July, 1944, when about 6,500 Gibraltarian evacuees had been moved into them. Since then, nine of the seventeen camps had been closed down as the number of evacuees had been slowly reduced as a result of repatriation.

The Camp accommodation consisted of Nissen huts and with the exception of Camp 17 at Carryduff near Belfast, were all of a standard type. The huts were constructed of a thin gauge ungalvanised iron sheeting, and the floors consisted of concrete flags. The huts were entirely unlined, and the concrete floors uncovered. They were heated by means of coke-burning combustion stoves, and were illuminated by oil lamps. Electricity was generated in the camps but was restricted to the administration buildings, kitchen, dining rooms, sick bays and staff quarters. The Wardens were accommodated in small brick houses, and the staff quarters were centrally heated.

Each camp had a well-equipped kitchen with coke-burning ovens, dining rooms, sick-bays, school buildings, and ablution blocks. Water was pumped from rivers or brooks through a chlorination plant. Mr Keith observed that during cold weather the water supply was frequently frozen, and the evacuees were then compelled to fetch their water from the rivers, or break the ice on the brooks! In addition, there was no water-borne sewage in any of the camps. The dining rooms were apparently not used as the evacuees preferred to take their meals in the living huts.

Mr Keith also commented on the several clubs for young people of both sexes which were to be found in all the camps. The girls were trained in needlecraft and the boys in woodwork, and these activities were supervised by trained instructors. 'The standard of work which I saw was remarkably good.'

Nonetheless, an inspection of a representative collection of living huts and other buildings firmly convinced Mr Keith 'that the camps do not provide an adequate standard of comfort for the unfortunate inhabitants.' He highlighted the lack of employment at a time of acute shortage of manpower in England; some of the younger evacuees had been unemployed since leaving school.

Mr Keith's description of the living quarters certainly lent weight to the long-standing AACR contention that conditions in the camps were 'appalling'. 'Many of the living huts', he wrote, 'are in an advanced stage of deterioration, and can only be kept weatherproof by means of constant and expensive repairs, which are sometimes delayed through a lack of material. I saw a number of huts in use which were by no means weatherproof, where constant rain and damp had rusted holes in the iron sheets, and I was informed that this problem is becoming more acute. I am quite satisfied that life in these places during the winter months must occasion a considerable degree of hardship, particularly on the women and children, and old people.

The window space is inadequate to provide a reasonable standard of lighting, and the interior of most huts was very gloomy. For some strange reason the interior walls are painted black. I should not be surprised to find an undue proportion with defective sight.

I saw no covering on the concrete floors other than blankets which had been put down in certain huts by the people themselves.

The coke stoves in the huts are kept burning day and night throughout the year, and consume a large quantity of fuel .... In spite of this I am convinced that the huts must be very cold in winter, and totally unsuitable for people from a warmer climate.

The camps are pervaded by an atmosphere of defeat and depression, and this problem is likely to become more acute in the late autumn unless steps have been taken by that time to effect a partial or general transfer of the evacuees to this country.

The lavatory and ablution blocks are very primitive. They are not illuminated and quite a number have deteriorated badly. In one camp I saw a whole row of six lavatories lacking separate doors and partitions.

In certain camps there were groups of living huts on low ground, liable to be flooded in heavy rain. I noticed particularly at Camp 9 that several huts were very close to the banks of the River Braid. The question of keeping water out of the huts in heavy rain is a constant worry to the camp staffs.'

Mr Keith also surmised that the standard of education in the camp schools was of a very low order, and he was informed that very few of the children attended local schools. He was also given to understand that the camp schools were frequently closed in the winter months because of the intense cold.

One bright note in an otherwise gloomy report was the reference to Camp 17, 'by far the best camp.' There, the huts were electrically illuminated, had wooden floors, and the camp was connected to Belfast's water mains (but not to the sewage system). Residence there was restricted to evacuees employed in Belfast, or to those whose children attended schools in Belfast. A surprising observation was that there were a number of huts in this camp unoccupied!

Mr Keith summed up his impression of the camps by saying that they were, in his opinion, 'totally unsuitable for the housing of a colonial population, and I am satisfied that they ought to be closed down at the earliest opportunity. I do not think that any local authority or Government Department would be permitted to house people in similar conditions in this country and the continued retention of these camps exposes the Colonial Office to criticism to which there can be no effective reply.

It is quite clear that the evacuees are seething with unrest, and they are determined not to spend another winter under such conditions, and I consider that we shall be faced with very serious problems if other accommodation is not provided ....

.... The provision of accommodation in England, and preferably London, must be pressed with vigour, and I have asked my Department to make every effort to solve this problem. I am convinced that the problem is beyond the capacity of the Ministry of Works.'

The Acting Colonial Secretary commented to the Governor that Keith's report made 'most depressing reading' and he admitted that he had not realised before just how bad conditions were in the Northern Ireland Camps.

A few weeks later, the Executive Officer of the Resettlement Board in Gibraltar, Mr D Lucas, produced his report on the camps and much of what he had to say confirmed Keith's report. Lucas was in Northern Ireland from the 4th until the 22nd May (prior to Keith's visit), during which time he visited all the Camps. 'The outstanding impression it has left on me is of a community of people demoralised, pauperised and, I think I can say that they are all suffering from an inferiority complex which has sunk to its lowest depth ....

.... It is difficult to put on paper the many things which have so impressed me. Before I went away the complaints I heard in Gibraltar about the Camps were generally misconstrued and mountains made out of molehills, whilst the most shocking complaints had been overlooked.

First and foremost is undoubtedly the demoralised atmosphere of everybody. Very few are employed and yet I feel that many could, if not employed outside the Camps, be in the Camps, without really allowing the problem in Northern Ireland to be increased .... The question of food varies but, I think, generally, the food is not entirely satisfactory ....' Lucas also commented on the lack of electricity in the living quarters and felt that after such a long time the authorities might have done something about this.

These reports placed a great deal of pressure on the Colonial Office in London to get the evacuees out of Northern Ireland. The Governor of Gibraltar cabled:-

'Am frankly appalled at conditions in Camps as revealed in report by Head of Welfare Department ... and fully confirmed by personal observations of my Resettlement Officer, and I trust that no efforts will be spared to secure transfer of maximum possible number before advent of winter. For every imaginable reason of morale and health it is essential that all the camps be entirely closed before winter, but if this really proves quite impossible then the only camp which seems to offer humane conditions is No. 17 at Carryduff. I beg that all the rest be closed down completely unless urgent and radical improvements are made forthwith before advent of winter.'

The next contingent of repatriates, 179 of them, arrived in Gibraltar on the 24th July, 1947, on board the liner *Ascania;* 159 came from Northern Ireland Camps and 20 from London, and all had been away from their homes for seven years.

The Governor had been informed in late July that the Colonial Office were examining the possibility of obtaining two hostels in London to accommodate the Gibraltarians in Northern Ireland, but he was instructed not to publicise this. The news finally broke on Tuesday, 9th September, 1947, when at a reunion in London of one hundred evacuees who had already moved to England under the Government Work Scheme described above, Mr Keith stated:

'There is a reasonable prospect of a considerable number of evacuees coming to London from the Ulster Camps if certain negotiations which are now in progress are successful.'

This announcement, although non-committal as regards numbers involved, at least raised hopes that a number of the seven-year exiles would not have to face another winter in Ulster. It was anticipated that camps in England would enable workers to obtain employment, even at some distance from their families, but with the prospect of visiting them at weekends and leave periods.

Four days after this announcement, the Governor cabled London that news had reached him that the Ministry of Works were claiming that the remaining property at Fulham (where one of the hostels earmarked for the Gibraltarians was situated) was required for accommodating Poles. He commented: 'I cannot stress too strongly vital necessity to remove a high percentage of evacuees from Northern Ireland camps before winter on grounds of humanity . . . political effect locally of failure to achieve this would be very serious in view of hopes that have been raised particularly if it became known that preference had been given to Poles.' The Secretary of State for the Colonies assured the Governor that pressure was being exerted upon the Ministry of Works to provide accommodation in Fulham Road for Gibraltarians.

The position regarding repatriation on the 20th September, 1947, was as follows:

A. Evacuees in Camps in Northern Ireland	1,347
B. In hospitals and in employment in Northern Ireland	16
C. In Great Britain under new employment scheme	173

Apart from C above, 34 evacuees had rejoined the Camps in Northern Ireland having given up the Employment Scheme.

There were a further 1,250 (including aliens) in Britain in addition to those under C.

An official notice, issued by the Colonial Office simultaneously in Northern Ireland and in Gibraltar on the 11th October, 1947, announced that two large buildings, capable of accommodating 1,000 people, had been secured in London to take evacuees from Northern Ireland, and that every effort was being made to close the camps before the onset of winter.

The larger of the two buildings, capable of holding 600 evacuees in family groups, was the Fulham Road Hostel in south-west London. The hostel was owned by the London County Council. The other hostel was the Sussex Square Club in West London, close to the Bayswater Road and a few minutes from Hyde Park on the north side.

It was planned for the evacuees to start moving in to Fulham Road in early November on a system of priorities which would leave the non-Gibraltarians to the last.

A few days later, the unofficial members of the Resettlement Board wrote to the Governor expressing serious concern at the conditions of the evacuees in Northern Ireland and Madeira. They complained that repeated representations had not been accepted in the past: 'the official impression that statements were exaggerated has always predominated.' The Executive

Officer of the Resettlement Board, Mr Lucas, had now reported on his inspection of the Camps 'and his findings of the unwarranted and appalling conditions cannot be more conclusive.' This information had been confirmed by an official of the Ministry of Welfare in London specially sent out to Ireland to investigate the Executive Officer's findings. The letter concluded:

'In view of what has now transpired, it is respectfully submitted that every effort should be made for the earliest return to Gibraltar of as great a number of evacuees as possible, and this should be done irrespective of whatever other measures may be envisaged by HM Government in England of their transportation to improved conditions in the United Kingdom.'

The Governor then met the unofficial members of the Resettlement Board and he agreed to approach the Naval authorities in Gibraltar for the use of four large huts opposite the Naval Officers Pavilion for temporary civilian occupation. The possibility of more temporary houses near Glacis Site would be explored, and the Governor also undertook to look into the matter of RAF families taking up accommodation in the town. He would also investigate the use of part of the Spanish Pavilion. Regarding the 195 aliens (150 statutory aliens and 45 aliens) in Northern Ireland, they were to be told that they could not return to Gibraltar until all Gibraltarians had been repatriated and resettled; indeed, they were to be advised to settle in the United Kingdom.

Despite all these measures, the Governor informed the unofficial members of the Resettlement Board that no further evacuees could be repatriated in 1947. Some 200 could be brought back in the first quarter of 1948 if Shorthorn Farm could be completed. The question of the 290 Spanish refugees in Gibraltar was also raised, it being pointed out that most could return to Spain as they were not political refugees.

The Governor duly wrote to the Heads of Services in Gibraltar pleading with them to release accommodation for some 200 evacuees 'on grounds of common humanity'. 'I do not believe that hutments and space cannot be provided temporarily if there is a real will to help . . . for the well-being of Gibraltar.'

Meanwhile, hopes of eradicating the Ulster problem were high amongst officials in London, though the evacuees did not raise their own hopes too much, given the many previous rumours which had proved groundless. Nonetheless, the officials seemed to mean business this time and plans went ahead.

In mid-October, 1947, two members of the Colonial Welfare Department travelled to Northern Ireland for consultations with the Government there on the proposed transfer of the evacuees to London. Whilst there they met members of the Central Committee of the Camps, representatives of which were given an opportunity of going to London to see the Fulham Road premises. It was intended that those evacuees who were left behind—probably almost entirely non-Gibraltarian—would be transferred to Camp 17, one of the best camps in Belfast. As we have seen, this camp had the advantage of being directly connected to the Belfast electricity supply and it was also close enough to that city for any evacuees who could get jobs to commute there.

Back at the Fulham Road Hostel plans were being laid for a communal catering system. Meals would be served in a large dining hall, though the evacuees would be free to make other arrangements. There was also a promise of special allocations of cooking oil, garlic and other similar spices, though much would have to depend upon London's own food situation.

Later in the month Mr Keith visited Gibraltar. Speaking to a *Gibraltar Chronicle* reporter, he said: 'We at the Colonial Office are determined to get the evacuees over from Northern Ireland as soon as possible whatever difficulties may arise.' Mr Keith was asked to what extent difficulties were being experienced, in view of the housing position in England, in securing materials and licences to carry out the necessary alterations at Fulham Road and Sussex Square. He replied that part of Fulham Road was suitable for occupation by the evacuees without alteration. 'Even if it means others not being given accommodation as good as we would have wished, we shall not allow this to delay their coming over. If necessary we can bring material for partitions over from Northern Ireland camps, and engage the evacuees themselves to do some of the work of conversion. I know there are many willing helpers in the Camps anxious for such a job.'

Asked what were the reasons for his visit to Gibraltar, Mr Keith intimated that they were connected with the long-term view of how long it would be necessary to provide accommodation in London, and for how many.

The Gibraltar City Council meeting of the 6th November, 1947, was informed that a letter had been received from the Colonial Secretary intimating that the possibility of converting the former Royal Naval Air Station at North Front for the purpose of housing temporarily 250 evacuees was being investigated, and enquiring whether the Council's sewer at North Front could take the additional load which would be involved by the increase in the population of the area.

The Chairman of the Council, Mr J A Hassan, stated that the City Engineer had reported that, though the sewer was at present overloaded, he could recommend that the Council accepted the additional load, especially since it would permit the return of evacuees.

The repatriation of a further 250 evacuees as a result of this latest development, together with the proposed transfer of 1,000 to London, would, it was anticipated, leave the Northern Ireland camps empty.

Work on Fulham Road meanwhile continued. By mid-November, a working party, consisting of Gibraltarians already in London and thirteen from Ulster, were beginning to make the Fulham Road hostel more habitable for family groups. The hope was still being expressed that the first party would arrive to take up residence by the end of the month. It was planned to bring over from Northern Ireland a stock of furniture which had been there in reserve and not in use in the camps.

November gave way to December and the anticipated move was not forthcoming! Official sources remained silent on the matter, and the advance party at Fulham Road was beginning to get restless. Discussions were said to be going on in 'the highest circles'. Rumour had it that Mr Creech-Jones, Secretary of State for the Colonies, had personally activated the placing of inter-departmental difficulties before the Cabinet. Certainly, something had gone wrong, and the Gibraltar periodical *El Calpense* voiced the feelings of many on the 8th December, 1947.

'Many promises have been made to the Gibraltarians evacuated in Northern Ireland but their sufferings, due to their long exile, are every day greater and the promises have not yet been fulfilled. 1,400 of our people are still in those frozen plains of Ulster, no measures having yet been found to make their stay less burdensome.

It is illogical to say that accommodation has not yet been found in Gibraltar, even though of a temporary nature, for these 1,400 persons, but it is even more ridiculous and absurd to say that accommodation cannot be found for them in England where at any rate they could live in cities and work, helping themselves and at the same time helping England, where the shortage of labour is every day more acute.

It is indisputable that in England, in common with many other places, there exists a housing problem, but such a problem in a country whose population numbers fifty millions cannot be so acute as to render it impossible to find accommodation for a handful of persons. The most absurd part of the matter is that there is a continuous flow of displaced persons arriving in the United Kingdom under the pretext that they are joining the labour ranks. If it is an easy matter to find accommodation for these people irrespective of the class to which they belong it is even more difficult for us to understand the gravity of the situation when it comes to housing Gibraltarians.

The authorities should bear in mind that Gibraltarians did not leave their homes because they so willed, nor did they leave of their own free will. They were forcibly removed under the greatest of threats if they did not obey the evacuation orders. Let it not be said that they were removed for their own safety, even though this may have been part of the reason, but that they were forced to leave their homes for military reasons. It is therefore only just that they should be adequately compensated by making an extra effort so that they may now be rehabilitated.

After prolonged suffering there was born a hope a few months ago when it was announced that facilities would be given to those who wished to go to England to work there. At long last the day was in sight when their long exile was coming to an end. But that promise, like so many others, has come to a dead end. The months have passed and our brothers remain in complete loneliness in those frozen and inhospitable plains living in huts lacking all kind of comfort and what is still worse having to depend on what we may call charity. The long years of inactivity are bound to affect the morale of those 1,400 persons who have always longed for the day when they could earn their daily bread with the sweat of their brow and who naturally enough are gradually losing their keenness to work as the days go by.

Gibraltarians do not ask for charity. They want to show that given an opportunity and far from becoming a burden to the rest they can be of use to the nation. They want from those who forced them to leave their homes a chance to build new homes. They only ask for justice and not compassion. If there is no room for them in Gibraltar they should at least be accommodated in some urban district of Great Britain until such time as their repatriation to Gibraltar can be undertaken.

There is nothing more cruel than to ostracise a man. That form of cruelty is sometimes necessary to punish certain crimes, but why punish a handful of Gibraltarians in such a way especially when they have not merited such treatment. Their only crime consisted in having been born in a fortress and being thus subjected to so-called military requirements.

It is shameful that so many requests are necessary to achieve what is required from those who can easily solve the problem. We do not for a moment think that the transfer of Gibraltarians to England would have brought protests from the hospitable English people, especially when they are tolerating the influx of all those persons who for diverse reasons refuse to return to their own country.' (translated from the Spanish).

Whilst the Ulster evacuees were discussing plans for a Gibraltarian protest outside those Government Offices responsible for the transfer hold-up, presumed to be the Ministry of Works and the Treasury, the Governor was being informed officially that difficulties had in fact arisen in connection with the transfer. A telegram from the Secretary of State for the Colonies stated that the future of the Gibraltarians remaining in Northern Ireland had recently been considered by the Ministers concerned who had raised strong objection to the transfer of these people to London as hitherto intended. Since it was accepted that existing accommodation in Northern Ireland was most unsatisfactory for winter conditions, the Ministers had agreed that a further effort should be made to discover how many could be accommodated in Gibraltar in the near future if everything possible were done by Service and Civil authorities in Gibraltar to make available additional accommodation. It would appear that the buck was being well and truly passed!

The Governor's response was immediate and unequivocal:

'Am appalled at unexpected opposition to move of evacuees to London. These unfortunate people are indeed being ill used and I must vehemently protest against attempt of Minister to cancel present plans both personally and on behaf of Government and citizens of Gibraltar.' (8th December, 1947).

On the 11th December, a party of twenty evacuees left Ulster for London. Reinforced by a number of Gibraltarians already in London, the intention was to demand an audience with the Secretary of State for the Colonies. The deputation was given moral support by Governor Anderson, who sent them a cablegram saying: 'I am doing all I can', and by the AACR.

Mr Thomas of the Colonial Office Welfare Department explained to the deputation that the Secretary of State was fully occupied with the Palestine debate, but that the Under-Secretary, Mr Rees Williams, would see them the following day. That meeting, on Friday, 12th December, 1947, coincided with the official announcement that the Cabinet had decided to abandon the scheme to transfer the Gibraltar evacuees from Northern Ireland to hostels in Fulham Road and Sussex Gardens on the grounds that 'London is overcrowded and unable to assimilate further inhabitants.'

Mr Rees Williams tried to soften the blow when he met the deputation of evacuees. Repatriation was to be accelerated towards which end Service Departments, notably the War Office, were releasing accommodation in Gibraltar. In addition, every effort was being made to give priority to Gibraltar's building requirements, and in the meantime the search for accommodation in Great Britain outside London would continue.

The *Gibraltar Chronicle* picked on two 'amazing' incidents which occurred during this interview. According to the newspaper's correspondent in London, the evacuees' leader, Mr Jones, had obtained Mr Rees Williams' permission to ask Mr Keith, head of the Colonial Office Welfare Department, his opinion of the Ulster Camps. Mr Keith had replied: 'Deplorable. Unfit for human habitation', and Mr Thomas of the same department had agreed. Jones had then turned to Rees Williams who, greatly discomfited had evaded the issue.

The other incident during the meeting had occurred when things were warming up and Rees Williams was being very hard pressed. Mr Creech-Jones opened the door, had a look round, saw what was going on and walked out again!

How would the evacuees react to this latest development? The deputation were bitterly disappointed and described the action of His Majesty's Government as a 'breach of faith and sustained inhumanity.' The *Gibraltar Chronicle* speculated that the Gibraltarians already in Fulham Road might decide to sit tight and defy ejection, thereby forcing the Government into a difficult position.

The same periodical claimed that the Cabinet's decision had been taken without full knowledge of the essential facts. 'It would appear impossible for responsible Ministers to decide on a deliberate breach of faith with both Ulster and Gibraltar, and the maintenance of a camp position which their own high officials frankly call "deplorable".'

The *Chronicle* was inclined to blame the Ministry of Works, 'which had always disliked the scheme'. This Ministry was the only source which could supply the actual material to put the hostels in order, or from the Colonial Office could obtain permits to buy their own material. They had clearly been sitting on the materials and refusing the permits. The Treasury, claimed the newspaper, had not stood in the way, and the London County Council, who owned the Fulham Road hostel, had all along been co-operative and sympathetic. 'The whole trouble seems to be due to the Ministry of Works, which is so all-powerful that they have blocked the scheme over the heads of the Colonial Office.'

The report added that Creech-Jones was a poor fighter in the House of Commons when it came to standing up against the heavy guns like Aneurin Bevan and Herbert Morrison, who had been members of the Cabinet Committee which had turned the scheme down (the Minister of Works, Alderman Key, did not have a seat in the Cabinet and had been represented by Bevan).

The newspaper further speculated that Key's brief to Bevan, neither of whom had seen the official report on conditions in Ulster, must have been on the lines that essential works were difficult, the housing situation was bad and being deferred, and that it would therefore be a bad political move to bring the evacuees to London. It was suggested that Bevan had persuaded Morrison that votes might be lost in Fulham if a large number of Gibraltarians were suddenly sent there.

Whatever the reasons for the Government's decision, it was not well received by the evacuees or in Gibraltar! The Gibraltarians already in Fulham Road decided to organise a 'sit-in' with reinforcements expected from Ulster. Although they had been officially given notice to leave, they had informed Mr Keith that they would not give up the Hostel and that they were seeking legal advice. Questions were tabled in the House of Commons, whilst in Gibraltar an AACR deputation met the Governor on the 15th December, 1947.

The deputation, consisting of Messrs A Risso, J Hassan and J T Ellicott, informed the Governor that the AACR would be taking steps locally to impress upon the Imperial Government the deep resentment felt by all classes in Gibraltar at this latest breach of faith towards the evacuees in Northern Ireland. This action took the form of a public demonstration three days later. With all shops closed, a large crowd assembled in John Mackintosh Square. Speeches were followed by two resolutions, which were passed unanimously:

1. 'This meeting records its most energetic protest and deep resentment at the action of the British Government in breaking its promise to the Gibraltarian evacuees to remove them from the inhuman camps in Northern Ireland and bring them over to London this winter.

2. This meeting supports the action already taken by His Excellency the Governor on behalf of the evacuees, and urges His Excellency to take drastic measures to ensure that in addition to the efforts already made all accommodation in Gibraltar which can be procured and made available be used for the earliest repatriation of all our evacuees.'

The tone of the interview of the 15th December, and the wording of the second resolution were indicative of the new and much more cordial relations now existing between the Governor and local representatives. At the end of the demonstration, General Anderson appeared on the portico of the Convent and he was greeted with loud applause from the demonstrators. Writing to the Secretary of State for the colonies about the demonstration, the Governor remarked that the AACR had kindly given him prior notice that it was not directed against him or the Government of Gibraltar. *El Calpense* carried an article soon after entitled:

'A GOVERNOR WHO INTERESTS HIMSELF
ON BEHALF OF HIS PEOPLE'

'. . . Everybody knows . . . that General Anderson is interesting himself in every way possible to correct the mistakes committed by the high authorities in England . . . The gratitude of the people to their Governor was shown at the manifestation held last week when he was cheered as for a long time no Governor here had been cheered.

Setting aside the attitude of some of his predecessors who were more concerned with their personal comfort rather than the needs of those below, the Governor has renounced some of his privileges so that they may alleviate in some measure the housing problem, with which is closely connected that of public health. That gesture is one to be remembered, more than nothing else for its spontaneity which clearly indicates that our Governor is inspired by human sentiments.

At the manifestation . . ., the public had the satisfaction of hearing how each and every one of the speakers was unanimously of the opinion that we are fortunate in these difficult times in having a Governor who has arrived, not with the intention of having a pleasant time and enjoying as best he can the privileges of his post, but inspired by the desire of ruling and of looking after the welfare of those under him.'

Meantime, the 'sit-in' at Fulham Road Hostel grew as more and more 'squatters' arrived there from Ulster. The *Chronicle* reported that a mass movement was taking place in the Gibraltar evacuee camps in Northern Ireland to obtain travel certificates for England to reinforce the Fulham squatters. The attitude of the evacuees at Fulham was reported to be one of absolute determination, with no confidence in the Commons' assurances that something was going to be done.

On the 18th December, 1947, the same day as the AACR demonstration, Sir Walter Smiles, Unionist MP for County Down, asked the Secretary of State for the Colonies what steps he was taking to implement the pledges given to the Gibraltarians, still living in Ulster, to transfer them to London that winter.

Mr Creech-Jones replied that the Government was deeply concerned about the Gibraltarians still living in camps in Ulster and was doing everything possible to repatriate the remaining 1,340 Gibraltarians as soon as accommodation could be made available in the Colony. Regarding the 700 or so who would have to remain in the United Kingdom for some time yet, every effort was being made to secure accommodation for them in London. 'Owing to practical difficulties, I regret our hopes have not been fulfilled, and my officers are exploring with all expedition, with the Ministries concerned, arrangements for settling them in other parts of Great Britain outside the London area.'

In a supplementary question, Smiles asked: 'Is the Secretary of State aware that the Gibraltar people feel that he has let them down, broken his word, and that the Ministry of Works is responsible for this?' A politician's reply ensued!

While 'reinforcements' from Ulster continued to arrive at Fulham, the London County Council adopted a new policy at the hostel. It had been customary for young men from the Prince's Gate hostel to visit their sisters and 'novias' (girl-friends) at Fulham. On the 18th December, police arrived at Fulham and prevented the visitors from entering. They were informed that hotel residents could enter and leave, but that visitors were forbidden.

The Irish edition of *The Daily Mail* carried a big article on the evacuees on Friday, 19th December, 1947. Beneath the headline: 'Despair grips men of Britain's lost colony. Eighth Christmas in exile', the article described how the evacuees from Gibraltar sat in dreary corrugated huts lit by oil lamps.

'They feel bitter, hopeless and tired. I saw a score of boys and girls wearing clothes made from blankets taken off their parents' beds. The children wear clogs and many of the parents are nearly barefooted.

The pocket money of 8/6 a week allowed by the Colonial Office does not run to luxuries. They live on the poverty line. The biggest grumble was about the food, on which the evacuees say it is only just possible to live. The children are pasty-faced and listless and there are not enough plates to go around.

Men and women from many walks of life make up the colony—shopkeepers, commission agents, waiters, skilled tradesmen, a boxer and a ballerina. Six hundred able-bodied men in the seven camps are bored, restless and frustrated—there is no work for them.

Mr B Martinez said: "It is painful living on charity. I am able to work. I want work. There is no education and no future for the children here." '

On Saturday, 27th December, 1947, came good news for the evacuees. Mr Keith, acting on personal instructions from Mr Creech-Jones, announced to over one hundred Gibraltarians assembled outside the Fulham Road hostel that the Colonial Office had accepted responsibility for the building, which would now be out of the hands of the London County Council. All Gibraltarians who had arrived from Ulster were now admitted into the hostel as would all others who opted to come. The ban on visitors was also ceased. The battle for Fulham Road had been won. Or had it . . .?

A few days after Mr Keith's announcement it was revealed that the Colonial Office was still not fully responsible for Fulham Road hostel, and that the London County Council had reimposed the ban on visitors. However, the hostel was finally taken over formally by the Colonial Office on New Year's Eve.

CHAPTER EIGHTEEN

The End of an Ordeal

The year 1948 witnessed the end of the Northern Ireland ordeal, eight further repatriation parties from the United Kingdom (about 750 persons all told), plus one from Madeira and several from Tangier. Conditions at the Fulham Road and Prince's Gate hostels posed problems.

Despite the formal take-over of Fulham Road hostel, there was no question of the evacuees being officially transferred from Ulster to London. The Colonial Office was not allowed to implement the originally worked out scheme which had provided for the transfer of small, properly accompanied parties, with luggage an official responsibility. This meant that the evacuees had to make their own private travel arrangements and pay their own fares. Women with children faced tough journeys, and there was no option but to leave heavy luggage in Ulster. This was to lead to untold problems! Old peoples' allowances were not being paid on the grounds that the evacuees were moving of their own volition and were therefore no longer a Government responsibility.

At Fulham Road the evacuees already there were working hard to make the place habitable, despite the fact that no materials were forthcoming from the Ministry of Works. They were trying to work out methods of screening so as to make some sort of family privacy with make-shift materials, including blankets being distributed by the Warden. The Colonial Office was meanwhile distributing whatever furniture was available from Ulster.

The evacuees were clearly facing an uphill struggle to get the hostel ship-shape. Although the Welfare officers were doing their utmost, the Government process was rotating very slowly. There were still no medical arrangements, no educational facilities, no children's nursery, and the lack of partitioning material was causing disruption of family arrangements, and was straining sanitary and washing facilities. Overcrowding was soon to add to the difficulties; a population of 250 on the 7th January, 1948, had risen to 421 by the middle of the month, and to 631 by the end of it!

The AACR, informed by the Evacuees' Executive Committee that the Ministry of Health and Local Government in Northern Ireland were refusing to accept any responsibility in respect of the heavy luggage left in the camps by the Gibraltarians who had left for London, appealed to the Governor. It was, the Association argued, unjust that the Northern Ireland Government should now decide to waive all responsibility for the care of this luggage, thereby increasing the worries of the evacuees which, as a result of recent events, had been greatly accentuated. It was also alleged that some camp wardens were threatening to throw the luggage out of the camps.

The Governor transmitted these complaints to London, saying that whilst it might be argued that by leaving the camps on their own initiative the evacuees had technically made themselves responsible for the safety of their own belongings, he felt that 'having regard to the protracted period of hardship which they have had to endure, it would be both justifiable and wise not to insist too strongly on the technical position.'

A Gibraltarian named Frank Brew, whilst in London on business, visited the Fulham Road Hostel and was appalled by the conditions under which the evacuees were living. The majority, he wrote, had had to leave their belongings in Northern Ireland and consequently were undergoing great privations. Moreover, as the numbers in the hostel increased so conditions worsened, and, claimed Brew, the Government department concerned was deliberately withholding materials with which partitions could be made. He concluded: 'My interest in this matter is that of a Gibraltarian. I had not seen them for six years and I was horrified to see how they are living and what they have gone through. The young people amongst them seem to be growing old rapidly, the youngest of them are growing illiterate ....'

The Governor wrote at some length to the Secretary of State for the Colonies. '.... This Fulham episode has revived here hostility and resentment against His Majesty's Government in a greater degree than ever before I arrived. The universal local feeling, with which I agree, was that the honour of His Majesty's Government was at stake over this matter.

.... the people feel really hurt and will not easily forget the treatment their compatriots have received, despite the compromise ending as regards Fulham.

I am desperately anxious to solve the whole problem as a matter of urgency. It is an ulcer poisoning our whole political life and relationship, and although active agitation rises and falls with the varying crises as they occur, yet so long as the ulcer remains one never knows when it is going to flare up again to irritate relations between people, classes and Government.

I have concentrated since I came here on trying to improve the atmosphere of resentment and suspicion which I found existing in the place, not without some success I think; but every time this cursed problem comes to the boil I lose some of the ground gained!'

His Excellency then referred to a change of policy at the Gibraltar end regarding the aliens and statutory aliens amongst the evacuees. He said that he had recently learnt that the families of Gibraltarians and statutory aliens who had lived in Spain before the war had also been evacuated by sanction in 1940, under the threat that if they did not go their bread-winners would cease to be given employment in Gibraltar. They had all now lost their houses and homes in Spain so the Governor felt that the British Government was under a very strong moral obligation to bring them back to Gibraltar, although they had never lived there before.

'We must of course deal first with Gibraltarians but we do feel that we ought to take a rather less uncompromising line with the others, especially as many of the statutory aliens are really Gibraltarians in all but name.'

This certainly represented a fundamental change from the earlier attitude that the return of these people should be postponed until, if ever, proper housing conditions were available for them in Gibraltar.

Regarding those evacuees still in Northern Ireland, the Governor had this to say: 'I most earnestly beg you to insist that (they) are treated as British subjects and as human beings. It really is imperative that you move them at once to decent accommodation in England.'

Whilst the Governor was thus strongly voicing the Gibraltarian cause, the Unofficial Members of the Resettlement Board were planning a Memorial to His Majesty the King in Council, to be signed by as many Gibraltarians as possible.

The Memorial, which contained twenty clauses, began by referring to the forcible nature of the evacuations, first to Morocco, then to London, Madeira and Jamaica and to the later removal of the London evacuees to Northern Ireland. It pointed out that although 15,000 had been returned, there were still 1,334 in Northern Ireland and another 1,400 in the United Kingdom not under the Government scheme, as well as a few still in Madeira and Tangier.

After references to the appalling conditions in the Northern Ireland camps, the Memorial stressed the deep regret of the evacuees and of the loyal people of Gibraltar at the failure of His Majesty's Government to implement its promise to transfer the evacuees to more humane conditions. This was followed by a reminder that both the well-to-do and the poor had without hesitation borne the heavy expenses of an evacuation carried out for military reasons.

Referring to local housing conditions, the Memorial said that the Government of Gibraltar, with the co-operation of the Services, had now exhausted all immediate possible means of accommodating more people in Gibraltar without the urgent further erection of temporary buildings, the material for the construction of which was unobtainable, and the cost of which could hardly be met by local resources which had been most severely drained.

'A building scheme involving the erection of blocks of flats at the instigation of the Local Government, with the concurrence of the Home Government, has had to be considerably curtailed owing to conditions imposed by the Home Government in connection with the tendering and carrying out of such work, which was eventually entrusted to an English firm at the minimum staggering cost of about £2,000,000 and this to build only one half of the originally planned blocks of flats which were in fact estimated to cost very much below the high figure referred to. The cost of such buildings has been strongly criticised by the people of Gibraltar as being out of all proportion to the size and resources of this small Colony.'

The Memorial concluded: 'Taking the foregoing facts into consideration, the people of Gibraltar, en masse, feel that it is inconsistent with the principles of justice and equity, and even of human feeling, to allow the grievances of their compatriot evacuees to remain unredressed and, therefore, that as a last resort they are in duty bound to appeal to Your Gracious Majesty in Council for a redress of such grievances.'

Forty-six repatriates from Northern Ireland Camps arrived in Gibraltar on the 15th January, 1948, on board the British ss *Orbita.* The majority were accommodated in the Little Sisters of the Poor Evacuation Centre. The ages of the repatriates varied from four months to about eighty years. This was the twentieth party to return since the commencement of repatriation.

At Fulham Road, apart from the problem of luggage already noted, a strong grievance was the refusal of the Ulster Government to surrender the evacuees' food and clothing ration books to their owners. It was believed that such action was illegal, as these books were the property of the individual concerned, and Fulham evacuees were sending a telegram of protest to the Ministry of Food. On a brighter note, partitioning was likely to be erected shortly, a sick bay was being set up, and nursing staff were due to come over from Ulster to take charge.

At the end of January, 1948, an official communique from the Colonial Secretariat announced that a sum of £5,000 had been allocated by the Lord Mayor's Air Raid Distress Fund to help evacuees who decided to settle permanently in the United Kingdom.

As more and more evacuees left Northern Ireland for London, the authorities decided to close down Camp No. 5 at Tawneybrack, Antrim. The evacuees in London were worried because all those remaining in that camp were being sent to other Antrim camps further from civilisation, and they feared that the Government's policy was to transfer the inhabitants of camps as they closed into Antrim, whence transfer to Britain was more difficult. The evacuees' appeal to the Ministry of Food about ration books had evoked an official reply that all evacuees had to be given their ration books when they left the camps, but the Ulster Government was being slow to comply with this. Concerning the luggage left in the camps, the authorities in Ulster had by the end of January agreed to store it, but without responsibility. At the same time, the Colonial Office had agreed to transfer to London most of the luggage left at Camp No. 17, accepting an undertaking by the Central Executive to reimburse expenses.

On the 4th February, 1948, the *Gibraltar Chronicle* reported that patience at Fulham Road Hostel was becoming exhausted by what the newspaper described as 'the stupid pinpricks of the Ulster and British Governments'. The latest grievance concerned the scale of charges being made by the Treasury for the accommodation at Fulham Road, a matter which was to give rise to many problems.

The charges were:

Single man	31/- weekly
Single woman	25/- weekly
Married couple	47/-; plus 7/- weekly for each child of school age and 17/6 weekly for juveniles under eighteen.

Such amounts were regarded as excessive by the evacuees in view of the current wage scales, and iniquitous in view of the lack of the most elementary amenities at Fulham. They were therefore refusing to pay. Regarding the clothing coupons, the Ulster Government had returned each evacuee one page, but not their whole books! This was considered to be illegal by the evacuees.

The Fulham population had risen to 660 by early February, with amenities still totally lacking, though the sick-bay nursing staff were due any day. The congestion was hardly affected by the next repatriation party of 102 which left the United Kingdom aboard the *Franconia* on the 21st February, since the bulk of this came from Ulster and only included fifteen persons from Fulham Road.

The month of March, 1948, brought fresh developments in the evacuee hostels in London. At Prince's Gate, the Colonial Office issued new regulations under which it ceased to cater for the residents, who were now to have their own ration books and the ability to buy and cook their own rations their own way. Additional gas-rings were installed and another kitchen was equipped. The previous charge of thirty shillings a week for board and lodgings became ten shillings a week for lodgings only, including room, furniture, clean linen, light and heat.

The new arrangement, for which the evacuees had been fighting for a long time, was naturally warmly welcomed by them.

At Fulham Road Hostel, the erection of partitioning finally got under way on the 9th March, with heavy fire-proof material being used. The sick-bays were now manned by three nurses, whilst the evacuees' luggage from Ulster had been safely stored in Fulham.

In Ulster, three Antrim camps, numbers nine, ten and eleven, were due to close soon and the remaining evacuees (less than 500 were expected to remain by the end of March) were to be concentrated in the three Down camps. The Colonial Office's opinion was that all the camps would be closed before September, and probably sooner.

Another repatriation party left the United Kingdom on the 22nd March aboard the *Franconia*. The party of 140 had a Gibraltarian as assistant supervisor—Mr Luis Castro, who had been evacuated as a boy of fourteen in 1940; it was his first visit back to the Rock. The majority of the repatriates (about one hundred came from Northern Ireland camps) were accommodated at the Royal Naval Air Station at North Front, which had been specially converted. There were about forty children in the party, a number of whom had been born in the United Kingdom.

Families were allotted in two or three rooms according to the size of the family. The *Gibraltar Chronicle* reported that the rooms were well ventilated and recently painted, and fitted with beds, chairs, tables, mattresses, blankets and pillows. There was also a spacious patio which the children used as a playground.

The feeding arrangements were initially in the hands of the contractor, Mr P Montegriffo. A motor-van arrived three times a day: at about 8.30 am to distribute breakfast, at midday to serve a hot meal and for supper at 6.30 pm. The head of the family would go to the kitchen and he would be issued with food according to the number of coupons. The food was taken away in casseroles and the repatriates ate in their own apartments.

This system was discontinued after a couple of weeks, unemployed repatriates receiving an allowance for food and fuel from the Government. The scale of family allowances was as follows:-

Married couple 25 shillings; for each child seven shillings and sixpence or five shillings according to age; each additional adult ten shillings.

When the Governor visited these repatriates on the 13th April, 1948, he found that all 110 of them—with one exception—were very happy to be back home, despite a howling Levanter! The exception was 60-year-old John Sanchez, who told the Governor that Northern Ireland suited his bronchitis better! He had only come back, he said, because his family had insisted.

Complaints voiced, most of which His Excellency was told had already been taken in hand, concerned diversion of the Catalan Bay bus to stop nearer the settlement, education arrangements and a request that the paraffin cart should call once a week instead of their having to into town to get oil.

The Governor also saw the huts being prepared to receive the next party of about 200 repatriates, due at the end of April.

At the Fulham Road hostel a complete block had already been partitioned and about 200 evacuees were employed in diverse occupations. There was a mild rebellion going on about the boarding charges, but despite this the atmosphere was extremely happy.

In mid-April the Colonial Office announced the formation of a committee to help with the resettlement of those evacuees who did not wish to return to Gibraltar. The Committee's main function would be to submit recommendations to the Head of the Welfare Department regarding the donation of £5,000 received from the Lord Mayor's Empire Air Raid Distress Fund and any other funds which might be received for the same purpose.

The main aim of this 'Resettlement Fund' would be to assist evacuees to purchase furniture and linen, and to help them to transfer their furniture from Gibraltar to the United Kingdom.

The Colonial Office statement added: 'Evacuees in receipt of grants from the Fund will thereby become ineligible for free passages to Gibraltar at a later date, and will be deemed to have automatically terminated their association with the Evacuation Scheme as from the date of receiving assistance in any form from the Fund.'

The point was also made that the £5,000 donated would not be enough to meet all claims, and that it was hoped that monetary support would be forthcoming from the Rock since 'obviously every man, woman and child who can be permanently settled here will lessen the potential overcrowding in already overcrowded Gibraltar.'

On the 23rd April, 1948, a further 190 repatriates embarked in the *Orbita* at Liverpool, 98 of them from London and 92 from Ulster. On the same day, Camp Number Two at Cargagh closed down, leaving only Camps Number One and Number Seventeen with a total of 385 evacuees. The *Gibraltar Chronicle's'* London correspondent observed that whilst the older evacuees seemed thrilled at the prospect of returning home, many of the younger generation, especially the girls, would have chosen to stay in London.

This party of repatriates arrived in Gibraltar three days later. The *Chronicle* reported that there were enthusiastic scenes when the fleet of Gibraltar Motorways buses arrived at the Repatriation Centre at North Front, a hot meal being served to the majority as soon as they arrived.

Mr Manuel Xerri, who returned with the largest family, six boys and two girls (his wife had died in Northern Ireland) told a *Chronicle* reporter:

'I am glad to be back in my native place. All my children are happy to return, but if I or any of the children have a chance of returning to England, we won't miss it.

Since I left Gibraltar some eight years ago I have had not the slightest reason for any complaint about any place that I have been sent to. I am sure there are many others who feel like myself.' An interesting comment!

The Colonial Office now informed the Governor that the transfer of evacuees from Northern Ireland to Fulham Road, up to the capacity of the hostel, had been agreed. Accommodation was immediately available for 200 and transfers would commence in May and be completed within two weeks. This would enable Northern Ireland to close Camp Number One the following month, and the remaining evacuees (most of whom would be prospective repatriates) would be concentrated at Camp Number Seventeen. Further transfers would be arranged if necessary as and when vacancies arose at Fulham Road and Prince's Gate.

Further details were supplied a few days later by Mr Thomas to the Fulham Central Executive Committee. Mr Thomas said that 200 evacuees would be brought over from Ulster in four parties of 50 between May 7th and 10th. People on repatriation lists would not be transferred. The hope was to completely close the Ulster Camps by the summer. Anyone unwilling to leave Ulster would be obliged to find their own accommodation there.

The first of these parties from Ulster, numbering 59 and including many children, arrived at Fulham Road on the 7th May, 1948. A second party, totalling 62, arrived on the 12th May, and a further 71 on the 20th May. The population of Gibraltarians in Northern Ireland was thereby decreased to 190, with about 70 due to be repatriated in early June.

This new influx into Fulham Road hostel brought its own problems. The *Gibraltar Chronicle's'* London correspondent pointed out that Fulham was clearly going to be extremely full after the middle of June and that public attention should now be focussed upon the state of 'welfare' there and the need to do something to increase amenities at the hostel. The correspondent claimed that, despite the fact that a fluctuating population of several hundreds had been in residence in the hostel since the beginning of the year, welfare facilities were still lacking. Thus, there were no Clubs, no Scouts or Guides, no organised recreational activities apart from the usual weekly dances, there were obvious problems connected with the old people, and the distribution of food had not yet been satisfactorily resolved.

A new twist to the story now emerged: it seemed that some evacuees who did not wish to return to Gibraltar were being pressurised to do so! The story broke with the publication at Fulham Road hostel of the following official notice:-

'As from the 19th May, 1948, all evacuees who are selected for repatriation to Gibraltar will be expected to return home, or alternatively to make arrangements for private accommodation. It will not be possible to permit evacuees who do not now accept repatriation to continue in residence at this Hostel.'

The *Gibraltar Chronicle's'* London correspondent followed up the matter. 'I talked to a man who was on the list for repatriation, but who, having for some months held a job as a stoker under the Ministry of Works, was moving heaven and earth to stay here.

He said: 'When I was in Ireland, I saw no future for myself or my people, and wanted to get back to Gibraltar. Now I see a chance of living here with good prospects, I want to take it.

Why can't some of those who are longing to go, but who are not on the list, go instead of me and those like me, who have made an effort to become self-supporting here and who see a chance to take root in this country?'

These remarks represented the feelings of a section of the evacuees who could not understand why the repatriation lists often contained the names of good workmen who were making a successful effort to fit in and make homes for themselves in England. On the occasions when such a person decided not to return to Gibraltar and found his own accommodation in England, the passage arranged for him was wasted. The *Chronicle* claimed that there had been a number of instances in which there had been empty berths owing to the people for whom they had been arranged falling out—

and those empty berths had not been filled. Not surprisingly, when those evacuees who were longing to return heard about these empty berths they wondered why they could not have used them! The great cry at Fulham Road was: 'Why should not those who want to go, go; and those who want to stay, stay?'

The evacuees laid the responsibility for such a state of affairs on the shoulders of the Repatriation Committee in Gibraltar, who, they claimed, were working on a census taken in Northern Ireland, at a time when they would have gone anywhere to get out of the Camps. The situation had now changed, and it was therefore felt that the selection of repatriates should be arranged in London, where officials were in much closer touch with the progress of those being dealt with.

The *Chronicle* stated that it was becoming more and more difficult to get people to go back. Each time a list of repatriates went up on the board at Fulham Road, there were many protests.

The Governor contacted the Colonial Office, saying that the revelations in the *Gibraltar Chronicle* had given rise to local public comment, and pointing out that if the notice referred to was strictly enforced, it might have the effect of causing persons who had obtained employment and who, subject to finding other accommodation, would be likely to remain permanently in the United Kingdom, to relinquish employment and accept repatriation to some extent against their will. Whilst appreciating that Fulham Road hostel could not continue indefinitely, the Governor said that 'it would be advantageous if only those who really wish to return are repatriated.'

He therefore suggested 'that no obstacle should be placed in the way of any evacuees who have obtained employment and wish to settle in the United Kingdom and that if any such persons are included in future repatriation lists they should be allowed to withdraw and be substituted by others who do wish to return.

It is suggested for consideration that those who so withdraw might not at present be required on that account to leave Fulham Road, although it might be made clear to them that they would be expected to find accommodation elsewhere . . . within a reasonable period, say six months. Should they still be in Fulham Road when the time comes to close the Hostel they could then be required to leave or be repatriated.'

The Secretary of State for the Colonies agreed that it was undesirable that certain evacuees should return under a degree of pressure while others who wished to return were kept in London. He explained that the notice in question had been issued to encourage the evacuees to make greater efforts to secure accommodation for themselves by making it clear that they could not remain in Fulham Road indefinitely. He now suggested that a questionnaire should be prepared for distribution amongst the evacuees in order to establish which Gibraltarians wished to return and which wished to remain in the United Kingdom.

By the beginning of June, 1948, the population at Fulham Road had reached an all-time high—740! The end of the Northern Ireland saga was not only in sight, but just round the corner. On the 4th June, the *Empress of Australia* crossed from Belfast to Liverpool with 71 repatriates; the number would have been one more but for the untimely and sudden death from natural causes of Mr Louis Martin aged 62. The ship left the United Kingdom on the 7th and arrived in Gibraltar on the 11th.

The total Gibraltarian population in the Northern Ireland Camps was now down to 113, with 100 due to transfer to Fulham Road as soon as the next repatriation party left later in June. Of the remaining thirteen in Northern Ireland then, twelve would be joining the repatriation party, leaving just one evacuee, a mental case whose future had not yet been decided.

Battles continued to be waged at Fulham Road Hostel. One concerned the distribution of rations, which the evacuees wanted on an individual basis rather than in bulk through the communal kitchen. By mid-June this had been achieved, the evacuees then having, individually, all that they had had when last in London. The only items distributed through the kitchens were those which it would have been impossible to distribute individually, such as meat, bacon and cooking fats.

Another 'battle' was over the payment of the charges for board and lodging. A number of evacuees continued to refuse to pay these charges and a written protest had been sent to the Secretary of State for the Colonies. The leaders of the 'won't pay movement' felt that there was a very strong case in favour of reduction and adjustment of the charges, which weighed most heavily and unfairly in the case of large families. Statistics were being prepared to show that these charges were excessive in relation to the insufficient accommodation and amenities.

A further repatriation party, numbering 130, left Liverpool on the 29th June, 1948, aboard the *Scythia.* In charge of the party was Captain Bateman-Fox, the Warden at Fulham Road Hostel. He had had a long association with the Gibraltar evacuees: with them since their arrival in England in August, 1940, through the bombings, in the Northern Ireland Camps and right through to the triumph of Fulham Road. He was now paying his first visit to Gibraltar. His assistant for the trip was the Gibraltarian Luis de Castro, who had accompanied an earlier repatriation party. The nurses accompanying the party—Mackintosh, Baker and Orfila—were also Gibraltarians, currently training at Croydon General Hospital. Since only 90 evacuees were expected at Fulham Road from Ulster in the near future, this meant that the hostel would be less crowded, and it was rumoured that a further small repatriation party would be leaving during July.

The first use to be made of the extra room, reported the *Gibraltar Chronicle's'* London correspondent, would be to extend the present schoolroom accommodation to one more much-needed classroom. This latest repatriation party also brought nearer the end of the Northern Ireland ordeal with the final evacuation of the Camps due to begin on the 6th July and timed to be completed on the 20th.

The matter of accommodation charges at Fulham Road continued to fester. The appeal made to the Secretary of State for the Colonies received an adverse reply, and deadlock ensued. Among those refusing to pay were some of the evacuees who had been listed in the *Scythia* party and had refused to return to Gibraltar.

More evacuees returned on the 12th July, 1948, aboard the ss *Asturias*. A few days earlier, Mr Rees Williams, Under-Secretary of State for the Colonies, answering a series of questions in the House of Commons, had stated that there were only 78 Gibraltarian evacuees remaining in Northern Ireland and that they would be out before the end of the month, when the remaining camp would be closed. The Under-Secretary had also stated that more than 600 evacuees had already been repatriated in 1948, and that there were 605 in Fulham Road Hostel, 205 of whom were in employment, the remainder being mostly dependents and persons incapable of work.

The following cable from the Colonial Office reached Gibraltar on the 23rd July, 1948: 'Final party of evacuees left Belfast for London on July 21st. All Northern Ireland camps now closed.'

The ordeal of Northern Ireland was over!

CHAPTER NINETEEN

The Residue

Seventeen months were to pass after the ending of the Northern Ireland chapter before the evacuation scheme was officially declared closed, and a further fourteen months elapsed before all Gibraltarians who wished to return home had been repatriated. The situation at Fulham Road Hostel continued to pose problems, and the emphasis now began to change from repatriation to resettlement in the United Kingdom.

At about the same time that the Northern Ireland camps were closing down, the Governor of Gibraltar travelled to London and visited the hostels at Fulham Road and Prince's Gate. At Fulham Road, His Excellency had informal talks with the Warden, staff and officials of the Colonial Office Welfare Department. He visited some of the rooms in the building, talked to the families and saw their actual living conditions. Some to whom he spoke were anxious for immediate repatriation, but the majority wished to settle permanently in the United Kingdom.

The Governor referred to the difficult conditions under which many people in Gibraltar were living, and he pointed to the wisdom of staying in London and saving money. When an evacuee said that he hoped to stay on account of the better prospects for his children, General Anderson praised his intention and determination. The Governor also visited the children's nursery, sickbay, dining room, kitchen and food stores.

At Prince's Gate, the Governor was visibly impressed at the great difference in living conditions and the complete lack of enthusiasm about repatriation. Every family said that they wanted to stay and they were unanimous in their praise of the Colonial Office Welfare Officers.

On that same day, the 23rd July, 1948, twenty repatriates sailed from the United Kingdom aboard the ss *Orbita.* The party, which was unescorted, arrived at Gibraltar on the 28th. They were mostly elderly people without dependents, but there was a family of four. One man—well-known to the older generation—was Harry Zammitt, once a celebrated jockey. He was rather worried when the Governor told him that the race-course at North Front was now an aerodrome! This party officially brought to a close the repatriation programme for 1948, but there was to be a further party of thirteen who arrived at Gibraltar aboard the *Empire Deben* on the 18th September.

There was movement in the opposite direction. Two people who had been repatriated in Captain Bateman Fox's party on the 28th June, Miss Mary Simoni and her brother, returned to the United Kingdom in August under their own steam. Their return caused a deep impression at Fulham Road, who now heard something of the impossibility of getting jobs in Gibraltar equal to those available in London. The Simonis claimed that there were others who would have liked to have returned, but who could not raise the fare.

Mr Thomas of the Colonial Office Welfare Department visited Gibraltar from the 27th September to the 14th October to discuss with local officials questions relating to the repatriation of evacuees in 1949, the possibility of disposing of luggage and furniture problems, the recovery of debts incurred by repatriates, and to report on the progress made with the plans to resettle evacuees in the United Kingdom.

He reported that on the 1st August, 1948, there were 713 evacuees in the Colonial Office hostels (629 in Fulham Road and 84 in Prince's Gate). A large number of those at Fulham Road were statutory aliens, that is persons not automatically entitled to reside in Gibraltar; most of them had lived in Spain before the evacuation. However, as has been seen, the Gibraltar Government had already decided to disregard the question of nationality or place of previous residence, and to draw repatriates from the list of people who had expressed a definite wish to return to the Rock.

The census completed in August, 1948, had established that of 713 evacuees living in the two hostels, 283 were anxious to return under any conditions, 285 wished to stay in the United Kingdom, and 145 were uncertain. This last group consisted, in the main, of people who would have liked to return to Gibraltar but not to the temporary type of accommodation being offered there.

In addition to the population of the hostels, it was estimated that about 1,500 Gibraltarians were living in private accommodation in various parts of the United Kingdom, but chiefly in London. An attempt to get these people to fill the census forms had proved singularly unsuccessful, only 60 doing so, of whom 59 had expressed a wish to be repatriated. It might be assumed that those who had not bothered to apply were not really interested in returning. On the other hand, some might not have heard about the census, and in any case all had a right to return to Gibraltar should they so wish. The existence of this group, scattered over different parts of the country, was to cause officials trying to wind up the evacuation scheme many headaches.

Mr Thomas pointed out to Gibraltar Government officials that Fulham Road Hostel had been leased from the London County Council and had to be vacated by the 30th September, 1949. There was no prospect of a lease extension and in any case the hostel was costing the British Government £50,000 a year. There was not the same urgency as regards Prince's Gate, which was under requisition, but the Colonial Office did not propose to hold the building for longer than was necessary.

It was explained to the Gibraltar Government that the Colonial Office would want repatriation completed before the expiry of the Fulham Road tenancy, but the Colonial Secretary of Gibraltar expressed doubt as to whether this would be feasible. He reminded Mr Thomas that the temporary loan of the Royal Naval Air Station, in which 250 repatriates were accommodated, was due to expire in June, 1949, and that the people there would then have to be rehoused. Furthermore, there were hundreds of families in Gibraltar living in grossly overcrowded conditions, and the only assurance that he could give Mr Thomas was that the repatriation of the 283 evacuees in the London hostels who had expressed a wish to return could be completed by June, 1950. It was highly unlikely, he added, that any repatriation could take place before June, 1949.

The views of the Colonial Office and the Government of Gibraltar were clearly incompatible! Mr Thomas conceded the point made to him about overcrowding in Gibraltar. 'I am satisfied .... that there are very genuine grounds for disquiet in regard to the general standard of accommodation in the Colony.' One possible way out of the impasse suggested by Mr Thomas was an approach to the Air Ministry for an extension of the loan of the RNAS until June, 1950. 'If this cannot be done, I would be most reluctant to suggest that any effort should be made to foist people on the Colony. It would be unwise from every point of view, and apart from overloading the health services to a dangerous degree, it would lead to a measure of social and political unrest, and still further retard the efforts of the Governor to cope with the housing situation. There is a danger of overcrowding the Colony to such an extent that rehousing measures would be defeated.'

As yet another Christmas approached, the inmates at Fulham Road Hostel awaited a new system of food distribution, under which they would be getting and cooking their own rations instead of having some through the communal kitchen. Such a system had been in operation at Prince's Gate Hostel since March, 1948.

Gas rings and individual cooking points had been installed for some time, and there were ample facilities for individual washing-up. However, as the month of November, 1948, slipped away no announcement was forthcoming regarding the implementation of the new scheme of things. The evacuees began to wonder whether they would be having their Christmas dinner communally again, instead of individually as had been hoped for.

The *Gibraltar Chronicle's'* London correspondent speculated that the Colonial Office was having a tussle with some other Department whose full acceptance of the self-feeding scheme had to be obtained. Was the problem over future lodging rates? The move from partly communal to wholly individual feeding would unquestionably be the most popular thing to have happened at Fulham Road hostel since its inception and, provided the new rates and charges were reasonable the *Chronicle* reporter felt that it would solve the whole problem of payments at the hostel. But whatever happened, Christmas 1948 would not be anything like the previous one when evacuees had been squatting in the hostel under siege conditions!

At about this time great difficulty was being experienced in getting passages to Gibraltar, and further repatriation parties had to be very small. Thus, on the 24th November, 1948, five repatriates arrived in Gibraltar on board the *Empire Test*. Four were from Fulham Road and the fifth a cured hospital patient. Two of these were young men—Manuel and Peter Alecio—who had been trained by the firm of Lipton and were now joining their branch in Gibraltar.

There were a number of evacuees who had been officially approved for repatriation, and several hospital patients, now fit and anxious to return before Christmas. However, although officials were doing their best it seemed unlikely that they could be got away before the New Year since there were so few ships and all were so heavily booked.

Towards the end of November, 1948, the Secretary of State for the Colonies again raised the matter of Gibraltar's repatriation plans. He informed the Governor that the future of the Gibraltar evacuees in the London hostels was due to come up again for discussion, that there was bound to be strong pressure to wind up the evacuation scheme entirely in 1949, and that its extension into 1950—ten years after it had started—should be avoided at all costs.

In his reply, the Governor explained that the new flats under construction would accommodate a minimum of 2,500 persons. The architect had estimated that three blocks (with a maximum capacity of 1,129) would be ready by the end of March, 1949, two further blocks (maximum capacity 720) by the end of July, 1949, one block (maximum capacity 476) by the end of September, 1949, and a final block (maximum capacity 588) by the end of March, 1950. These new flats would not solve the problem of overcrowding, and the only accommodation available for new repatriates would be in Government Centres where they would have to remain indefinitely. The maximum number of further repatriates which could be received would be 350, and there would be no room in Government Centres before November, 1949. On the other hand, if the Air Ministry were to agree to an extension of the loan of the RNAS for a further nine months, then it would be possible to take 300 repatriates between July and September, 1949, and another 50 later.

The Governor concluded: 'I am fully in accord with your desire to see the early end of the evacuation scheme. The sole limiting factor is Gibraltar's capacity of reception. I shall be in a much better position to assess possibilities about the middle of next year. It is clear however that the only means by which substantial progress could be guaranteed in 1949 is if you can obtain from the Air Ministry an extension of the period for which the RNAS can be made available to this Government as above suggested.'

While this impasse continued, the feeling within the Colonial Office was that emphasis had to gradually change from repatriation to resettlement. With half the evacuees at Fulham Road wanting to remain in the United Kingdom it seemed unlikely that the £5,000 originally donated for resettlement would be sufficient. The question was now raised as to whether Gibraltar should make some contribution to the Fund.

The new rationing system by which evacuees would provide for themselves, and the resultant new charges at Fulham Road hostel were finally announced in early December, to come into effect on the 12th. For self-contained accommodation the charge was to be fifteen shillings per room, and for partitioned accommodation 12/6 per room. Families requiring two or more rooms would be charged at an additional nominal rate. All rates included heat, light and laundry for impersonal articles such as bedding. The large majority of the evacuees welcomed the new system.

The problem of the residue of evacuees in the United Kingdom continued to occupy the minds of officials both in London and Gibraltar throughout the year 1949. On the 3rd January, the Secretary of State for the Colonies, Lord Listowel, put the problem to the Governor. The Fulham Road lease would expire on the 29th September, 1949. What was to happen then to the 616 Gibraltar evacuees living there? Three alternatives presented themselves to the Secretary of State: repatriation, rehousing in another hostel, or absorption into the ordinary civilian population of the United Kingdom. Gibraltar insisted that all the evacuees who had opted for repatriation could not return in 1949, there was no prospect of obtaining another hostel the size of that at Fulham Road, and the process of absorption was bound to be slow and difficult. So what could be done?

Lord Listowel suggested trying all three alternatives simultaneously. Since about 375 of the evacuees had opted for repatriation, this would leave 241 to be provided with private accommodation in the United Kingdom. There was no chance of achieving this before September given the long waiting lists for houses in Britain; since the move from Northern Ireland at the end of 1947 only about thirty evacuees had found homes of their own! The liklihood was, therefore, that when the Fulham Road lease ended accommodation would still be required for about 200 Gibraltarians—it might just be possible to obtain another hostel for these but certainly not for double that number, which would be the requirement based on the present repatriation programme.

(Prince's Gate, with a capacity for about 80, could be retained after September, 1949).

The conclusion drawn by the Secretary of State from all this was that there was no alternative but to press Gibraltar to take all those of the hostel dwellers who had opted for repatriation (about 375) before the Fulham Road lease ended. Referring to the Governor's earlier request for an extension of the loan of the RNAS (which would have solved the problem), the Secretary of State commented that if the Station was retained by the Gibraltar Government until 1950, then the Air Ministry's building programme would have to be entirely recast. He doubted whether they could be asked to do this!

The Governor remained adamant: Gibraltar could *NOT* take 375 persons by the end of September, 1949, unless the RNAS could be retained until May, 1950, or unless further accommodation could be built (which the Government of Gibraltar could not afford!). The Air Ministry subsequently agreed to extend the loan of the RNAS until December, 1949, which gesture the Governor described as 'helpful but inadequate'.

Lord Listowel insisted. In a cable dated the 19th March, 1949, he stated: 'While I realise your difficulties I must make it clear that I personally attach great importance to winding-up the evacuation scheme this year. I must therefore press you to undertake at this stage to repatriate from this country, before the end of September, all those who wish to leave (up to a maximum of 375).' He added that if necessary the Gibraltar Government should erect more Nissen huts—but this would have to be done at their own expense since the United Kingdom could not afford to contribute!

The Governor gave in: 'In the circumstances I have no alternative but under duress to agree to meet the cost of the extra Nissen huts from Gibraltar funds. Their erection is quite essential if your wishes regarding the completion of repatriation are to be met. I cannot however give a categorical undertaking at this stage to repatriate from the United Kingdom, before the end of September, all who wish to leave up to a maximum of 375.' The reason given for this was a delay in the construction of the new flats. 'Provided no further delays occur, it should just be possible, with the Nissen hut scheme, to accept 375 repatriates by the end of September.'

That, then, remained the question: could Gibraltar absorb up to a maximum of 375 repatriates by the end of September, 1949? Owing to shipping difficulties, the first parties of that year were of necessity small: less than twenty embarked at Southampton on the 2nd February aboard the *Empire Trooper*, eight left the United Kingdom on the *Empress of Australia* on the 25th March, and another small group left by the same ship on the 30th May. A larger party, numbering about 100, left on the 1st July, again aboard the *Empress of Australia.*

The next repatriation party had something of a different aspect to it, part of the journey being done by an overland route. On the 4th June, the Governor was informed that no further passages would be available, after the July sailing, before October, but that offers had been received for 150 passages on the Argentinian ship *Cordoba* leaving Southampton for Bilbao on the 27th July. Agents could arrange rail passages from Bilbao to Algeciras. The Governor agreed to accept such a party provided the numbers did not exceed 150.

The *Cordoba* party, numbering 140, arrived at Santurce, the landing station for transatlantic liners, some ten miles down stream from Bilbao, on the morning of the 29th July, 1949. The Customs and Migration authorities, who had been previously contacted, made no difficulties and by midday all the repatriates were installed in the carriages of the special train. They were given lunch in two relays at a restaurant half a mile from the landing stage. The special train left at 4 pm for Miranda del Ebro, where it arrived three hours later. Arrangements had been made for dinner to be provided them in two restaurants near to the railway station there.

The coaches were coupled to the Morocco express when it passed through Miranda early next morning. Meals on the 30th were provided in a restaurant car for the exclusive use of the Gibraltarians, which the Madrid Embassy had arranged to be attached to the train at Valladolid. The repatriates arrived at Algeciras on the morning of the 31st and there board the *Mary Claire* for the final lap. According to the *Gibraltar Chronicle,* the repatriates found 'their beloved ''Peñon'' looking much the same as when they left it nine years ago—wrapped in a misty levanter.'

The British Consul at Bilbao, Hugh McErlean, commented thus on this voyage:-

'I was surprised and relieved that the movement of these people was thus carried out without a hitch. It is to the simple and effective arrangements made by the Consular section of the Madrid Embassy that this satisfactory outcome may chiefly be attributed. But credit is also due to the Spanish National Railways (RENFE) .... to the guides provided by the Colonial Office and Gibraltar; and finally to the repatriates themselves, who were orderly, well-behaved and good-humoured.'

The 29th September, 1949, came and the Fulham Road Hostel did not close! The Secretary of State informed the Governor that since the number of evacuees remaining was higher than expected, the Ministry of Health, who was to assume responsibility after the 29th September, had been unable to provide alternative accommodation pending individual re-housing and that a further limited tenancy had been arranged at Fulham Road. Both hostels would be administered by the London County Council. The hostels by then only contained those who had elected to stay in the United Kingdom permanently.

Another small repatriation party, numbering 25, left Liverpool aboard the *Oxfordshire* on the 13th October, 1949, arriving at Gibraltar four days later. At about the same time, a notice was posted up at the hostels in London, announcing that the evacuation scheme would end officially on the 31st December, 1949. Free passages would be provided for those wishing to be repatriated up to but in no case after a period of two years after that date. The notice added that it would not be possible for any evacuees to be repatriated until accommodation was available in Gibraltar, but that those who elected to be repatriated had to be prepared to return to Gibraltar when passages were arranged for them. Evacuees who declined to accept repatriation when offered, would be regarded as having finally forfeited all right to repatriation at Government expense at a later date.

It was hoped that this statement would reach the many Gibraltarians, estimated at around 2,000, who were living in private accommodation but who still had the right to repatriation if they wished to exercise it. It was for their benefit in particular that the two-years extension of the free passages arrangement was being made.

On the 16th January, 1950, the Secretary of State for the Colonies sent the Governor of Gibraltar a provisional list of 131 names of evacuees who had applied for repatriation under the terms of the notice published the previous October. He was anxious to send as many of these as possible to Gibraltar before the end of March, 1950. A few days later the opportunity arose of sending the entire party in a troopship leaving the United Kingdom in late February.

The Governor replied that, regretfully, he could not accept the repatriation of any of these persons at the moment except those whose repatriation under Government Notice 214 had been authorised (eight of the 131 in fact!). He explained that no accommodation was available, delays had occurred in the building of the permanent blocks of flats, and the Government had been unable to implement its promise to evacuate the RNAS by the end of 1949. The position would be reviewed by the Resettlement Board during the second half of the year. In the circumstances, the Secretary of State agreed that the matter should rest for six months.

Seven months later the Secretary of State was asking for the result of the Resettlement Board's review of the situation, saying that he was particularly anxious to complete the repatriation before the 31st March, 1951! In conclusion he said:

'I am convinced that if you would agree to accept all the families concerned in one party at an early date quite a number would refuse to travel and would thus forfeit their repatriation rights.'

The Resettlement Board discussed the matter on the 15th November, 1950, and agreed that sixty repatriates could now be fitted in the Little Sisters of the Poor. In actual fact, only 28 evacuees were repatriated in that year.

And so the repatriation spilled over into yet another year! On the 9th February, 1951, a party of 29 repatriates left London heading for Gibraltar by overland route, due to the lack of sea passages. The party comprised five complete families and a few individuals, and they were to be accommodated in the Little Sisters of the Poor Centre, pending resettlement.

The *Gibraltar Chronicle* again looked for the personal angles. 'One of the families, named Rocca, broke up at Victoria Station when the train steamed out. Frank and Thomas Rocca were on the train. On the platform was father Antonio Rocca and a younger brother and sister. Mrs Rocca was at home in Kentish Town.'

Rocca told why the family split up. 'There is no accommodation for people going back to Gibraltar. All this party will go into rest homes when they get there. As we have a house in London there is no point in giving it up. After six or seven months the boys will get a place out there. If they can't, they will come back here.'

The party arrived home on the 11th February, 1951, thereby closing a chapter in the history of Gibraltar. The repatriation programme had been officially completed, apart from the mental patients at Cane Hill Hospital.

However, this was not the end of the story, for one family, Juana Llambias and her five children, had been inadvertently omitted. They should have returned in April, 1951, but their repatriation had to be further deferred when the Naval armament supply ship, the *Bedenham* caught fire at the Gun Wharf and blew up during unloading on the 27th April. Due to the explosion all available accommodation, including that earmarked for the Llambias family, had to be brought temporarily into use to house families removed from their homes on account of blast damage. Juana Llambias and family duly sailed on the *Batory* on the 21st August, 1951. Of all Gibraltarians evacuated, about 2,000 had chosen to stay in Britain permanently.

CHAPTER TWENTY

Epilogue

What effects did the experiences just related have upon the character and development of the civilian population of Gibraltar? In general terms one may point to a 'widening of horizons', particularly amongst the younger evacuees. The Gibraltarians had been removed from the narrow confines of an extremely small Fortress/Colony community and exposed to more modern living facilities (in London at any rate), a closer contact with the English language and British Institutions. The struggles arising out of the running of the Evacuation Centres and Camps, over conditions in Northern Ireland, and, above all, from the long-protracted and vexed question of repatriation taught the Gibraltarians, it would seem, to fight officialdom at the highest levels. This in turn was to give rise to demands for a greater say in the running of their own affairs in the immediate post-war period.

Overcrowding had been a problem in Gibraltar since time immemorial. The fact that many of the repatriates who had previously lived in Spain would now have to be accommodated in Gibraltar created, as has been seen, many problems. Nor would many of the returning Gibraltarians be content to accept the poor quality accommodation they had tolerated before the War. Those who had been billetted in the 'better' areas of London had sampled the luxuries of modern-style housing, and they would naturally hanker after similar amenities on their return to the Rock. As one evacuee put it: 'there will be a lot of changes to be made in Gibraltar when we go back.' All this gave a tremendous boost to the house-building programme, and led to the erection of many blocks of flats with up-to-date amenities. The construction of such self-contained flats also had an interesting side-effect—the old 'patio' mentality, where neighbours would sit at their front doors in the evenings and chat for hours on end (a practice still prevalent in the smaller towns and villages of Spain) gradually diminished.

Another interesting sociological side-effect of the war years was the change which was brought about in the women of Gibraltar. Before the war, the place of the Gibraltarian woman was very much 'in the home'—very few would have dreamt of going out to work. The war changed all that! It has been seen how many Gibraltarian women evacuees worked in munition factories and other essential war-work whilst in London. It is not, I think, to stretch the point too far to say that the war years 'emancipated' the Gibraltarian woman. She is still today very much the centre of the home, mother and wife above all else, but she also goes out to work and many have mapped out useful careers for themselves.

The experience gained by some evacuees in the fight for better conditions for themselves and for their compatriots gave a considerable impetus to the demand for greater self-government in the Colony. Familiarity, it is said, breeds contempt, and the closer contacts which the Gibraltarian evacuees had with Englishmen of all classes buried once and for all the old colonial subservient attitude to one's 'superiors'. No longer were the decisions of the Colonial Government accepted without question. The Gibraltarians had learned well the workings of British democracy. As R A Preston put it in a pamphlet entitled 'Gibraltar, Colony and Fortress': 'for the first time in its history Gibraltar began to witness the resurgence of complaints and grievances leading to co-ordinated action and the founding of the Association for the Advancement of Civil Rights specifically designed to foster Gibraltarian public opinion.' (quoted in The *Gibraltar Chronicle,* 8th April, 1947).

The Association for the Advancement of Civil Rights had been formed in Gibraltar at the end of 1942, and it was to play an important role in the fight for greater self-government. An early success was the reconstitution of the City Council (suspended in 1939) in 1945, for the first time with an elected majority. Five years later, in November 1950, Gibraltar was given its own Constitution with Legislative and Executive Councils. In both these bodies elected members were numerically balanced by official members nominated by the Governor who also could veto any decisions taken. Further developments came in 1956 (when the number of elected members was increased from five to seven), and in 1964 (when the number was again increased to eleven and a Council of Ministers was created). However, limited as such concessions were, they represented an important step along the road to greater self-government, and further changes were to come in 1969.

The evacuation also had the effect of knitting the Gibratarians into a closer community than ever before. Be they in London, Northern Ireland, Jamaica or Madeira, they were made much more aware of the fact that they were 'different', a community, indeed almost a nation! As has been seen, the desire to return to 'El Peñon', the 'fatherland', became an obsession with many. The Gibraltarian identity had undoubtedly been strengthened.

Linguistically, although Spanish was to continue as the language of most homes, the greater contact with the English language during these years was to have a profound effect, particularly upon the younger generation. This was to be strengthened by the great strides made in educational facilities after the war.

A Committee appointed by the Governor to consider the post-war educational needs of Gibraltar (in relation to pre-war facilities) reported in 1943:-

'No visitor to Gibraltar, whatever his calling, however brief his stay, can fail to be impressed by the generally poor standard of education of its people and this conclusion has formed the leitmotif of the many criticisms which have been levelled at its administration; it is a melancholy fact of which the Gibraltarian himself must be only too well aware for the 1931 census recorded that approximately 20% were wholly illiterate. The evacuation of the civil population and consequent closure of the schools presents an opportunity such as may never occur again of overhauling the entire educational machinery and that is the task which has confronted this Committee.' The opportunity, thankfully, was not lost!

Thus out of so much that was bad came some good. The Gibraltarians had suffered displacement from their homes and separation from their families, some of them had endured years of waiting for a return to 'normality'. But when that came, Gibraltar was to be a much better place in which to live.

Gibraltar Government Files Referred To

MP S14/1939	Evacuation of Civil Population (Main File) Medical arrangements Madeira.
MP 519/1940	Reports from Major Patron and Mr Dryburgh.
MP 421/1940	Reports from Mr Dryburgh.
MP 568/1940	Madeira Reports.
MP 24/1941	The British School for Gibraltar Children, Funchal. Report by HBM Consul.
MP 329/1942	Club for Gibraltarian Youths in London.
MP 226/1943	Evacuees Committee in London. Representations by AACR
MP 369/1942	Memorial to Secretary of State by AACR regarding Jamaica evacuees.
MP 0029	Resettlement Board (four volumes).
MP 0502	Transfer of evacuees in London to Northern Ireland.
MP 325F	Air Raid Casualties in UK (Evacuees).
MP 1907	Transfer of evacuees from Northern Ireland to London (three volumes).
MP S61/1940	Raids in Gibraltar.
MP 0048 series:	00481—First UK Party.
	0048V—Second UK Party.
	0048W—Third UK Party.
	0048Y—Repatriation of evacuees in Northern Ireland.
	0048AA—Fourth UK Party.
	0048AB—Fifth UK Party.
	0048AH—Sixth UK Party.
	0048AJ—Luggage aboard ss *Silver Teak*.
	0048AX—Seventh UK Party.
	0048AZ—Eighth UK Party.
	0048BA—Ninth UK Party.
	0048BF—Tenth UK Party.
	0048BG—Eleventh UK Party.
	0048BH—Twelfth UK Party.
	0048BI—Thirteenth UK Party.
	0048BJ—Fourteenth UK Party.
	0048BN—Fifteenth UK Party.
	0048BP—Sixteenth UK Party.
	0048BS—Seventeenth UK Party.
	0048BT—Eighteenth UK Party.
	0048BX—Twentieth UK Party.
	0048BY—Nineteenth UK Party.
	0048BZ—22nd UK Party.
	0048CA—23rd UK Party.
	0048CB—24th UK Party.

0048CC—25th UK Party.
0048CD—26th UK Party.
0048CF—27th UK Party.
0048CG—28th UK Party.
0048CH—29th and 30th Parties.
0048CI—31st UK Party.
0048CJ—32nd UK Party.
0048CK—33rd UK Party.

MP 192/1941	Educational facilities for children of Gibraltar Evacuees in the UK, Madeira and Jamaica.
MP 99/1941	Gibraltar Evacuees Liaison Committee Minutes.
MP 101/1941	Inter Departmental Committee on the Welfare of Evacuees from Gibraltar. Minutes.
MP 340/1940	Amenities for Evacuees. Formation of a Committee for the provision of a fund entitled the Gibraltar War Relief Fund.
MP 523/1940	Baggage belonging to Evacuees. Questions re.

MP 101/1941 Inter Departmental Committee on the Welfare of Evacuees from Gibraltar. Minutes.
MP 340/1940 Amenities for Evacuees. Formation of a Committee for the provision of a fund entitled the Gibraltar War Relief Fund.
MP 523/1940 Baggage belonging to Evacuees. Questions re.

APPENDIX A

Schedule of Evacuation to French Morocco

May/June, 1940

Contingent number	Name of Ship	Date of Departure	Number of Evacuees
*	Gibel Dersa	21st May, 1940	494
1	Mohamed Ali Kebir	22nd May, 1940	950
2	Mohamed Ali Kebir	24th May, 1940	850
3	Mohamed Ali Kebir	26th May, 1940	908
4	Mohamed Ali Kebir	30th May, 1940	920
5	Mohamed Ali Kebir	1st June, 1940	1,111
6	Mohamed Ali Kebir	3rd June, 1940	1,279
7	Mohamed Ali Kebir	6th June, 1940	1,183
8	Mohamed Ali Kebir	9th June, 1940	1,020
9	Mohamed Ali Kebir	12th June, 1940	1,410
10	Mohamed Ali Kebir	17th June, 1940	896
*	Gibel Dersa	19th June, 1940	544
11	Mohamed Ali Kebir	19th June, 1940	924
12	Mohamed Ali Kebir	24th June, 1940	593

GRAND TOTAL EVACUATED: 13,082

*denotes voluntary evacuees outside Government Scheme

APPENDIX B

Schedule of Evacuation to the United Kingdom, Madeira and Jamaica

July, 1940 to July, 1941

Contingent number	Name of Ship	Date of Departure	Number of Evacuees
1M	Royal Ulsterman	19th July, 1940	449
1UK	Avoceta Clan McBean Bactria	21st July, 1940	499
2UK	Athlone Castle	26th July, 1940	1,597
3UK	Ulster Monarch Royal Ulsterman Royal Scotsman	27th July, 1940	1,923
4UK	Large convoy	30th July, 1940	5,010
2M	Neuralia	10th August, 1940	1,248
5UK	Neuralia	20th August, 1940	1,786
1J	Neuralia	9th October, 1940	1,093
2J	Thysville	31st October, 1940	393
6UK	Arundel Castle	22nd May, 1940	349
7UK	Nea Hellas	30th May, 1941	500
8UK		4th July, 1941	152
			TOTAL: 14,999

M=Madeira UK=United Kingdom J=Jamaica

APPENDIX C

Schedule of Repatriation

April, 1944 to August, 1951

Contingent number	Name of Ship	Date of Arrival	Number of Repatriates
1UK	Duchess of Richmond Antenor	6th April, 1944	1,367
1M	Indrapoera	31st May, 1944	977
2UK	Stirling Castle	2nd August, 1944	3,161
3UK	?	2nd September, 1944	488
2M	?	? September, 1944	36
4UK	?	5th October, 1944	437
3M	?	? October, 1944	76
5UK	Elizabethville	25th October, 1944	150
1J	?	26th October, 1944	c.1,500
4M	?	? November, 1944	21
6UK	?	15th January, 1945	c.170
5M	Cabo de Hornos	? April, 1945	134
7UK	Carthage	23rd April, 1945	285
8UK	?	11th May, 1945	282
6M	Carvalho Araujo	? May, 1945	99
9UK	Batory	22nd June, 1945	778
7M	Batory	24th June 1945	193
At this point, 10,950 were back out of a total of 16,700 evacuated.			
10UK	Bergensfjord	23rd July, 1945	c.40
11UK	Ascania	26th July, 1945	423

Contingent number	Name of Ship	Date of Arrival	Number of Repatriates
12UK	Eastern Prince	? September, 1945	236
13UK	Celicia	22nd November, 1945	503
14UK	Devonshire	3rd March, 1946	c.250
8M	?	? March, 1946	c.31
15UK	City of Paris	17th April, 1946	259
At this point, 12,847 back—c.2,500 still to come			
16UK	Ascania	29th June, 1946	175
17UK	Cheshire	24th September, 1946	c.177
At this point, 13,188 back			
18UK	Samaria	18th January, 1947	246
19UK	Ascania	20th March, 1947	115
20UK	Ascania	24th July, 1947	179
21UK	Orbita	15th January, 1948	46
22UK	Franconia	25th February, 1948	102
23UK	Franconia	27th March, 1948	144
24UK	Orbita	27th April, 1948	190
25UK	Empress of Australia	11th June, 1948	71
26UK	Scythia	June, 1948	130
27UK	Asturias	9th July, 1948	34
28UK	Orbita	28th July, 1948	20
29Uk	Empire Deben	18th September, 1948	13
30UK	Empire Test	24th November, 1948	5
31UK	Empire Trooper	2nd February, 1949	c.20
32UK	Empress of Australia	March, 1949	8
33UK	Empress of Australia	June, 1949	c.20
34UK	Empress of Australia	July, 1949	c.100

Contingent number	Name of Ship	Date of Arrival	Number of Repatriates
35UK	Cordoba	31st July, 1949	140
36UK	Oxfordshire	17th October, 1949	25
37UK	?	11th February, 1951	29
38UK	Batory	August, 1951	6

Total repatriated: c. 13,911
Remaining in UK: c. 2,000

Index

M

N